FANTASY
OF THE 20TH CENTURY

| AN ILLUSTRATED HISTORY | BY RANDY BROECKER |

FOR ALL THOSE WHO, WITH WORD AND BRUSH, HAVE SHAPED THE WORLD OF FANTASY;
AND FOR SARA, WITH LOVE, WHO MEANS ALL THE WORLD TO ME.

Copyright ©2001 Randy Broecker

Cover design LISA M. DOUGLASS, COLLECTORS PRESS, INC.
Based upon cover design concepts by DRIVE COMMUNICATIONS, NEW YORK
Book design DRIVE COMMUNICATIONS, NEW YORK
Copy editing LORI STEPHENS

This edition published exclusively for
Barnes & Noble, Inc., by Collectors Press, Inc.

Printed in China

9 8 7 6 5 4 3 2 1

ISBN   0-7607-6571-5

FANTASY

OF THE 20TH CENTURY

| AN ILLUSTRATED HISTORY | BY RANDY BROECKER |

BARNES
& NOBLE
BOOKS
NEW YORK

TABLE OF

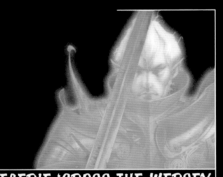

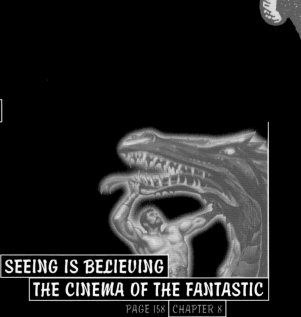

BETTER LIVING
THROUGH FANTASY

1001 DELIGHTS

LOST WORLDS, LOST RACES

CONTENTS

THE PULP ALCHEMISTS

COMPLETE ENCHANTERS

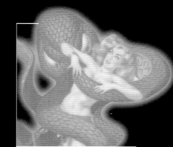

A GOOD STORY
IS WORTH REPRINTING

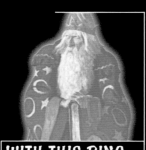

WITH THIS RING...

BETTER LIVING

THROUGH FANTASY

Once upon a time—long before these days where people line up around the block in front of airplane hanger-size chain bookstores, waiting for the clock to strike midnight (the witching hour) so they can be first to purchase the latest installment of *Harry Potter*—there was *fantasy*.

Back in those day of yore, far removed from the aforementioned bookstores of today, where one can sip a cappuccino, nestled in an overstuffed chair, and read the entire book (never mind buying it!) there was *fantasy*.

And it was *good*.

Often *great*.

It still is.

It can take you to places you could never visit, no matter how well connected a travel agent you have. It's changed a little like most things but, also like most things, a lot of it is still the same. And it's been with us for a long, long time. Fantasy literature, like its siblings horror and science fiction, has been around since the earliest recorded histories of the world. My own interest in the field doesn't go quite as far back as that, but it has been pretty much life-long nonetheless. And what an extensive field it is! There are more than enough subgenres to keep any-one interested. It's not an easy subject to pigeonhole, stamp, catalog, file, and index.

Consider the popular young adult variety, perhaps best exemplified today by the *Harry Potter* books by J. K. Rowling. But don't forget the others. There are

AVON FANTASY READER #18
1952
ARTIST UNKNOWN

An unpublished story by Robert E. Howard, creator of Conan the barbarian, some great pulp reprints, and a cover that defines sword and sorcery. What more could you ask for?

Is there a dragon in the house? You'd better believe it. In this part of town they walk, they talk, and sometimes they even crawl on their bellies like reptiles.

THE SWINE OF AEAEA
the story of a modern Circe
By CLIFFORD BALL

THE RETURN OF HASTUR
a tale of the Ancient Ones
By AUGUST W. DERLETH

SEABURY QUINN
H. P. LOVECRAFT
EDMOND HAMILTON
and others

160 pages of unusual fiction

MARCH
25¢

2
WEIRD TALES
MARCH 1939
VIRGIL FINLAY

Circe, one of the earliest practicing sorceresses, makes a rare pulp appearance, and she's in good company.

fairy tales, Arthurian legends, heroic fantasy, sword and sorcery adventures, humorous fantasy, Arabian Nights-styled tales, and lost race fables, any of which could fill a book this size and more. Too much fantasy, too little space. And these are just some of the subgenres of fantasy readers have encountered in a field whose boundaries are only those of the imagination itself.

It is a field that has greatly enriched my own life. I *can't* tell you that during campus riots back in the 1960s a stray bullet from a National Guardsman's rifle lodged itself in a copy of the Ace paperback edition of *The Fellowship of the Ring* by J. R. R. Tolkien that I happened to have in my top pocket, thus saving my life. Nothing quite that dramatic. But I *can* tell you that it has introduced me, in one way or another, to many extremely talented individuals that I am lucky enough to count as good friends and colleagues (including my wife), provided me with the opportunity to make artistic contributions to the genre in my own way, and given to me what it gives to anyone who takes the time to open a book and read: entertainment. And it has delivered those things to me in spades for quite a while.

Now I'm hoping to return the favor and do the fantasy genre some justice with the following illustrated history. But be warned, as we set out on our quest "Here there be dragons…"

Randy Broecker
Chicago, Illinois
September 2000

APR. 22

10¢

FOREIGN LEGION
NOVELET

Robert Carse

ARGOSY

RED STAR MAGAZINE
4-22

WEEKLY

When the World Ends
—What Next?

An Amazing
New Novel

MINIONS
OF THE MOON

CHAPTER 1
1001 DELIGHTS

The earliest roots of fantasy literature can be found in the epic poem *Gilgamesh* circa 2000 B.C. and in other classical works such as Homer's *Iliad* and *Odyssey* and Virgil's *Aeneid*. These, along with the mythologies of the Greeks, Romans, Celts, and Germanic peoples all with their various deities, form the basis of heroic fantasy. It is quite possibly the oldest theme in literature. Epics like the Finnish *Kalevala* and the stories of the Welsh *Mabinogion* contain gods and monsters, warriors and wizards. The German tale *The Niebelungenlied* centers on the heroic Siegfried, a dragon, giants, dwarves, *and* a magic sword—all major elements still being penned by fantasy writers today. *Beowulf,* another epic poem, also deals in heroes and monsters and yet another enchanted sword. Then there is the British war- lord Arthur, the magician Merlin, and a certain sword by the name of Excalibur.

DIE ODYSSEE
HOMER TRANSLATED BY
JOHANN HEINRICH VOSS
DATE UNKNOWN
ALFRED RENZ

German edition of the
early heroic fantasy.

With its romantic quest elements, the Arthurian legend is a rich fantasy vein that is mined to this day.

One Thousand Nights and a Night, the original translation of which has become known as *The Arabian Nights,* can be traced back as early as A.D. 800. Its framing device is Scheherazade who nightly told tales to the Sultan (who had made a vow to marry a virgin each night and behead her the following morning because of an earlier wife's betrayal) but stopped each dawn before she finished them, thus sustaining his interest and postponing her demise one thousand and one times. It remains an influential body of work, composed of romantic and magical adventures from "Aladdin" to the "Seven Voyages of Sinbad". And Scheherazade might just be the first recorded storyteller to really sweat over a deadline!

Other early influential writings include *The Voyages and Travels of Sir John Mandeville* (circa 1360) with its fantastic exploits, *The Faerie Queene* (1590–1609) by Edmund Spenser, and *Le Morte Darthur* (1485) by Sir Thomas Malory whose Arthurian legends were later used by Alfred, Lord Tennyson as the basis for his epic Victorian poem *Idylls of the King* (1859).

English playwright William Shakespeare mixed fantasy with romance in both *A Midsummer Night's Dream* (1595) and *The Tempest* (1611), while *Gulliver's Travels* (1726) by Jonathan Swift incorporated giants, talking animals, flying islands, and other fantastic entertainments enfolded in political and religious satire.

A major work in the early history of the fantasy novel is *Vathek* (1786) by William Beckford. In Arabian Nights fashion, it is richly imaginative and decadent—not unlike its author. Through a family inheritance, Beckford was the wealthiest commoner

THE WANDERINGS OF ODYSSEUS
ROSEMARY SUTCLIFF
1995
ALAN LEE

A re-telling of one of the earliest fantastic voyages, beautifully illustrated by Alan Lee.

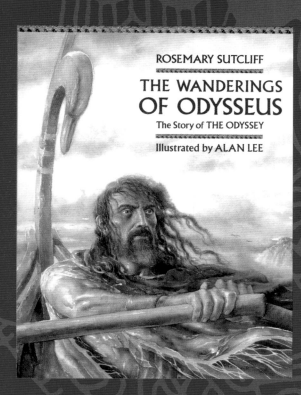

THE MABINOGION
TRANSLATED BY GWYN JONES AND THOMAS JONES
1982
ALAN LEE

The epic collection of Welsh mythology and Alan Lee's masterpiece.

THE SAMPO
JAMES BALDWIN
1912
N. C. WYETH

Heroic adventures from the Finnish *Kalevala*.

Billowy black, and the three Rhine-daughters
Sink in the gulf of the Rhine below,
And worlds of waters fail and fall—
Light is lost in the purple pall,
Gone the Rhine-gold's gleam and glow.
Wakes the woe of the wan world's will,
Laughs the Nibelung far and shrill—
He who the light of love renouncing
Wins the will of the world his own,
Works of the red Rhine-gold his ring!]

[End of first scene ; the Rhine is black ; the stars come out in the sky.]

5
WAGNER'S RING OF THE NIEBELUNG PART I – THE RAPE OF THE RHINE-GOLD

F. J. STIMSON
SCRIBNER'S MAGAZINE
DECEMBER 1898
MAXFIELD PARRISH

Alberich the Niebelung steals one of fantasy's first rings.

6
SIEGFRIED

THE ILLUSTRATED LONDON NEWS
CHRISTMAS 1933
JOSÉ SEGRELLES

Segrelles' dramatic rendition of the legendary hero.

7
DAS RHEINGOLD

THE ILLUSTRATED LONDON NEWS
CHRISTMAS 1933
JOSÉ SEGRELLES

Giants battle while the gods look on.

8
ARTHUR RACKHAM'S
COLOR ILLUSTRATIONS
FOR WAGNER'S "RING"
1979 REPRINT
ARTHUR RACKHAM
Reprint of Rackham's
1911–12 illustrations
based on Richard Wagner's
operatic interpretation of
The Neibelungenlied.

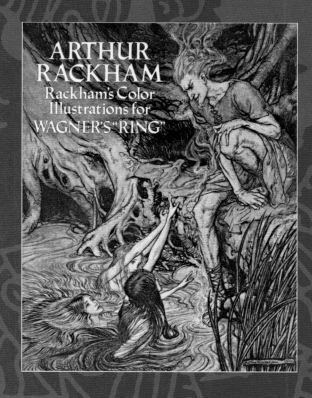

in England. He lived as he pleased in his own "stately pleasure dome", Fonthill Abbey, which he had built to house himself and his collection of acquired art treasures. Charles Foster Kane would have approved.

Folk legends in Europe and America were the source of many popular tales, and one of the most famous is "Rip Van Winkle" (1819–20). Its American author, Washington Irving, collected German folk legends while living in England, and their influence can clearly be seen in the aforementioned story and the author's equally famous "The Legend of Sleepy Hollow", originally published in the same collection.

In *A Christmas Carol* (1843), Charles Dickens established the idea of the man who finds redemption through otherworldly guidance. Scottish poet and author of children's fairy tales and adult fantasy George MacDonald created a haunting faerie dreamworld with *Phantastes, a Faerie Romance for Men and Women* (1858). He also produced another symbolic otherworld adult fantasy in *Lilith* (1895). A friend of Lewis Carroll (a.k.a. Charles Lutwidge Dodgson), MacDonald read the original manuscript for *Alice's Adventures in Wonderland* (1865). The story may have influenced his own books for children which include *At the Back of the North Wind* (1871), *The Princess and the Goblin* (1872), and *The Princess and Curdie* (1883).

L. (Lyman) Frank Baum was an author also known for his children's books including *Mother Goose in Prose* (1899), illustrated by Maxfield Parrish. In 1900 he created one of fantasy's best loved worlds in *The Wonderful Wizard of Oz.* It was the beginning of an immensely popular series for Baum and the basis for one of the most famous fantasy films of all time: *The Wizard of Oz* (1939).

The beginning of the popularity of the "lost race" adventure can be traced back to 1885 and *King*

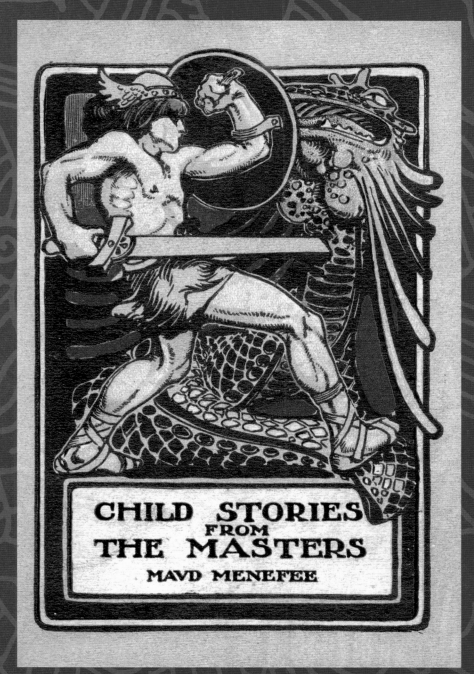

9
CHILD STORIES FROM THE MASTERS
MAUD MENEFEE
1899
ARTIST UNKNOWN
Two staples of heroic fantasy literature—the sword and the dragon—from a version of *Siegfried* aimed at children.

LEGENDS · OF · CHARLEMAGNE

ILLVSTRATED BY N·C·WYETH

LEGENDS OF CHARLEMAGNE
THOMAS BULFINCH
1924
N. C. WYETH

Based partly on the 1516 poem *Orlando Furioso* by Lodovico Ariosto. I warned you about the dragons…

Solomon's Mines by H. Rider Haggard. *The Wonderful Adventures of Phra the Phoenician* (1891), the story of an immortal reborn through the years, was the brainchild of Edwin Lester Arnold. The son of a poet and philosopher, he also wrote *Lieutenant Gulliver Jones: His Vacation* (1905), an early Martian fantasy that may have influenced Edgar Rice Burroughs' later adventures set on that red planet.

Arthur Machen is well known as a supernatural storyteller through such novels as *The Great God Pan* (1894), but he also wrote fantastic tales inspired by the Welsh legends of his homeland, including *The Hill of Dreams* (1907). H. P. Lovecraft was one of the many writers influenced by Machen's work.

Much of the great early fantasy writing came out of Europe, and the source of a good deal of it can be clearly traced to folk stories, myths, and legends. So it should come as no surprise that the writer widely regarded as the founding father of modern fantasy fiction was born in London, England in 1834.

William Morris—designer, poet, artist, and writer—was influential in a growing movement to return to the beauty of times past in art and design, along with such other creative talents as the artist Edward Burne-Jones and artist and poet Dante Gabriel Rossetti. Morris established his own company to design and make furniture, stained glass, fabric, tiles, carpet, jewelry, and hand-printed wallpaper, helping to transform Victorian design sensibilities into those of the Arts and Crafts movement and Art Nouveau. In the later part of his life he established his own publishing imprint, Kelmscott Press, devoted to printing beautifully illustrated and designed editions. The first book off the press was Morris' own novella *The Story of the Glittering Plain* (1891). Having previously written several short fantasies and

THE ARABIAN NIGHTS ENTERTAINMENTS
SELECTED AND EDITED BY ANDREW LANG
1898
H. J. FORD

One of countless versions, this has a brilliant gold-embossed cover design reflecting Ford's detailed interior illustrations.

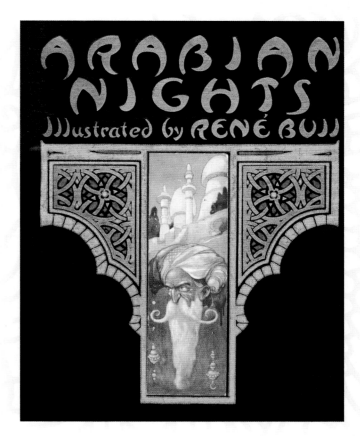

THE ARABIAN NIGHTS
1917
RENÉ BULL

Scheherazade's bedtime stories, nicely illustrated by Bull.

THE FAERIE QUEENE

EDMUND SPENSER
1590–1609 (1894–96 REPRINT)
WALTER CRANE

Just one of the many detailed
illustrations for Spenser's verse.

RIP VAN WINKLE

WASHINGTON IRVING
1819–20 (1939 REPRINT)
EVERETT SHINN

An early American fantasy on
the dangers of oversleeping!

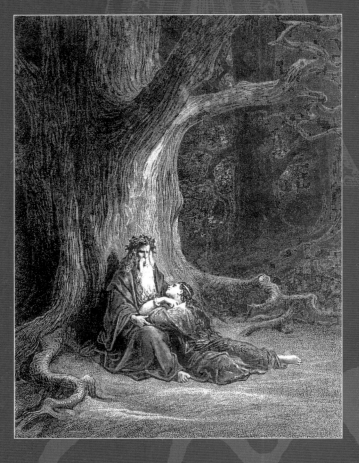

IDYLLS OF THE KING

ALFRED, LORD TENNYSON
1859 (1868 REPRINT)
GUSTAVE DORÉ

One of Doré's moody engravings
for the Arthurian poem.

VATHEK

WILLIAM BECKFORD
1786 (1928 REPRINT)
MAHLON BLAINE

Blaine's artwork perfectly
complements Beckford's
decadent prose.

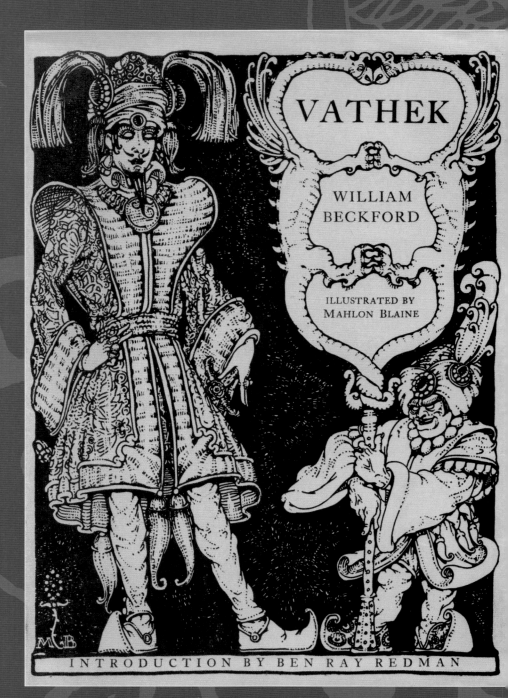

VATHEK

WILLIAM BECKFORD

ILLUSTRATED BY
MAHLON BLAINE

INTRODUCTION BY BEN RAY REDMAN

Rip Van Winkle

WASHINGTON IRVING

ILLUSTRATED

EVERETT SHINN

translated classics like *The Odyssey* and some Icelandic sagas, he now published major fantasy novels through Kelmscott.

His novel *The Wood Beyond the World* (1894), with its imaginary mediaeval world tapestry, filled with eldritch magic and beauty, is often considered the first modern fantasy novel. It is written in the nature of a quest: a young hero journeying from the city to unknown realms encounters three mysterious figures—a young girl, captive to and mistreated by an ogre-ish creature, in the service of a beautiful woman, The Mistress. Our hero ultimately dispatches the ogre through his love for the maiden and the two of them run off together to his world, far away from the sorceress Mistress. Morris followed it with the epic-length fantasy *The Well at the World's End* (1896), another quest, this time for the well by the world's edge where those who drink from it shall find peace. The posthumously published novels *The Water of the Wondrous Isle* and *The Story of the Sundering Flood* (both 1897) were to be the last of the magic. William Morris died on October 3, 1896.

The fine binding and design of the Kelmscott Press books served as inspiration and then became a staple in fantasy publishing, especially in illustrated books.

Gustave Doré's folios of engravings illustrating works like Dante's *Inferno, Don Quixote,* The Bible, *The Adventures of Baron Munchausen,* the works of Milton, and numerous fairy tales were extremely popular—first in his native France, then in the 1860s in London. They were incredibly detailed and wildly imaginative. Aubrey Beardsley, best known for his decadently erotic black and white illustrations for *Salome,* had his first illustrated book published in 1894 (an edition of *Le Morte Darthur* by Malory). Book illustration in England and Europe

THE WONDERFUL WIZARD OF OZ
L. FRANK BAUM
1900
W. W. DENSLOW

Title page of the first edition
of a fantasy favorite.

THE WONDERFUL WIZARD OF OZ
L. FRANK BAUM
1900 (1965 REPRINT)
ROY G. KRENKEL
(AND FRIEND)

Another look at one of the most
popular tales of all time.

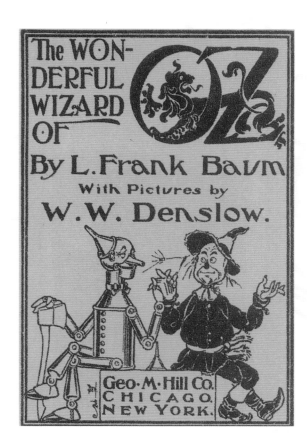

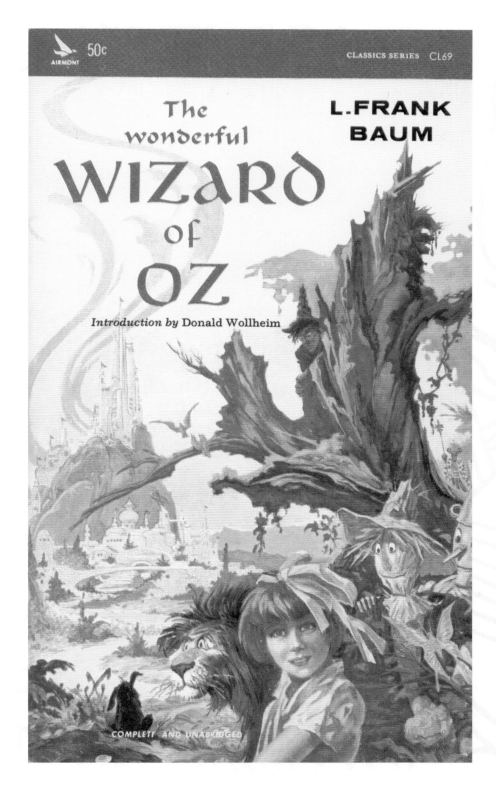

was not only popular but the books themselves, in most cases, were beautifully designed and bound. This combination of imaginative artwork and exquisite production reached a high point with limited gift editions published in Britain during the early 1900s.

Sidney H. Sime contributed illustrations to London magazines such as *The Pall Mall, The Sketch,* and *The Strand.* He did caricatures but also leaned toward the macabre and fanciful. His career as a book illustrator started when a very particular author sought him out to provide drawings for a new collection of stories.

That author was Edward John Moreton Drax Plunkett, 18th Lord Dunsany, known professionally simply as Lord Dunsany. Tall in stature, a veteran of both the Boer War and World War I and wounded in

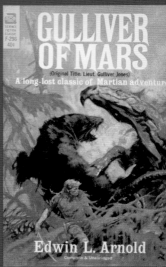

GULLIVER OF MARS

EDWIN LESTER ARNOLD
1905 (1964 REPRINT)
FRANK FRAZETTA

Later re-titling of an early planetary fantasy.

PHRA THE PHOENICIAN

EDWIN LESTER ARNOLD
1891 (SEPTEMBER 1945 REPRINT)
LAWRENCE STERNE STEVENS

Pulp reprint of Arnold's H. Rider Haggard-inspired story.

THE MYSTERIOUS STRANGER

MARK TWAIN
1897–1908 (1916 REPRINT)
N. C. WYETH

Abbreviated version of Twain's early fantasy with Wyeth's astrologer cutting a fine wizard-like figure.

THE WOOD BEYOND THE WORLD

WILLIAM MORRIS
1894
SIR EDWARD BURNE-JONES

One of the exquisite illustrations from what is considered to be the first modern fantasy novel.

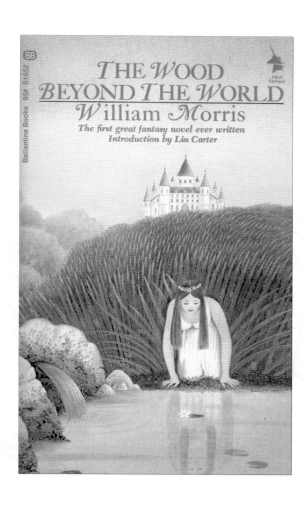

the Easter Rebellion of 1916, Dunsany was a prolific writer, producing novels, plays and short stories. However, he still found time for big game hunting in Africa. Stories relating our world to that of faerie, and fantasy lands created out of whole cloth, like those of J. R. R. Tolkien, all owe an enormous debt to Dunsany. While William Morris is considered to be the initiator of the otherworld fantasy in novel form, Dunsany receives that credit for the short story.

Dunsany's first collection of stories, *The Gods of Pegána,* was published in 1905. It contained eight illustrations by Sime and signaled the beginning of a collaboration between author and artist that produced many wonderful volumes. At times they even reversed the usual process, with Dunsany writing stories based around Sime's imaginative illustrations. Further collections soon followed, starting with *Time and the Gods* in 1906 and continuing through *The Sword of Welleran and Other Stories* (1908), *A Dreamer's Tales* (1910), *The Book of Wonder* (1912), and *The Last Book of Wonder* (1916). A story from *The Sword of Welleran*

♛ 25

THE WOOD BEYOND THE WORLD
WILLIAM MORRIS
1894 (1969 REPRINT)
GERVASIO GALLARDO

A well-deserved part of Lin Carter's Adult Fantasy line-up.

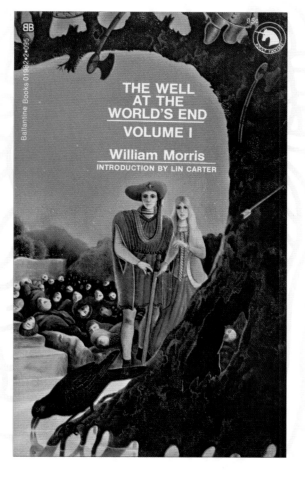

♛ 26

THE WELL AT THE WORLD'S END
WILLIAM MORRIS
1896 (1970 REPRINT)
GERVASIO GALLARDO

William Morris' follow-up to *The Wood Beyond the World,* here published in two volumes.

♛ 27

THE WATER OF THE WONDROUS ISLES
WILLIAM MORRIS
1897 (1971 REPRINT)
GERVASIO GALLARDO

One of the last of Morris' fantasy novels.

LA DIVINA COMMEDIA
DANTE ALIGHIERI
1472 (1921 REPRINT)
FRANZ VON BAYROS

Another look at
the stunning work
of Von Bayros.

LA DIVINA COMMEDIA
DANTE ALIGHIERI
1472 (1921 REPRINT)
FRANZ VON BAYROS

The most beautifully illustrated
edition of Dante's masterpiece
which is comprised of *Inferno*,
Purgatorio and *Paradiso*.

THE BOOK OF WONDER
LORD DUNSANY
1912
SIDNEY H. SIME

Sime illustrates
"The City of Never".

entitled "The Fortress Unvanquishable, Save for Sacnoth" might be the earliest example of the sword and sorcery subgenre of fantasy. It was reprinted almost sixty years later, during the 1960s revival of the genre, in one of the seminal heroic fantasy anthologies.

Dunsany wrote over forty plays, many of a fantasy nature, and at one time had five of them running simultaneously on Broadway. After his experiences in World War I, lighter fantasies gave way to those of a darker nature in both his short stories and novels. Collections such as *Tales of War* (1918) and *Tales of Three Hemispheres* (1919), and the novels *The Chronicles of Rodriguez* (1922) and *The King of Elfland's Daughter* (1924)—perhaps his best-known work—were all darker in tone.

Dunsany's later stories were written in a more humorous vein; many of them concerned Mr. Joseph Jorkens, an old codger who related tall tales in exchange for drinks from his fellow cronies at their gentlemen's club. The Jorkens stories were collected in several volumes, including *The Travel Tales of Mr. Joseph Jorkens* (1931), *Jorkens Remembers Africa* (1934) and *Jorkens Borrows Another Whisky* (1954).

Both William Morris and Lord Dunsany had a profound influence on other writers in the field, and both helped shape the modern adult heroic fantasy tale.

In 1914, Welsh writer Kenneth Morris began a series of Celtic fantasies with *The Fates of the Princes of Dyfed*. Drawing upon branches of the *Mabinogion,* this faerie tale entertainment continued in *Books of the Three Dragons* (1930). Almost unknown, compared to writers such as Lord Dunsany and William Morris, he is considered by some today to be one of the outstanding contributors to the genre. His pre-Columbian fantasy novel *The Chalchiuhite Dragon: A Tale of Toltec Times* was posthumously published in 1992.

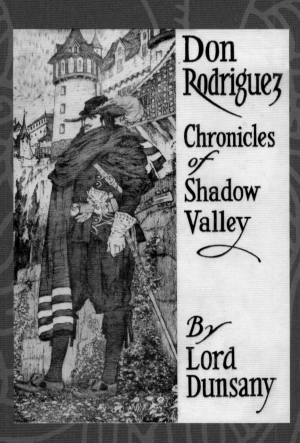

31
TIME AND THE GODS
LORD DUNSANY
2000
JOHN WILLIAM WATERHOUSE

Omnibus volume of several Dunsany collections, including the above.

32
DON RODRIGUEZ: CHRONICLES OF SHADOW VALLEY
LORD DUNSANY
1922 (1928 REPRINT)
SIDNEY H. SIME

Lord Dunsany's first novel, also known as *The Chronicles of Rodriguez.*

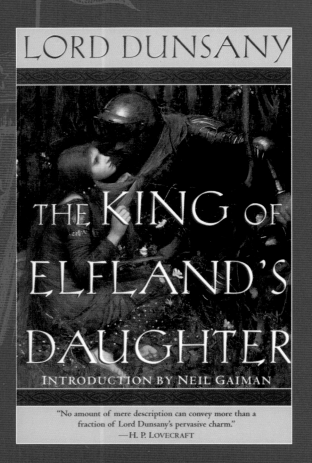

33
**THE KING OF ELFLAND'S
DAUGHTER**
LORD DUNSANY
1924 (1999 REPRINT)
JOHN WILLIAM WATERHOUSE

A seminal fantasy novel.

34
**THE FATES OF THE PRINCES
OF DYFED**
KENNETH MORRIS
1914 (1978 REPRINT)
GEORGE BARR

A neglected Celtic
heroic fantasy.

Before shifting gears and subgenres, I should also
mention one other British fantasist who found fame
with an amazing fantasy epic: Eric Rucker Eddison.
Like Morris, he was interested in Norse sagas, and in
1930 he translated *Egil's Saga*. He is more famous for
one novel, *The Worm Ouroboros* (1922) and a major
related trilogy, the 'Zimiamvia' series which comprised *Mistress of Mistresses* (1935), *A Fish Dinner in
Memison* (1941) and the unfinished *The Mezentian
Gate* (1958). *The Worm Ouroboros* had little impact
when it was originally published but garnered a following over the years, especially from many fantasy
writers. In the book, a man dreams he flies by a hip-
pogriff-drawn chariot to Mercury where demons
and witches wage a war of sorcery. Quests, adventures, and battles abound in an heroic fantasy years
ahead of its time. The world of the worm was revisited
and finally recognized as a classic during the 1960s
when epic fantasy flourished.

Although most of the fantasy writers of the early
twentieth century mentioned in this chapter were
European, the reading-for-entertainment arena in
the U.S. was richly imaginative as well.

Pulp magazines were a cheap alternative to buying
hardcover fiction, and they delivered the goods, especially, as they developed, to those looking for
adventure, science fiction, horror, and fantasy. Lost
city adventures were an early fantasy favorite, as
were interplanetary science fiction stories. Every so
often an author's creation would strike the public's
fancy and spark the imagination. Did you ever hear
the one about the English Lord who was raised as a
child by apes?

35
METROPOLITAN
AUGUST 1916
WILLY POGÁNY

Mainstream magazines frequently
used fantastic images on their covers.
Pogány presents a variation on the
mermaid—a familiar fantasy figure.

ROOSEVELT in the
Metropolitan
AUGUST
15 Cents
Willy Pogány
LONG EVER AGO
by Rupert Hughes
and other short stories

In 1885 the lost race fantasy adventure was "discovered" with the publication of *King Solomon's Mines* by Henry Rider Haggard. Haggard, a British civil servant, barrister, and writer, served time in the Colonial Service in South Africa. As far as his writing career is concerned, it was obviously time well spent, providing him with ample material on the "mysterious dark continent" for his high adventure stories. His tale of treasure and pagan magic in a lost city deep in the African continent was a bestseller and launched a trend, although Hollywood eliminated the mystical aspects when it eventually got its hands on the story. The hero, Allan Quatermain, returned in several novels over the course of the next forty years, even though he was killed off in the sequel *Allan Quatermain* (1887). Such was the popularity of the character that Haggard featured him in other books, at different periods in his life, and even brought him back through dreams to visit ancient times.

CHAPTER 2
LOST WORLDS, LOST RACES

2

THE ANCIENT ALLAN
H. RIDER HAGGARD
1920 (DECEMBER 1945 REPRINT)
LAWRENCE STERNE STEVENS

Dreams take Allan to
ancient Egypt.

1

**ALLAN QUATERMAIN/
KING SOLOMON'S MINES**
H. RIDER HAGGARD
1887/1885
(REPRINT DATE UNKNOWN)
ARTIST UNKNOWN

A double dose of H. Rider
Haggard adventure for fifty cents!

3

SHE
H. RIDER HAGGARD
1886 (1926 REPRINT)
ARTIST UNKNOWN

Movie photoplay edition
of Haggard's influential
fantasy.

Themes of racial or ancestral memory, reincarnation, and immortality play important roles in some of Haggard's best writing and were blended to great effect in *She* (1886), his most influential novel. The story of Ayesha, "She-Who-Must-Be-Obeyed", tells of the discovery of the lost African city of Kor by Leo Vincey and his expedition. It turns out that Vincey is a reincarnation of Kallikrates, a high priest loved and then killed by Ayesha. Resisting the dual temptations of Ayesha and immortality, Vincey refuses to enter the sacred Pillar of Life. However, when Ayesha returns to the pillar's flames she instantly ages hundreds of years and her beauty and life are destroyed. No less than seven film versions of *She* were made between 1908 and 1965.

The hardcover and magazine publication of several of Haggard's novels were enhanced by Maurice Greiffenhagen's beautiful black and white paintings.

The adventures of Allan Quatermain can be found in several volumes including *The Ancient Allan* (1920), *Heu-Heu, or The Monster* (1924), *Allan and the Ice-Gods: A Tale of Beginnings* (1927), and in 1921 readers were treated to the double threat of *She and Allan*. Ayesha also featured in two sequels of her own, *Ayesha: The Return of She* (1905) and *Wisdom's Daughter* (1923).

Haggard wrote many other non-series adventure fantasies. *The World's Desire* (1890), co-written with Andrew Lang, recounted further tales of Odysseus and an Ayesha-like Helen of Troy. *Eric Brighteyes* (1891) was a Viking fantasy, *The People of the Mist* (1894) explored yet another lost city, and ancient Egypt was the setting for *Morning Star* (1910). Switching from Africa to South America, Haggard delivered Aztec action in *Montezuma's Daughter*

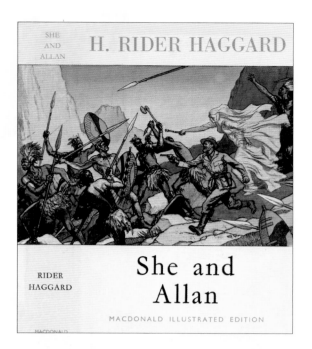

(1893) and discovered a hidden Mayan city at the *Heart of the World* (1895).

H. Rider Haggard is almost singlehandedly responsible for the extreme popularity of this type of story: lost cities, deep in subtropical jungles, where ancient races dwelled, or fabulous treasures are buried beneath Atlantean ruins, guarded by subhuman beings patiently awaiting the promised return of their god (whom they seem to think might be the tall, blond, pith-helmeted stranger who has stumbled upon their hidden city). Magic, excitement, and adventure were to be had, and from the 1880s through to the 1930s this formula enjoyed a long run in novels, serials, and the pulp magazines which catered to a wide variety of fiction tastes.

Rudyard Kipling, a friend of Haggard's, wrote his famous *Jungle Book*(s) in 1894–95. Kipling's early childhood was spent in India and formed a background for his work, much of which used fantasy and supernatural themes. The two collections of stories about Mowgli, a boy raised by wolves, and his coming-of-age tests to learn the laws of the jungle, have been adapted for film four times to date, including an animated Disney musical. Kipling was awarded the Nobel Prize for Literature in 1907; he was the first British author to receive such an honor.

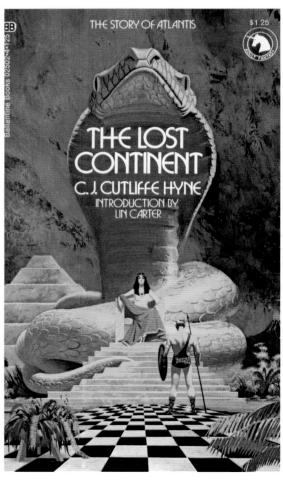

5

MORNING STAR
H. RIDER HAGGARD
1910 (FEBRUARY 1950 REPRINT)
LAWRENCE STERNE STEVENS

A striking cover portrait
by Lawrence.

6

THE LOST CONTINENT
C. J. CUTCLIFFE HYNE
1899 (1972 REPRINT)
DEAN ELLIS

A Haggard-inspired novel
of Atlantis.

In 1899, C. J. Cutcliffe Hyne wrote of *The Lost Continent,* an adventure set during the final days of Atlantis. Hyne's work was published in *Pall Mall,* along with that of Kipling, and *Pearson's* magazine. *Pearson's* also published Haggard and some of H. G. Wells' science fiction. From July to December 1899, *The Lost Continent* was successfully serialized in *Pearson's* and a hardcover publication by Harper's appeared the following year. The story unfolds from a manuscript found in a cave and develops into a rousing adventure of magic, mystery, and romance.

In 1912, Sir Arthur Conan Doyle, the creator of Sherlock Holmes, introduced another memorable character—Professor George Edward Challenger—and his scientific discovery of a plateau populated by prehistoric animals in the novel *The Lost World.* Joseph Clement Coll provided some inspired pen-and-ink drawings for the book, which remains a thrilling adventure. It was filmed several times, but the 1925 silent version, with its brilliant stop-motion effects by Willis O'Brien, the genius behind the original *King Kong* (1933), still remains the best.

There was also plenty of adventure to be had in the U.S. during this period. In 1896 the Frank A. Munsey Company published *The Argosy,* the first "pulp" magazine—so-called because of the cheap paper it was printed on. It featured a wide variety of stories, including some strange and fantastic adventures. Another Munsey title, *The All-Story,* ran even more fantasy material. In 1912 it published a first novel by an unknown writer titled *Under the Moons of Mars.* It was not the usual type of science fiction found at the time—no scientific mumbo jumbo here. This was more a romantic-fantastic adventure with interplanetary trappings, and reader response was overwhelmingly positive.

Sir Arthur Conan Doyle

THE LOST WORLD

A fantastic
expedition
back to the
dawn of time

See Irwin Allen's thrilling film production of "The Lost World"
in CinemaScope and color. Released through 20th Century-Fox.

G514

PYRAMID
PB
35¢

❼
THE LOST WORLD
SIR ARTHUR CONAN DOYLE
1912 (1960 REPRINT)
TOM BEECHAM

They don't get any more
lost than this one; a great
cover for the Irwin Allen
1960 movie tie-in.

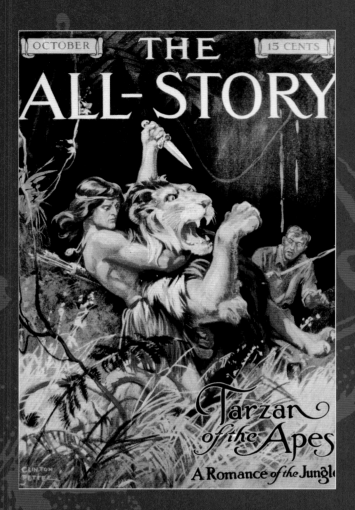

THE ALL-STORY

OCTOBER   15 CENTS

Tarzan of the Apes

A Romance of the Jungle

⑩ TARZAN AT THE EARTH'S CORE
EDGAR RICE BURROUGHS
MARCH 1930
FRANK HOBAN

Tarzan meets *The Lost World* in one of his best adventures.

⑧ TARZAN OF THE APES
EDGAR RICE BURROUGHS
OCTOBER 1912
CLINTON PETTEE

The lord of the jungle makes his first appearance.

⑨ TARZAN AT THE EARTH'S CORE
EDGAR RICE BURROUGHS
1929–30 (REPRINT DATE UNKNOWN)
J. ALLEN ST. JOHN

One of many great cover paintings St. John did for Burroughs.

TARZAN
AT THE
EARTH'S
CORE

EDGAR
RICE
BURROUGHS

BURROUGHS

TARZAN
AT THE EARTH'S CORE

by

EDGAR·RICE·BURROUGH
AUTHOR OF "TARZAN OF THE APES,"
"TARZAN AND THE LOST EMPIRE,"
"TANAR OF PELLUCIDAR " etc.

Price 25 Cents
Thirty Cents in Canada

MARCH 1930

THE
BLUE BOOK
MAGAZINE
(ILLUSTRATED)

TARZAN
AT THE EARTH'S CORE
by EDGAR RICE BURROUGHS
'The Hazardous Highway'
by Frederick R. Bechdolt
$500.
IN CASH PRIZES
FOR REAL EXPERIENCES

The author was one Norman Bean—not a name that really fits the creator of the heroic John Carter and his fantastic exploits on the red planet and with good reason, because it was not the author's real name. It was the pen name of Edgar Rice Burroughs. Retitled *A Princess of Mars* for its hardcover publication in 1912, it was the first of almost a dozen 'John Carter of Mars' adventures written over the next thirty years.

Burroughs was born in Chicago in 1875 and had had a number of different jobs before turning to writing in his mid-thirties. It was a career that seemed to suit him. In those early days of the pulps he was a resourceful businessman as well as a popular and prolific writer. His second novel, published complete in the October 1912 issue of *The All-Story,* was a little jungle romp called *Tarzan of the Apes* and the rest, as they say, is history!

The story of a human child raised in the jungle by apes was even more popular than the Mars adventure, and Tarzan would go on to become one of the most famous and beloved characters in popular fiction—and the maker of Burroughs' fortune. Tarzan has appeared in every medium, from movies to comic books and become an icon of popular culture. Many of the more than twenty Tarzan novels featured lost cities and their denizens: Tarzan encountered surviving Atlanteans, cities of Amazons, ancient Romans, and even a lost Mayan civilization.

Like Haggard before him, Burroughs' fantastic romance was very successful with the reading public. In addition to the Tarzan and Mars books, Burroughs wrote some lost race stories, such as *The Cave Girl* (1925) and a series of novels about Pellucidar. This was a world within the hollow Earth inhabited by both prehistoric animals and people; it started with

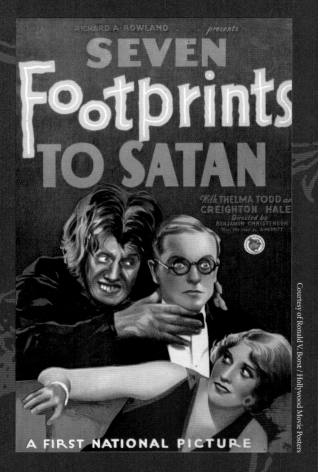

RICHARD A. ROWLAND ... presents

SEVEN
Footprints
TO SATAN

With THELMA TODD and
CREIGHTON HALE
Directed by
BENJAMIN CHRISTENSEN
from the novel by A. MERRITT

A FIRST NATIONAL PICTURE

Courtesy of Ronald V. Borst / Hollywood Movie Posters

14

**SEVEN FOOTPRINTS
TO SATAN**

FIRST NATIONAL PICTURES
1929
ONE-SHEET POSTER

Film version of the
only non-fantasy
A. Merritt novel.

At the Earth's Core (1914) and continued with the cross-over novel *Tarzan at the Earth's Core* (1930). In two other series the author took readers on adventures to Venus and the Moon, and he also produced a slew of fantastic novels with such titles as *The Land That Time Forgot* (1924) and *The Monster Men* (1929).

Throughout his career, one artist would become recognized and associated for life with Burroughs' work—James Allen St. John. St. John produced numerous covers and interior illustrations for the pulps, along with dust jackets for a wide range of hardcover titles for Westerns, science fiction, and romances but, above all, adventure. An accomplished painter, pen-and-ink illustrator, and designer, he was a tremendous influence on future fantasy artists. Burroughs is often thought of as a science fiction and adventure writer, but there is much in the way of fantasy in his work and St. John was able to bring out this aspect in his exquisite paintings and drawings.

Soon after Tarzan made his pulp debut, *The All-Story* published another first story by an author destined to be as important as Burroughs, especially when it came to the all-out fantasy adventure tale. In November 1917 the short fantasy "Through the Dragon Glass" by Abraham—or simply "A."— Merritt appeared.

Merritt was born in 1884 and was something of an adventurer himself before he turned his hand to writing. After dropping out of high school he went hunting for treasure in the Yucatan jungle. In his late teens he started a career as a newspaper reporter in Philadelphia, progressing to night editor before moving to the William Randolph Hearst empire where he earned a very good salary as editor of the well-respected *The American Weekly*. He held the position until his untimely death from a heart attack robbed the fantasy field of one of its finest craftsmen.

Whereas Burroughs completed more than sixty books, Merritt left us with less than a dozen, eight of which were novels. But what a legacy it was. That short story of a journey through a jewel into a fantasy world was just a taste of what was to come.

In 1918 *The All-Story* published *The Moon Pool* and cemented Merritt's reputation as a major talent. Its sequel, *Conquest of the Moon Pool*, was published in six weekly installments in 1919. The "combined" novel was printed in hardcover that same year with an outstanding illustration by Joseph Clement Coll.

The Moon Pool tells of a living energy force that uses a South Seas island pool as a gateway between our world and another, through which several characters are taken. More adventurous romantic fantasy elements were brought to play in *Conquest of the Moon Pool*, including the introduction of Lakla, a beautiful handmaiden to a race of intelligent frog people; the villainous priestess Yolara; and Larry O'Keefe, of the handsome, heroic O'Keefes. It is, amongst other things, another lost race story.

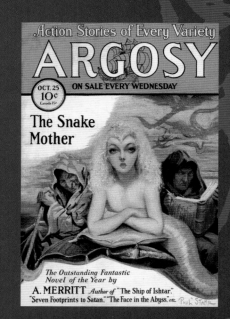

⑮ THE SNAKE MOTHER
A. MERRITT
OCTOBER 25, 1930
PAUL STAHR

One of Merritt's most memorable creations.

⑰ THE SHIP OF ISHTAR
A. MERRITT
NOVEMBER 8, 1924
MODEST STEIN

Something other-worldly is about to happen; you can sense it in this cover.

⑯ THE DWELLERS IN THE MIRAGE
A. MERRITT
JANUARY 23, 1932
ROBERT A. GRAEF

More rousing adventure from Merritt with a beautiful cover by Graef.

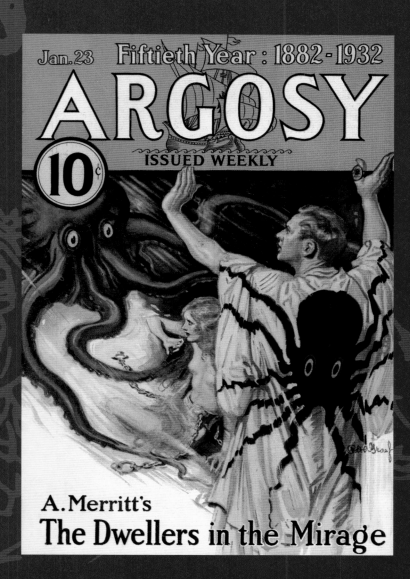

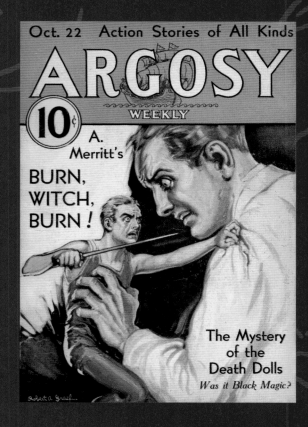

⑱ BURN, WITCH, BURN!
A. MERRITT
OCTOBER 22, 1932
ROBERT A. GRAEF

A fantasy thriller about a witch and her murderous "dolls".

Courtesy of Ronald V. Borst / Hollywood Movie Posters

Although it couldn't justifiably be pigeon-holed as science fiction, Hugo Gernsback reprinted it in his *Amazing Stories* pulp over the course of three issues in 1927, proclaiming it "a classic"—something he did infrequently, but when he did, he was usually spot on.

Considering that Merritt only began to write fiction after he started to work for *The American Weekly*, the craftsmanship and originality in his relatively small body of work is all the more impressive. The handful of short stories he wrote are mini-gems as well, beginning with his first, "Through the Dragon Glass". Among the others are "The People of the Pit", a suspenseful tale of an underground world of strange creatures and their human captives, and "Three Lines of Old French", a beautiful story about a fatigued soldier in World War I and an experiment that succeeds only too well. Merritt received many letters from England from those who had lost sons in the war, praising "Three Lines of Old French" and its life-affirming message.

His next novel, *The Metal Monster*, appeared in installments in *Argosy All-Story Weekly*, starting with the August 7, 1920 issue. Merritt brought back the character of Dr. Walter P. Goodwin from *The Moon Pool* to give some scientific weight to the proceedings. It was an incredible tale featuring a lost race adventure and another of Merritt's striking females: Norhala of the Lightnings, able to summon metallic shapes, (parts of a greater sentient metal city that draws power from the sun), to do her bidding. Merritt wasn't entirely happy with the novel, stating that while it contained some of his best writing, it also revealed some of his worst. Be that as it may, it is some of the best "worst" you'll ever read! And more of his best was yet to come.

⑳

CREEP, SHADOW!
A. MERRITT
SEPTEMBER 8, 1934
ROBERT A. GRAEF

Sequel to *Burn, Witch, Burn!* and even more of a fantasy.

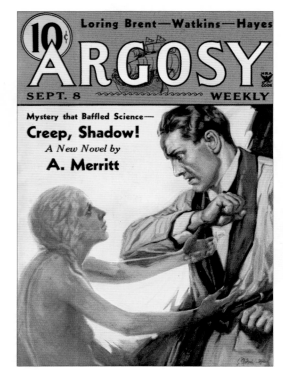

21

CREEP, SHADOW!
A. MERRITT
1934 (AUGUST 1942 REPRINT)
VIRGIL FINLAY

A perfect example of what Finlay brought to Merritt, not to mention stunning interior illustrations.

22

**THE FOX WOMAN/
THE BLUE PAGODA**
A. MERRITT AND HANNES BOK
1946
HANNES BOK

Title page illustration by artist and Merritt fan Hannes Bok who completed the unfinished novel and illustrated it.

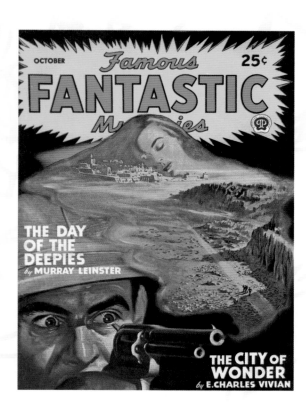

24

THE CITY OF WONDER
E. CHARLES VIVIAN
1922 (OCTOBER 1947 REPRINT)
LAWRENCE STERNE STEVENS

From the smoking barrel of a gun, a great symbolic lost city cover.

23

LAND OF THE SHADOW PEOPLE
CHARLES B. STILSON
JUNE 26, 1920
P. J. MONAHAN

Stilson specialized in lost race adventures.

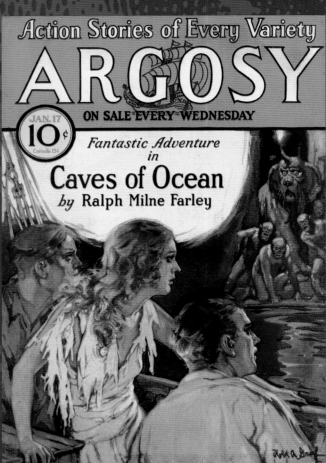

The Face in the Abyss, published in *Argosy All-Story Weekly* in September 1923, may well be the quintessential Merritt novel. It offered a dazzling story and cast: a treasure hunt in the Peruvian mountains uncovers a lost land; a race of immortals, invisible flying serpents, and humanoid spider creatures; the beautiful Suarra; harnessed and ridden dinosaurs; the Snake Mother, (part-woman and part-serpent); and The Face itself, a tremendous bodiless visage on the wall of a giant cavern whose flowing tears are liquid gold. A sequel, *The Snake Mother,* was written but did not see print for several years. A hardcover combining the two revised parts was eventually published in 1931.

Merritt christened *The Ship of Ishtar* over six installments in *Argosy All-Story Weekly* in 1924. In the story, an invalid finds himself restored and transported on deck to fight a pre-ordained battle of Good vs. Evil on a ship which sails upon a timeless sea. Other novels of Merritt (pun most definitely intended) included *Seven Footprints to Satan* (1927), the only non-fantasy he wrote. An entertaining mystery, it was filmed as a comedy by First National Pictures in 1929.

The January 1932 issue of *Argosy* contained *The Dwellers in the Mirage,* a story consisting of not one but several lost races—Nordic, Pygmy, and Mongolian. Also along for the adventure were Lur, the Witch Queen, with her pack of white wolves; Our Hero, Leif Langdon, a possible reincarnation of one of the Nordic race; and the Great Khalk'ru the Kraken, an ancient octopus-like creature from Norse legend, always on cue for a sacrifice. That sacrifice was depicted on a beautiful cover by Robert A. Graef.

Burn, Witch, Burn! followed in 1932, again in six installments. A supernatural thriller, it involved a witch posing as the owner of a doll shop; her living dolls are past victims that she arms with poisoned needles and uses to do her evil bidding. Graef provided another crowd-pleasing cover. The novel was again issued in hardcover and, as with most of Merritt's work, met with very favorable reviews. In fact, it ran through several hardcover printings in England, where Merritt believed he was even more popular. A film version was released by MGM in 1936 under the title *The Devil-Doll,* directed by Tod Browning, who had directed *Dracula* with Bela Lugosi (1931). Although the changes made from book to film caused Merritt to dislike the result, it remains an enjoyable thriller with wonderful performances by Lionel Barrymore and Maureen O'Sulllivan and brilliant miniature effects.

An ironic cinematic sidenote is that in 1961, a film version of fantasy writer Fritz Leiber's novel *Conjure Wife* was filmed in England from a screenplay by genre writers Richard Matheson and Charles Beaumont. The British title was *Night of the Eagle* while the American title became *Burn, Witch, Burn!.*

Another cover by Graef, for the September 1934 issue of *Argosy,* illustrated Merritt's *Creep, Shadow!.* Combining elements of Breton folklore regarding the

29

THE GREATEST ADVENTURE
JOHN TAINE
1929
(REPRINT DATE UNKNOWN)
EMSH

More lost worlds
and dinosaurs!

legend of the ancient city of Ys, along with characters from *Burn, Witch, Burn!,* the author created a sequel of sorts that, in the end, delivered an even more liberal dose of fantasy than the previous book. A hardcover edition appeared soon after, to more excellent notices.

Some of Merritt's novels were reprinted again by *Argosy* in the late 1930s. When the pulp magazine conducted a poll, asking readers to pick the best stories the magazine had ever run, *The Ship of Ishtar* was voted above all the others.

Creep, Shadow! turned out to be Merritt's last fantasy, in part because of his increasing responsibilities at *The American Weekly.* He had reached the height of his popularity and his stories continued to be reprinted. Some of these reprints were accompanied by the work of artist Virgil Finlay. Finlay created masterpieces of color and detail in both cover and interior illustrations.

Merritt had seen some of Finlay's early, meticulous line and stipple work in the pulps and personally offered him a job with *The American Weekly* in 1938. When *Argosy* reprinted *Seven Footprints to Satan* the following year, Merritt championed Finlay as the only artist who could do his work justice. For his part, Finlay would prove up to the task, producing some of his finest work for Merritt's novels.

In 1943 at the age of fifty-nine, A. Merritt, the man who had written of so many fantastic other worlds, left for one himself.

Two uncompleted stories, "The Fox Woman" and "The Black Wheel" were published in limited edition hardcovers in 1946 and 1947 respectively. They were completed and illustrated by Hannes Bok, an imaginative pulp artist, fantasy writer, and Merritt admirer.

Many other authors developed a flair for the lost race story and, though never as popular as Merritt, managed to entertain in pure pulp adventure style.

Robert Ames Bennett wrote *Thyra: A Romance of the Polar Pit* (1901) and *The Bowl of Baal* (1916–17). H. Bedford-Jones, a prolific Canadian-born pulpster, created *The Seal of John Solomon* (1915) among other stories and erected *The Temple of the Ten* with W. C. Robertson in 1921.

The lost race was a specialty of Charles B. Stilson who wrote *Polaris of the Snows* (1915), *Polaris and the Goddess Glorian* (1917), and *Land of the Shadow People* (1920).

British writer E. C. Vivian (a.k.a. Charles Henry Cannell) wrote several adventures during the 1920s including *The City of Wonder* (1922), *Fields of Sleep* (1923), and *People of the Darkness* (1924).

One of the most famous lost race novels was *Lost Horizon* (1933) by British-born author James Hilton. The story of Shangri-La, a lamasery hidden for centuries in the Valley of the Blue Moon, is an exceptional book and was made into an equally exceptional film in 1937, directed by Frank Capra.

**"WONDERFUL AND TRAGIC ALLEGORY ...
AMAZING AND THRILLING."** —H. P. Lovecraft

In Tlapallan, lost city of an ancient race, lay the black stone of evil incarnate. And then a man from the outside world became the agent of its awful power. . . .

Printed in U.S.A.

65-401 95¢

paperback library · Fantasy novel

THE CITADEL OF FEAR
by Francis Stevens
Introduction by Sam Moscowitz

THE CITADEL OF FEAR
FRANCIS STEVENS
1918 (1970 REPRINT)
STEELE SAVAGE

A great Merritt-like fantasy.

THE SECRET PEOPLE
JOHN BEYNON
1935 (APRIL 1950 REPRINT)
LAWRENCE STERNE STEVENS

Lost race novel by science fiction author John Wyndham under the Beynon pseudonym.

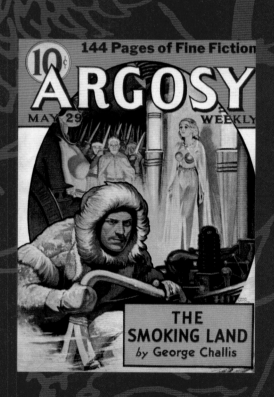

THE SMOKING LAND
GEORGE CHALLIS
MAY 29, 1937
RUDOLPH BELARSKI

Like Max Brand, Challis was another pseudonym of Frederick Faust and, from this cover, it looks like that lost race might soon be found.

During the early decades of the twentieth century there were still many undiscovered regions of the world, so great enjoyment could be gained from these lost lands stories, perhaps by those readers who dreamed of one day discovering such alluring places themselves.

A contemporary of A. Merritt and a writer of similar fantasies was Francis Stevens, the pseudonym of Gertrude Bennett. She wrote only a dozen stories for the pulps before she abruptly stopped writing altogether in 1920. Like Merritt, her stories were highly imaginative and vividly told. Unlike Merritt, her small output is sadly neglected. *The Citadel of Fear* (1918) is probably her best known tale. First published in *Argosy,* the reader accompanies a rugged Irish adventurer who journeys to a lost valley in Mexico's Collados del Demonio (The Hills of the Fiend), and through the Golden City in Tlapallan, land of Quetzalcoatl, where the evil god Nacoc-Yaotl is worshipped.

British-born writer Talbot Mundy (a.k.a. William Lancaster Gribbon), was the creator of *King-of the Khyber Rifles* (1916), which contains an underground world. Mundy wrote several such adventures featuring Athelstan King of the Secret Service. Most of his novels were set in the East and many contain hints of fantasy.

A favorite dweller of hidden valleys were dinosaurs and in *The Greatest Adventure* (1929), writer John Taine had fun discovering some.

Other "lost worlds" were still being discovered well into the 1940s. *Golden Blood* was spilled by Jack Williamson in 1933, John Wyndham (as John Beynon) revealed *The Secret People* (1935), and *Dian of the Lost Land* was found in 1935 by Edison Marshall. Max Brand (a.k.a. Frederick Faust), who earlier discovered *The Garden of Eden* in 1922 now found *The Smoking Land* (1937), which presumably had its own section.

Robert Moore Williams gave *Jongor of Lost Land* (1940) some room to roam and prehistoric monsters to encounter. Jongor liked it and came back for more.

By the 1950s most of the available lost worlds seemed to have been discovered but, in the 1960s, with the revival of Burroughs and others, newer pastiches were affectionately created, recalling the heydays of pulps past.

Newer works include bestselling author Michael Crichton's *Congo* (1980), *The Undying Land* (1985) by William Gilmor, *The Haunted Mesa* (1987) by Louis L'Amour, a series of books about *The Mountain Made of Light* begun in 1992 by Edward Myers, and *Down to Heaven* (1997) by Mark Canter.

The lost world was being discovered all over again, and in 1998 award-winning science fiction writer Greg Bear gave us a delightful *Dinosaur Summer*. Set in 1947, where Sir Arthur Conan Doyles' Professor Challenger and his lost world are historical fact, a young boy and his father experience some close encounters of the prehistoric kind.

Started by Haggard in more innocent times, developed and fine-tuned by Burroughs and Merritt, and seasoned by countless others, the lost race adventure, although not as prevalent as it once was, is not yet extinct. However, like those rugged pulp heroes, running low on water, food gone, clutching an old parchment map won in a poker game from some sailor out of Singapore, with visions of untold treasures awaiting in a long abandoned temple, never mind this Damballah god or whatever his name is…you just have to search a little harder.

㉟
AMAZING STORIES
APRIL 1941
J. ALLEN ST. JOHN

It may have primarily been a science fiction pulp, but borderline fantasies slipped in here and there and St. John helped with a visual push.

WEIRD TALES
MAY 1942
EDMOND GOOD

H. P. Lovecraft was one of the most celebrated writers for *Weird Tales,* but his stories never received a cover illustration except in this Canadian edition of the pulp.

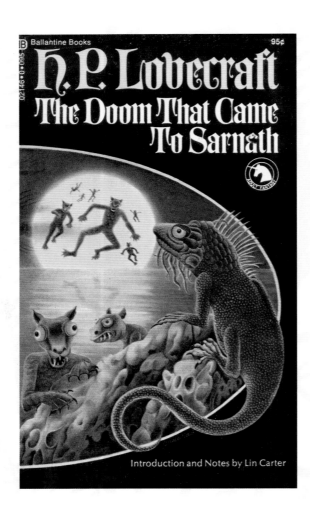

THE DOOM THAT CAME
TO SARNATH
H. P. LOVECRAFT
1971
GERVASIO GALLARDO

Some of those suspicious batrachians cavort on the cover of this collection of Lovecraft stories reprinted for Lin Carter's Adult Fantasy series.

DREAMS AND FANCIES
H. P. LOVECRAFT
1962
RICHARD TAYLOR

Arkham House collection of Lovecraft stories inspired or based on his dreams, which really must have been something.

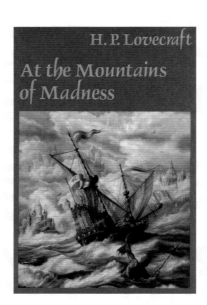

AT THE MOUNTAINS OF MADNESS
H. P. LOVECRAFT
1985
RAYMOND BAYLESS

One of Lovecraft's best tales is part of the newer, improved, definitive text collections from Arkham House, which first put his work into hardcover with the collection *The Outsider and Others* in 1939.

word rates. These included authors whose work would go on to be reprinted in more durable hardcover form, whose stories would see numerous printings to this very day, greatly influence other writers, and even be adapted for films and television.

Edgar Rice Burroughs and A. Merritt had already made names for themselves and were being paid top dollar, but the pulps were about to give birth to some of the finest fantasy practitioners the field would see, and some of their origins were, well, a little weird…

In 1919 *The Thrill Book,* a Street & Smith publication, was the first pulp to specialize in fantastic stories. It ran for only sixteen issues, but it got the ball rolling, publishing an off-the-wall mix of horror, science fiction, and strange adventures.

A new pulp appeared in March 1923 called *Weird Tales.* Its first year was shaky, to say the least, but it survived until it was finally laid to rest in 1954-279 issues later, an incredible record for any publication. There being no rest for the wicked, (or in this case, the weird), it has been revived over the years in various incarnations, one form of which is still published today.

Subtitled "The Unique Magazine", *Weird Tales* showcased some of the finest-ever fantastic fiction in its pulp pages. It had various editors over the years, beginning with Edwin Baird, a writer himself. He was assisted by Farnsworth Wright, who was, in fact, more knowledgeable when it came to this type of material.

The first of many writers to find a home in its pages and go on to a permanent position in the history books was Howard Phillips Lovecraft. Although a few of his early stories had been published elsewhere, most of Lovecraft's output was printed in the

WEIRD TALES
APRIL 1938
VIRGIL FINLAY

A nice cover by Finlay
that pefectly complements
Smith's tale of Zothique.

WEIRD TALES
JANUARY 1932
C. C. SENF

A wonderfully weird cover
and a first one for Clark
Ashton Smith.

WEIRD TALES
SEPTEMBER 1947
BORIS DOLGOV

Clark Ashton Smith excelled at exotic,
otherworldly fantasies and received
several fine cover interpretations of
his work in *Weird Tales*.

pages of *Weird Tales*. Today, the author is best remembered for his stories of cosmic horror centering on a mythology of The Great Old Ones, rulers of Earth aeons ago, now lurking at the threshold of our world, biding their time, waiting for the stars to properly align so they can return and enslave the human race. This so-called Cthulhu Mythos, named after one of its chief gods, was a unique concept that would be added to by other writers, with the cautious encouragement of H. P. L.

Although he is often considered to be a horror writer and justly regarded as the greatest writer of supernatural fiction since Edgar Allan Poe, Lovecraft also wrote a good deal of Lord Dunsany-influenced fantasy. In the late teens and early 1920s, many dream-like stories flowed from his pen. "The Doom That Came to Sarnath" (1919), "The Cats of Ulthar" (1920), and "Celephais" (1920) are just a few. Most of the early stories were published in small, limited editions from private presses. *Weird Tales* published some, including "The Strange High House in the Mist" (1926), "The White Ship" (1919), "The Statement of Randolph Carter" (1919), "The Silver Key" (1926), and "Through the Gates of the Silver Key" (1932), the latter co-written with E. Hoffmann Price. Price was another regular contributor to the magazine who also wrote hundreds of stories for the pulps and was still creating fantasy adventures as late as the 1980s.

Lovecraft's major Dunsanian fantasy, "The Dream-Quest of Unknown Kadath" (1943), in which the lead character journeys through the Gates of Deeper Slumber into the Land of Dreams itself, was not published until years after the author's death. Dunsany's own *The Gods of Pegána* (1905) was an obvious influence on H. P. L.'s pantheon of elder

gods that included Nyarlathotep (The Crawling Chaos) and Shub-Niggurath (The Black Goat of the Woods with a Thousand Young) among its colorful members.

Even in Lovecraft's horror stories there is much fantasy, whether conjured up from the *Necronomicon*—an ancient tome of eldritch magic written by that "mad Arab Abdul Alhazred"—or in the waters off the coastal town of Innsmouth, whose inbred citizens seem to have something "fishy" about them (and with good reason).

One of the few Lovecraft stories that had the misfortune of being rejected by *Weird Tales* is actually one of his best fantasies. "At the Mountains of Madness", considered to be too long by Farnsworth Wright (who took over editorship of the magazine from Edwin Baird) was eventually published in *Astounding Stories* in 1936. The story is about an expedition to the Antarctic and the discovery of colossal structures once inhabited by the Ancient Ones.

In 1939, two years after Lovecraft's premature death at the age of forty-six, friends and fellow writers Donald Wandrei and August Derleth founded

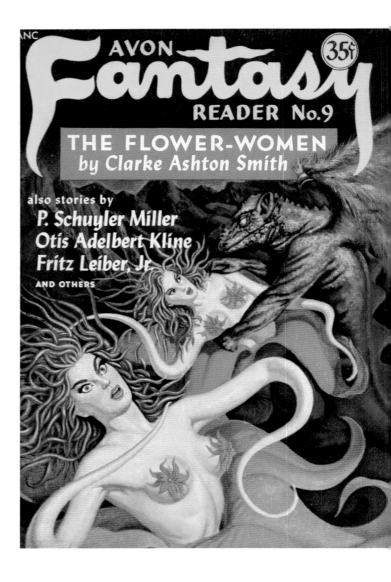

the publishing imprint Arkham House, named after Lovecraft's most famous fictional locale and based on his own home town of Providence, Rhode Island. *The Outsider and Others*, a collection of Lovecraft's stories, was the first of many hardcover volumes from the publisher that presented the works of major fantasy and horror authors. Arkham House is still publishing today and continues to keep Lovecraft's work in print, as well as giving many new talents their first book publication.

Lovecraft was an avid letter writer and kept up voluminous correspondence with many other authors of the period. Some of those within this circle were also contributors to *Weird Tales*.

No one wrote of strange, otherworldly vistas quite as exquisitely as Clark Ashton Smith. Lovecraft encouraged him to submit work to *Weird Tales*, and Smith's poetry was published in "The Unique Magazine" from 1923 onward. An artist as well as a poet, he was born near and lived most of his life in Auburn, California. Smith's verse had already been published in several volumes, including *The Star-Treader* (1912), *Odes and Sonnets* (1918), and *Ebony and Crystal* (1922) before he made his debut in *Weird Tales*.

The September 1928 issue of the magazine featured a short story by Smith called "The Ninth Skeleton", which marked the beginning of a brilliant storytelling career. In just a few years he was appearing on a regular basis in the magazine. During the 1930s he had over fifty stories published in *Weird Tales* alone. "The End of the Story", in the May 1930 issue, marked the start of a prolific period of writing in which he developed several different story cycles, each displaying his imaginative use of language and poetic descriptive passages. Smith turned his atten-

LOS MUNDOS PERDIDOS

... Y una selección de los mejores relatos de

CLARK ASHTON SMITH

11.

LOS MUNDOS PERDIDOS
CLARK ASHTON SMITH
1991
FRANK FRAZETTA

Inspired casting for the cover of a Spanish edition of Clark Ashton Smith stories.

12.

SKULL-FACE AND OTHERS
ROBERT E. HOWARD
1946
HANNES BOK

Ten years after his death, some of Howard's best stories were published in hardcover by Arkham House, with a beautiful (although not exactly Howard) cover by Hannes Bok.

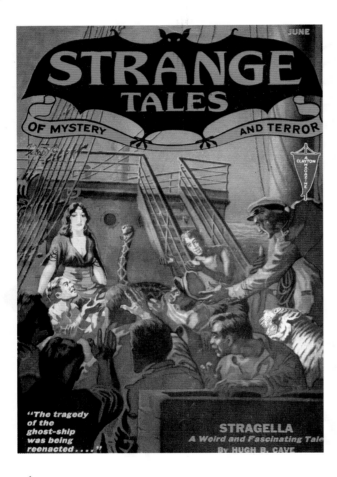

STRANGE TALES

JUNE 1932

H. W. WESSO

This issue of the short-lived pulp magazine published a racial memory story by Robert E. Howard with a character called "Conan of the Reavers". The Conan we know made his first bow soon afterwards in the pages of *Weird Tales*.

WEIRD TALES

DECEMBER 1932

J. ALLEN ST. JOHN

Conan's adventures begin in this issue with "The Phoenix on the Sword" and St. John paints a stunning cover for Otis Adelbert Kline's "Buccaneers of Venus".

tion from poetry to the short story form with brilliant results.

Many of his stories were set in fantastic locales. There were tales of Hyperborea, a lost polar continent; Poseidonis, an Atlantean isle; Averoigne, a mythical province in mediaeval France; and Zothique, an imaginary continent of future Earth where science slumbered and sorcerers' magic was awake, with dark gods summoned by the incantations of magicians and necromancers.

The titles of some of these stories alone conjured visions that the text delivered: "The Uncharted Isle", where a shipwrecked survivor encounters a strange race worshipping an even stranger "living" god; "The Testament of Athammaus", a story of Hyperborea, where an inhuman criminal has a most peculiar way of surviving repeat encounters with the headsman's blade, proving in the end, just how inhuman he really is; "The Weird of Avoosl Wuthoqquan" sounds quite Dunsanian; it is a tale in which a fat, greedy, money-lender is parted from his riches with a little help from a loathsome creature that is anything but money-hungry; and then there was "The Tale of Satampra Zeiros", the adventurous thief of Uzuldaroum who loses both his right-hand man and his right hand while attempting to steal a treasure from a temple of the dark god Tsathoggua.

Smith wrote science fiction in addition to his verse and fantasy pieces, and he appeared in many other pulps, although over half of his output was published in *Weird Tales*. His vivid imagination extented into illustration, painting, and sculpture, creatively interpreting some of the strange and wonderful beings in his own and H. P. Lovecraft's stories. Like Lovecraft, he influenced many other writers, and his verse and tales of magical worlds were collected in

several hardcover volumes from Arkham House, now long out of print. By the late 1930s he was writing less and less and he died in 1961, long after the flow of fiction had all but ceased.

Unlike Lovecraft, only a small portion of Clark Ashton Smith's work is readily available to the reading public today. This will hopefully be remedied soon, as it is a great loss to those who wish to read fantasy by one of the maestros of the genre.

Weird Tales, after a few initial problems, seemed to be hitting its stride. The early cover art was somewhat crude, but it gradually improved as different artists were called upon to display their talents.

Another writer began to appear in *Weird Tales* during the 1920s who, along with Lovecraft and Smith, formed such a creative backbone to the pulp that it is no small wonder it has achieved the legendary status it holds today. His name was Robert E. (Ervin) Howard.

His first story, submitted at the age of fifteen, was rejected by the pulp magazine *Adventure*. It was three years before he tried again, this time with a story of prehistoric man called "Spear and Fang". It was accepted by *Weird Tales* and appeared in the July 1925 issue. At half a cent per word, Howard became a published writer for the pulps.

WEIRD TALES
MAY 1934
MARGARET BRUNDAGE

Reader response to Conan was overwhelming and Howard obliged by giving them more of his exploits, with covers by Margaret Brundage, the First Lady of pulp art.

His early stories for the magazine, while entertaining, were more in the horror vein. With a story called "Red Shadows" in the August 1928 issue however, Howard began writing the type of material for which he would become famous.

Solomon Kane, a sixteenth century English puritan and unstoppable righter of wrongs, was the protaganist and the first of several memorable series characters Howard created. "Red Shadows", an adventure story with supernatural moments set in the African jungle, proved to be very popular with readers, so Howard brought back his brooding hero for other encounters with evil-doers, expanding the fantastic elements as the series developed. Tall, somber, dressed in black, and dealing out justice with his rapier, Solomon Kane swashbuckled his way through six more issues of *Weird Tales*, encountering cannibals, sorcery, and a race of winged demons.

Howard seemed at home with this type of fiction and soon other larger-than-life creations of his found a home in the pages of *Weird Tales*. In the August 1929 issue, one year after Solomon Kane first graced its pages, a new Howard character made his debut.

Kull of Atlantis, an exiled savage who seized the throne of the Kingdom of Valusia, battled the evil forces of "The Shadow Kingdom"—the title of this first adventure. It is a novelette of swords and sorcery, in which the barbarian-turned-king finds himself involved in the treacheries of an ancient shape-shifting race of serpent people. Kull returned the following month, gazing a little too deeply into "The Mirrors of Tuzun Thune", a wizard of an elder race who offers the ruler glimpses into other worlds but at a deadly price.

Howard then shifted gears to produce a three-part serial for *Weird Tales* in the then-popular Oriental Menace vein. "Skull-Face" (1929) was a sorcerer of Atlantis returned from the dead and, in the best Fu-Manchu tradition, thirsty for the blood of the white race. *Skull-Face and Others* was used as the title for the first hardcover collection of Howard's fantasy writing, published by Arkham House in 1946.

Kull was back in the November 1930 issue, as one of the "Kings of the Night", along with Bran Mak Morn, King of the Picts—yet another heroic figure from Howard's fertile imagination. Like Kull and Kane, Bran also returned, and in November 1932 he summoned up "Worms of the Earth" to help fight the Roman legions, although his "help" turned out to be a lot more than he bargained for in this effective horror/fantasy novella.

Howard had already built up a stable of strong characters whose stories were very popular with the readers of *Weird Tales*. With the December 1932 issue he played the final card of his career, never realizing just how celebrated and enduring his latest creation would become.

The title of the story was "The Phoenix on the Sword" and its hero was Conan, a Cimmerian barbarian who lived during the Hyborian Age, a fictional historical period after the fall of Atlantis, documented by Howard in an essay called, simply, "The Hyborian Age" (1936-38). Conan's adventures—and there were seventeen of them published in *Weird Tales*, although not in any chronological sequence—took him from a young thief of around seventeen years of age in "The Tower of the Elephant" (1933) to the older, battle-scarred warrior who takes his kingdom by force in "Phoenix". Kull was apparently a forerunner of Conan as "The Phoenix on the Sword" was actually a re-write of an unsold Kull tale.

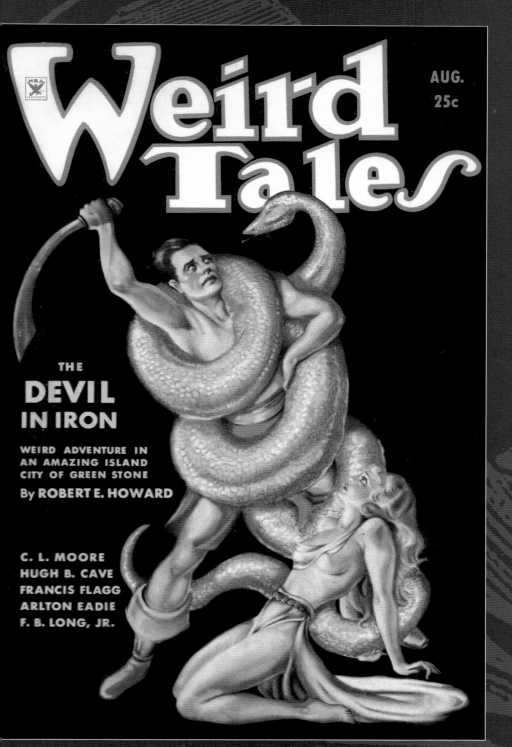

17

WEIRD TALES
NOVEMBER 1935
MARGARET BRUNDAGE

Naked, surrounded by cobras, her hair staying perfectly in place (or places). More Howard and Brundage.

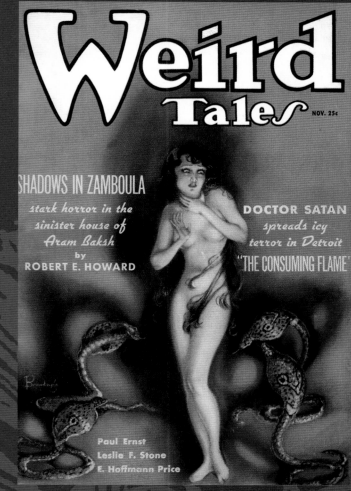

16

WEIRD TALES
AUGUST 1934
MARGARET BRUNDAGE

One of the more action-packed of the Brundage Conan covers, although I don't know about that snake's head.

18

AVON FANTASY READER
NO. 10
1949
ARTIST UNKNOWN

Another cover treatment of Conan, this time for Donald A. Wollheim's pulp reprint digest.

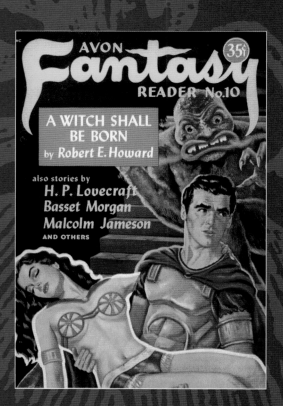

英雄コナン・シリーズ

狂戦士コナン

ロバート・E・ハワード —— 鏡 明訳

19.

CONAN THE BARBARIAN
ROBERT E. HOWARD
1954 (1971 REPRINT)
ICHIRO MOTO

Conan pulls the old "bite the vulture in the neck" routine, a famous Howard scene from "A Witch Shall be Born", on the cover of this Japanese reprint of the Gnome Press book.

20.

CONAN THE CONQUEROR
ROBERT E. HOWARD
1950 (1953 REPRINT)
NORMAN SAUNDERS

One half of an Ace Double Novel paperback, this was a reprint of the novel *The Hour of the Dragon* that Gnome Press retitled for its 1950 hard-cover publication.

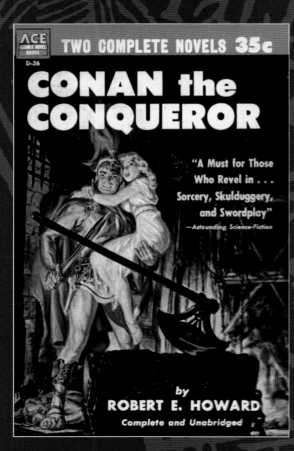

ACE DOUBLE NOVEL BOOKS
D-36

TWO COMPLETE NOVELS 35c

CONAN the CONQUEROR

"A Must for Those Who Revel in . . . Sorcery, Skulduggery, and Swordplay"
—*Astounding Science-Fiction*

by
ROBERT E. HOWARD
Complete and Unabridged

Weird Tales

THE HOUR OF THE DRAGON

a vivid weird story of a thousand eery thrills

by ROBERT E. HOWARD

DEC. 25c

Paul Ernst • Clark Ashton Smith
Edmond Hamilton • Harold Ward

21.

WEIRD TALES
DECEMBER 1935
MARGARET BRUNDAGE

The first installment of Howard's only Conan novel. If you think he looks a little pathetic here, just wait.

THE COMING OF CONAN
ROBERT E. HOWARD
1953
FRANK KELLY FREAS

One of the Gnome Press hardcover editions of Conan stories with a cover by acclaimed science fiction and fantasy artist Kelly Freas.

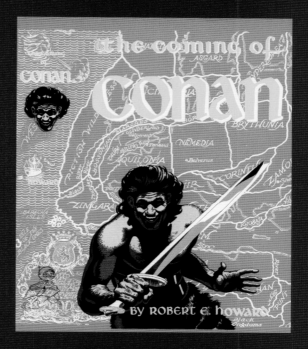

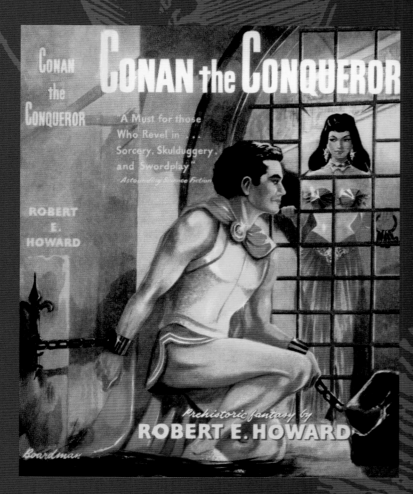

CONAN THE CONQUEROR
ROBERT E. HOWARD
1950 (1954 REPRINT)
ARTIST UNKNOWN

Look familiar? It's the same scene that Brundage portrayed, this time for a British hardcover reprint. Here Conan is an immaculately coiffed barbarian and—Crom's Devils! —where did he get those shoes?!

TALES OF CONAN
ROBERT E. HOWARD AND L. SPRAGUE DE CAMP
1955
EMSH

Another volume in the Gnome Press Conan series, edited and with collaborations by L. Sprague de Camp, with a cover by another respected science fiction and fantasy artist Ed Emshwiller.

Reader response to Conan in the pulp's letters column, "The Eyrie", confirmed that *Weird Tales* had a
hit on its hands.

In the January 1933 issue, Conan faced imprison-
ment, wizardry, and a monstrous serpent, along
with other inhabitants of "The Scarlet Citadel". With
the June issue the same year, the Conan story "Black
Colossus" received a cover illustration.

In the 1920s, cover art for *Weird Tales* was a mixed
bag. Between 1927 and 1932, Curtis C. Senf produced more than forty paintings for the magazine,
including one for Howard's "Red Shadows". A major
feature in most cases, and a selling point not lost on
Farnsworth Wright, was the inclusion of a nude or
nearly nude woman, preferably in distress.

Hugh Rankin, another cover artist, did more sim-
plified but colorfully stylish work, with again a good
emphasis on the female form. Both illustrators contributed interior work as well. By 1932, J. Allen St.
John, already known for his Burroughs illustration
work, joined the roster of regular cover artists, producing nine paintings, several of them considered to
be among the finest of his career. He also redesigned
the title logo, which has remained its recognizable
look ever since.

The cover illustration for "Black Colossus" was by a
relative newcomer to the magazine. Margaret
Brundage, a young fashion illustrator, had done two
popular covers in 1932, both featuring her trade-
mark: beautiful, near-nude women. She had also
supplied covers for *Oriental Stories* and *Magic
Carpet Magazine,* two short-lived companions to
Weird Tales. She created her pictures using pastel
chalks and, because of this, they were very delicate.
The magazine was impressed and so was Howard,
who wrote to say that her art for "Black Colossus"

was a favorite of his cover pieces. It would also be the first of thirty-nine consecutive covers she did for the magazine, nine of them for Conan stories.

The Conan stories were proving to be among the most popular published by *Weird Tales*. Fellow writers H. P. Lovecraft and Clark Ashton Smith praised the small-town Texan's writing. During 1935, Howard's stories in various genres appeared in several different pulps. He was seemingly at the top of his game.

Meanwhile, Conan the barbarian fought his way to a throne, along a dangerous route paved with wizards, demons, beautiful women, and reptilian monsters. Howard introduced him to "Rogues in the House" (1934) with its ape-creature in priest's clothing, "The People of the Black Circle" (1934) and their evil sorceries, and put him through the mill in "A Witch Shall be Born" (1934),—in this story an inquisitive vulture receives its come-uppance when a crucified Conan breaks the bird's neck with his bare teeth! The only Conan novel, *The Hour of the Dragon*, was a rousing piece, containing elements from other Conan stories, which appeared in five parts in *Weird Tales* from December 1935 to April 1936. It looked like there was no stopping Howard. But something did…

He was very close to his mother, Hester. Her health had been failing for quite some time and medical bills were taking their toll on the family's finances. On June 11th, 1936 he learned that she had slipped into a terminal coma. Howard had lived for his mother and on that day, after leaving her bedside, he died for her by putting a bullet in his head. He was just thirty years old. She died the following day.

However, despite the tragic death of his creator, Conan would return.

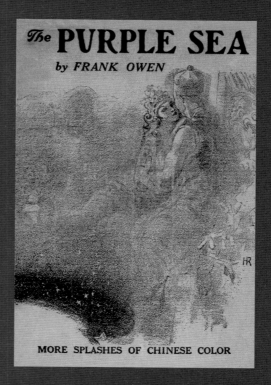

27

THE PURPLE SEA
FRANK OWEN
1930
HUGH RANKIN

Hardcover collection of Owen's Chinese fantasies, published by The Lantern Press.

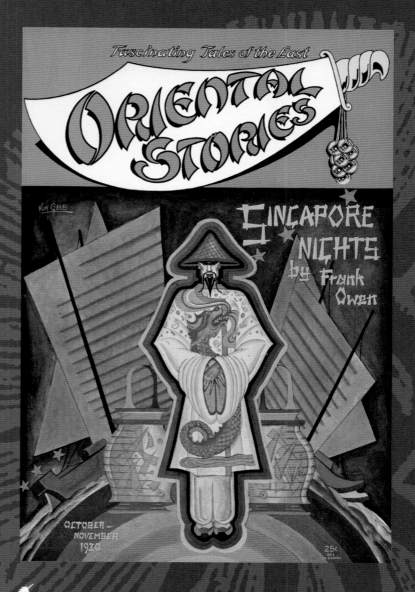

28

ORIENTAL STORIES
OCTOBER–NOVEMBER 1930
DONALD VON GELB

The first issue, from the people who brought you *Weird Tales,* with a stylish cover for Owen's "Singapore Nights".

THE
BLACK GOD'S KISS
the weirdest story
ever told
By C. L. MOORE
also
H. BEDFORD-JONES
and others

WEIRD TALES
OCTOBER 1934
MARGARET BRUNDAGE

A striking Brundage interpretation of
C. L. Moore's female warrior, Jirel of Joiry.

FEB.—25¢

THE SAPPHIRE GODDESS
By NICTZIN DYALHIS

ANTHONY M. RUD
EDMOND HAMILTON
WILLIAM H. POPE
DAVID H. KELLER
E. HOFFMANN PRICE

WEIRD TALES
FEBRUARY 1934
MARGARET BRUNDAGE

Sword and sorcery the Brundage
way for the cover story by the
appropriately exotically named
fantasy writer Nictzin Dyalhis.

WEIRD TALES
APRIL 1933
J. ALLEN ST. JOHN

A rousing adventure fantasy
from Jack Williamson and a
golden moment in St. John's
pulp cover painting career.

EDMOND HAMILTON • E. HOFFMANN PRICE • CLARK ASHTON SMITH

APRIL 25¢

Weird Tales

GOLDEN BLOOD
by Jack Williamson

Some unpublished manuscripts originally rejected by *Weird Tales* were revised and printed. During the 1950s Gnome Press published seven hardcover volumes of Conan stories, several of them edited by and featuring posthumous collaborations with fantasy writer L. Sprague de Camp. In 1953 Ace Books published Howard's Conan novel now retitled *Conan the Conqueror,* as one half of an Ace Double paperback. Conan kicked off the revival in heroic fantasy literature in 1966 with a series of paperbacks edited by de Camp that eventually included new adventures written by a number of fantasy writers. Pastiche novels, comic books, movies and television series followed, making Conan one of the best known fantasy fiction characters ever.

In his short life, Robert E. Howard created the sword and sorcery subgenre as we know it today, and he did so through his seemingly simple gift of passionate storytelling. His death was a shock to his fellow writers and readers and Lovecraft wrote of the injustice of it. But within a year he too would be gone.

Lovecraft, Smith, and Howard were the celebrated Three Musketeers of *Weird Tales,* but they weren't the only ones contributing popular fantasies to the pulp magazine. Otis Adelbert Kline appeared in the first of several early issues in the March 1923 *Weird Tales.* His serial, "Tam, Son of the Tiger", was an adventure fantasy in the Edgar Rice Burroughs tradition which ran over six issues in 1931. Another six-part serial, "Buccaneers of Venus", was published the following year and received some beautiful cover treatments by J. Allen St. John.

The pulp's earliest and most popular writer was Seabury Quinn; however, his stories were more in the weird horror vein, with his series character Jules de Grandin fighting the forces of evil.

Frank Owen was another popular fantasist, making his debut in the October 1923 issue with "The Man Who Owned the World". He went on to make nearly forty appearances in the magazine up until the early 1950s. Owen wrote colorful Oriental fantasies in imaginary China-like settings. Some of them were collected in the evocatively-titled *The Wind That Tramps the World* (1929) and *The Purple Sea* (1930). Several novels were also published during the 1930s, while some of his other *Weird Tales* stories included "The Dream Peddler" (1927), "The Tinkle of the Camel's Bell" (1928), "For Tomorrow We Die" (1942), "The Man Who Amazed Fish" (1943), and "The Gentleman with the Scarlet Umbrella" (1951) —the last three featuring the venerable Doctor Shen Fu, a Chinese alchemist.

Manly Wade Wellman made his first appearance in *Weird Tales* in 1927. He was a frequent contributor of supernatural fantasies to the pulp magazine, including a series about occult investigator Judge Pursuivant written under the byline of Gans T. Field. A prolific writer and a wonderful storyteller, his stories of John the Balladeer, or Silver John (a wandering minstrel who fights the forces of evil armed with his silver-stringed guitar), are a major contribution to the fantasy field. Several stories were collected as *Who Fears the Devil* (1963) from Arkham House. Other related novels followed in the 1980s.

The unlikely sounding but genuinely named Nictzin Dyalhis sold only eight stories to *Weird Tales,* but he made his mark nonetheless. His work was mainly in the romantic fantasy vein, often involving elements of reincarnation and the transmigration of souls, as in the case of "The Sapphire Goddess" (1934), "The Sea-Witch" (1937), and "Heart of Atlantan" (1940).

A. Merritt's only *Weird Tales* entry was extremely

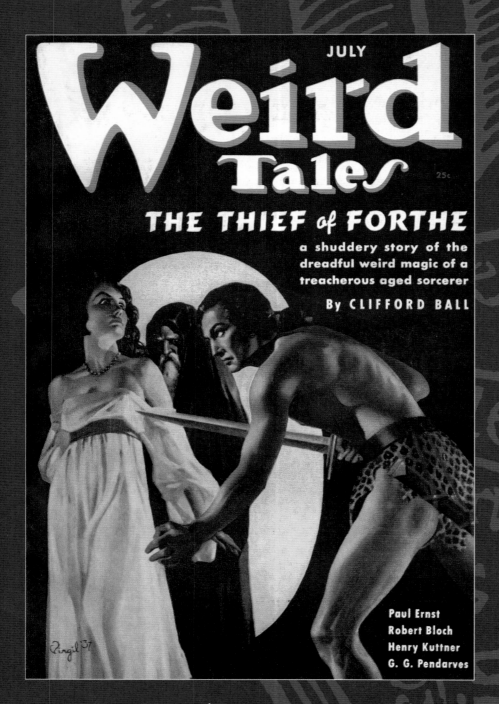

JULY

Weird Tales

25c

THE THIEF of FORTHE

a shuddery story of the
dreadful weird magic of a
treacherous aged sorcerer

By CLIFFORD BALL

Paul Ernst
Robert Bloch
Henry Kuttner
G. G. Pendarves

WEIRD TALES
JULY 1937
VIRGIL FINLAY

Clifford Ball's "The Thief
of Forthe" was one of many
attempts by writers to fill
the gap left by Robert E.
Howard's death, and Virgil
Finlay produced a cover
worthy of a Conan!

A. Merritt's only *Weird Tales* entry was extremely popular; the August 1926 issue featured "The Woman of the Wood", a story originally rejected by *Argosy* which Farnsworth Wright was only too happy to publish. A testament to Merritt's talent, it was one of the top stories ever to appear in the history of the magazine and was quickly reprinted in the January 1934 edition.

Celebrated science fiction writer Jack Williamson showed Merritt's influence in his early fantasy *Golden Blood*. It was serialized over six issues in 1933 and the first installment, in April, featured one of the best ever covers on a pulp, again courtesy of J. Allen St. John.

Contributing over a dozen stories in the 1930s, Catherine Lucille Moore, a young authoress, created two memorable series characters. Her first story, "Shambleau" (1933), a science fiction fantasy, had as its hero Northwest Smith, interplanetary adventurer. While on Mars he saves a girl from an angry mob, only to fall under the deadly spell of the "creature" herself—a sort of science fantasy version of the Medusa legend. Luckily he is saved before meeting his end beneath the Shambleau's living tresses. Northwest Smith would return, but in October 1934 Moore introduced a heroine from mediaeval France in the first of several historical fantasies. "The Black God's Kiss" was the story and Jirel of Joiry was the female fighter. Margaret Brundage provided the cover, depicting the Black God on the receiving end of that kiss.

Jirel was back in "Black God's Shadow" (1934), a sequel. Both the Northwest Smith and the Jirel stories were subsequently given hardcover publication and have been extensively reprinted over the years. Moore married Henry Kuttner, another *Weird Tales*

16th Year of Publication

Weird Tales

25c · OCT.

BEYOND THE PHOENIX

a tale of sorcery and thrilling action
By HENRY KUTTNER

WEIRD TALES
OCTOBER 1938
MARGARET BRUNDAGE

More adventures of Elak,
with a very nice heroic cover
by Brundage.

Weird Tales

16th Year of Publication

JULY

25c

SPAWN OF DAGON

By HENRY KUTTNER

Robert Bloch • **Seabury Quinn** • **Edmond Hamilton** • **David H. Keller**

WEIRD TALES
JULY 1938
VIRGIL FINLAY

More swords and sorcery
and another fine Finlay
cover for Henry Kuttner's
Elak of Atlantis story
"Spawn of Dagon".

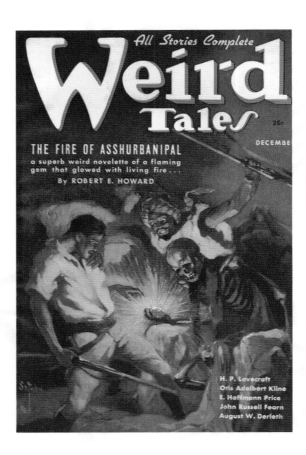

WEIRD TALES
DECEMBER 1936
J. ALLEN ST. JOHN

The late Robert E. Howard gets a St. John cover treatment, and one can only imagine how Conan might have looked in the hands of this brilliant artist.

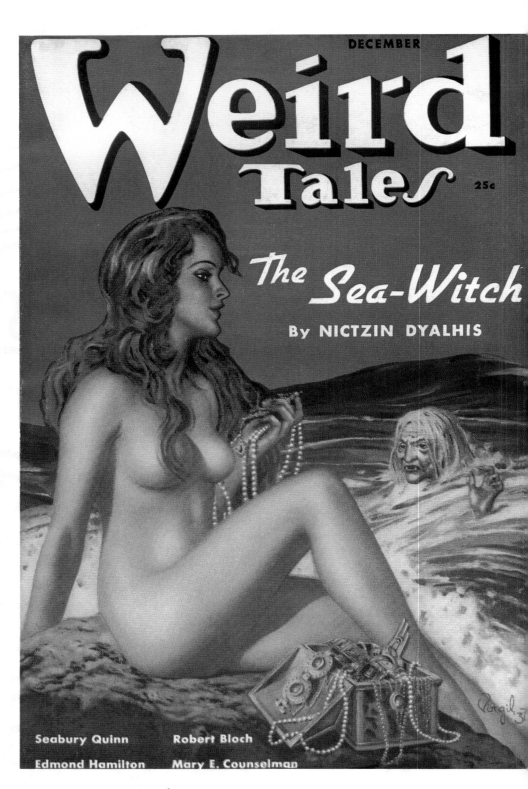

WEIRD TALES
DECEMBER 1937
VIRGIL FINLAY

Finlay beats Brundage at her own game with this cover for "The Sea-Witch".

writer, in 1940 and the two collaborated on much of their later work.

In 1938, Kuttner himself began a series of pulp stories about Elak of Atlantis, his version of a Conan-type character. Elak faced monsters and sorcery as best he could, in true pulp fashion, with a tip of his sword to Robert E. Howard.

Howard himself received posthumous publication with "The Fire of Asshurbanipal" in the December 1936 *Weird Tales,* accompanied by a great J. Allen St. John cover. One can only wish that St. John had done a Conan cover as he would have been ideal. In 1939, *Almuric,* a novel completed just before Howard's death, was serialized over three issues. More in the science fiction fantasy vein of Edgar Rice Burroughs, it was not as polished as most of the author's other work.

In the mid-1930s, a new artist started contributing beautifully detailed artwork to *Weird Tales.* Readers loved him and demanded more. H. P. Lovecraft even wrote a sonnet about one of his illustrations. The artist's name was Virgil Finlay, and by the late 1930s he was providing most of the interiors for "The Unique Magazine". He went on to do a tremendous amount of work for the pulps, in his meticulous stipple ink style that took days to execute – a staggering feat indeed, considering that he was paid between $5.00 and $8.00 per drawing.

Finlay was the king of the pulp artists when it came to black and white interiors, both in quality and quantity. It was only a matter of time before he took on cover assignments, and he made that transition in February 1937. Soon he was providing *Weird Tales* with more covers and nudes, *à là* Margaret Brundage.

In November 1938 *Weird Tales* had a new publisher and nudes on the cover became, well, old nudes.

WEIRD TALES
JULY 1939
VIRGIL FINLAY

A nice weird fantasy cover by Finlay, who produced beautiful work both inside and out for the pulps.

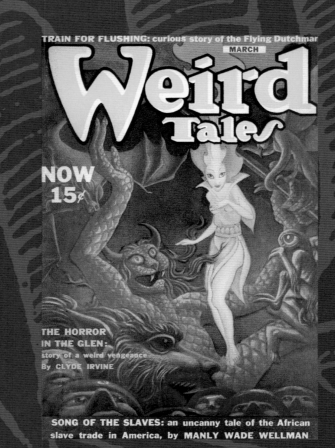

TRAIN FOR FLUSHING: curious story of the Flying Dutchman
MARCH

Weird Tales

NOW 15¢

THE HORROR
IN THE GLEN:
story of a weird vengeance
By CLYDE IRVINE

SONG OF THE SLAVES: an uncanny tale of the African
slave trade in America, by MANLY WADE WELLMAN

38.

WEIRD TALES
MARCH 1940
HANNES BOK

Another talented artist
doing stylish work in
the pulps, this was one
of Bok's more fanciful
covers for the magazine.

39.

WEIRD TALES
NOVEMBER 1946
BORIS DOLGOV

A first cover by artist
Dolgov. Dolgov and
Bok worked in somewhat
similar styles and collaborated on occasion.

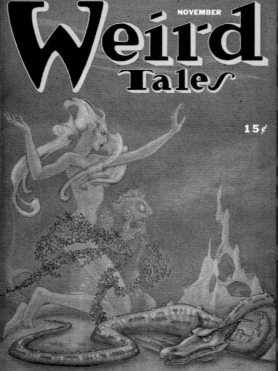

AUGUST DERLETH   ROBERT BLOCH
NOVEMBER

Weird Tales

15¢

"SPAWN OF THE GREEN ABYSS" by C. HALL THOMPSON

Brundage covers soon stopped (although she would later return) and Finlay took on more assignments, along with other new artists. One of those was Hannes Bok, who was destined to become another celebrated fantasy artist with his brightly colored cover paintings and stylish black and white interiors.

Finlay went to work for A. Merritt at *The American Weekly* and Bok moved into his place for a few years, producing lighter, fantasy-styled illustrations for the pulp.

Young science fiction and fantasy writer Ray Bradbury, who had his early horror/fantasy stories published in *Weird Tales,* championed Bok to editor Farnsworth Wright. Bok was heavily influenced by Maxfield Parrish in technique and compositional elements; combined with his own unique style, it made for some inspired illustrations.

A later cover and interior artist well-suited for fantasy work was Boris Dolgov. A friend of Bok's, Dolgov worked in a similar style and the two even collaborated, signing their work "Dolbokgov".

In 1940 *Weird Tales* had a new editor, Dorothy McIlwraith. Her first issue, in May, had a cover by Bok illustrating "The City from the Sea", a Merritt-styled lost race fantasy by Edmond Hamilton. Hamilton was a great pulp science fiction writer who dipped his pen into fantasy now and then.

The last of Henry Kuttner's Elak stories, "Dragon Moon", started the January 1941 issue off on the right track, with a wonderful cover by Harold De Lay, a contributor since the late 1930s, but it would mark a swan song for the sword and sorcery story in *Weird Tales.*

In 1942, horror writer Robert Bloch, later famous—or infamous—for *Psycho* (1959), wrote "Nursemaid to Nightmares", a humorous fantasy revolving around a keeper of various mythological

WEIRD TALES
MAY 1940
HANNES BOK

Another fine Bok cover for Edmond
Hamilton's lost race fantasy.

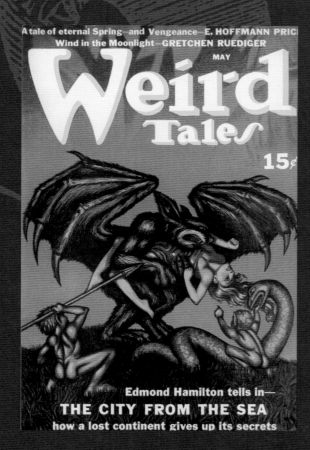

A tale of eternal Spring—and Vengeance—E. HOFFMANN PRICE

Wind in the Moonlight—GRETCHEN RUEDIGER

MAY

Weird Tales

15¢

Edmond Hamilton tells in—
THE CITY FROM THE SEA
how a lost continent gives up its secrets

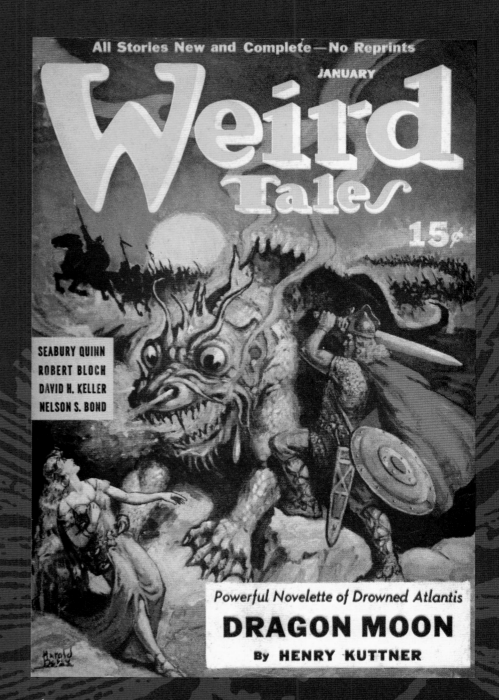

All Stories New and Complete—No Reprints

JANUARY

Weird Tales

15¢

SEABURY QUINN
ROBERT BLOCH
DAVID H. KELLER
NELSON S. BOND

Powerful Novelette of Drowned Atlantis
DRAGON MOON
By HENRY KUTTNER

WEIRD TALES
JANUARY 1941
HAROLD S. DE LAY

Heroic fantasy *Weird Tales*-style,
with a wonderful dragon cover
for Kuttner's final Elak story.

creatures. Bloch had a long run of horror stories
published in *Weird Tales* in the 1930s and 1940s but
now more humor was creeping into his writing.

Fritz Leiber, Jr. had more than half a dozen weird
stories published in the pulp from 1940 to 1950, but
he had been submitting heroic fantasy material to
them, unsuccessfully, since the late 1930s.

Weird Tales kept chugging along until 1954, publishing fewer and fewer diamonds amongst the
lumps of coal. In 1939 a new magazine specializing
in fantasy came along, paying good rates and only
too happy to take those rejected stories off Fritz
Leiber's hands. Indicative of the type of fiction it
would publish, this magazine didn't take itself
too seriously.

With the death of Robert E. Howard there were sporadic attempts by other writers to fill the gaps left by Conan and Co., but it didn't look as if anyone was going to take the tragic Texan's place. Farnsworth Wright told *Weird Tales* readers in no uncertain terms how he felt concerning their requests for other writers to continue with new Conan tales—a very polite "no way". The field could have used someone like Wright in the aftermath of the 1960s sword and sorcery revival. Then in 1939, fantasy was given a fresh coat of paint with a healthy dollop of humor added to the mix. John W. Campbell Jr., editor of *Astounding Science-Fiction*—a science fiction pulp —was publishing some of the

CHAPTER 4

COMPLETE ENCHANTERS

2

UNKNOWN
MAY 1939
H. W. SCOTT

L. Ron Hubbard, L. Sprague de Camp, and Robert Bloch all excelled at *Unknown*'s brand of fiction.

STREET & SMITH'S

UNKNOWN
FANTASY FICTION
20c
FEB. 1940

DEATH'S DEPUTY by **L. Ron Hubbard**

1

UNKNOWN
FEBRUARY 1940
EDD CARTIER

Imagination ran wild in the pages of *Unknown*.

STREET & SMITH'S

UNKNOWN
MAY
1939
20c

RETURNED FROM HELL
by **STEVE FISHER**

3

SLAVES OF SLEEP
L. RON HUBBARD
1939 (1948 REPRINT)
HANNES BOK

An Arabian Nights-styled dream fantasy with a fitting cover by Bok.

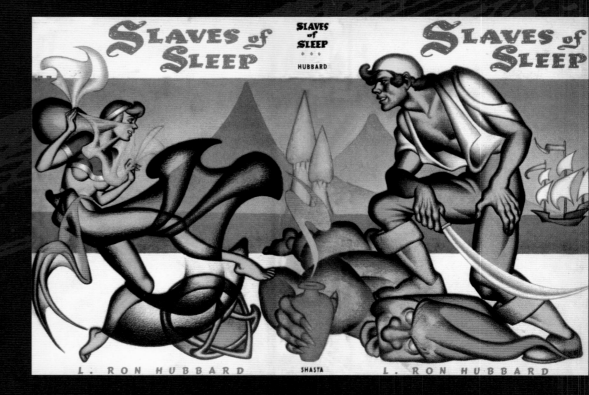

SLAVES of SLEEP

SLAVES of SLEEP

SLAVES of SLEEP
HUBBARD

L. RON HUBBARD   SHASTA   L. RON HUBBARD

best writers in the field and he wanted to do the same for fantasy fiction. But he didn't want his writers to do it in a *Weird Tales*-type of way, which he thought was now clichéd and outdated. He wanted solid writing and he wanted it to seem plausible, even in the face of the fantastic.

Campbell's new magazine was called *Unknown,* and the first issue came out in March 1939. Many of the tales he used took place in the reader's all-too-familiar contemporary world, making the intrusion of fantasy, no matter how incredible, seem all the more real. This grounding in reality gave the stories an entertaining spin and, more often than not, contained a good deal of humor, an element that had been missing from most fantastic fiction for years.

A number of established writers from Campbell's stable for *Astounding* contributed stories, as did several talented newcomers.

L. (Lafayette) Ron (Ronald) Hubbard, science fiction writer and later, Dianetics guru, contributed some early wild tales, his most famous being "Slaves of Sleep" (1939) which was later published in hardcover with a wonderful wraparound dust jacket by Hannes Bok. Its hero was mild-mannered Jan Palmer who lived a normal life in our world during his waking hours but, once asleep, became one with Tiger, an adventurer in the magical, Arabian Nights-like World of Sleep. "Death's Deputy" (1940) was another of Hubbard's humorous fantasies for *Unknown.*

Norvell W. (Wooten) Page (perhaps better known as Grant Stockbridge, author of *The Spider* pulps) was also present in those early issues with two short novels about an ancient crusader. The first was *Flame Winds* (1939) which introduced Hurricane John, a brawny, red-bearded, carousing adventurer.

He was back in *Unknown* the same year in *Sons of the Bear God,* where the character was revealed as being the genesis of the folk legend of Prester John, known as Wan Tengri or John of the Wind Devils to the Mongols in the East. The two novels were resurrected in paperback for new audiences in 1969.

In the August 1939 issue of *Unknown,* two unlikely heroes made their literary debut, breathing new life into the concept of the sword and sorcery adventure. The two rogues were Fafhrd, a seven-foot-tall, blond, Viking-like barbarian from out of the cold waste, complete with the appropriate accoutrements, including longsword; and the Gray Mouser, small, clever, gray-hooded, and as nimble and sharp as the rapier he carried. They fought man, magic, and frequently amongst themselves, becoming very real characters and endearing themselves to the readers.

"Two Sought Adventure" was the title of the first novelette and the author was Fritz Leiber, Jr. Farnsworth Wright had previously rejected these stories but *Weird Tales'* loss was *Unknown's* gain. Set around the fabled city of Lankhmar, Leiber chronicled five of the duo's tales for *Unknown* from 1939 – 43. To give an idea of just how different and entertaining the writing was, especially considering the genre and the time, picture the film *Butch Cassidy and the Sundance Kid* in the trappings of heroic fantasy, and you've got a pretty close idea.

The concept of Fafhrd and the Mouser, and Lankhmar, went back to 1934 to shared correspondence between Leiber and his friend Harry Fischer. Fischer sent Leiber an outline introducing the two characters and Leiber replied with one of his own. Further exchanges added bits and pieces, and then

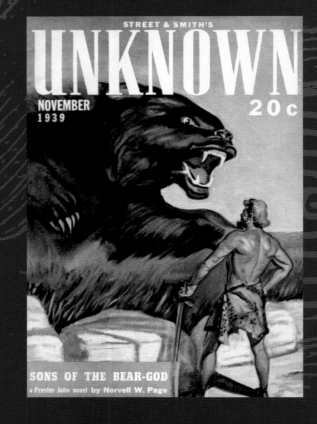

Leiber wrote his first novella about the two. He de-
liberately set about making his leads more human:
susceptible to temptations, surviving by luck in their
encounters with more obviously powerful oppo-
nents, human or otherwise.

The adventures of Fafhrd and the Gray Mouser
didn't end with *Unknown*. When Arkham House
published *Night's Black Agents* in 1947, a hardcover
collection of Leiber's weird stories, he dusted off that
early novella and polished up "Adepts Gambit", another gem in their chronicles. During the 1950s, a
few more stories found homes in fantasy digests and
in 1957 Gnome Press published a hardcover collection, *Two Sought Adventure*. A more celebrated Leiber
saw "Lean Times in Lankhmar" published in *Fantastic*
in 1959 and other new tales soon followed.

Prior to his death in 1992, Leiber received many
well-deserved honors including a Life Achievement
World Fantasy Award and a Hugo Award in 1971 for
"Ill Met in Lankhmar". His two adventurers continue
to entertain readers today, their original escapades
receiving numerous paperback and hardcover reprint-
ings, and Robin Wayne Bailey continued their
exploits in the novel *Swords Against the Shadowland*
in 1998.

In addition to Leiber, Campbell had more literary
tricks up his sleeve for *Unknown*. In the December
1939 issue, he published L. (Lyon) Sprague de Camp's
"Lest Darkness Fall", in which a man accidentally
time travels to Ancient Rome. Five months later he
hit readers with the double whammy of the writing
team L. Sprague de Camp and Fletcher Pratt. The
memorable duo were a perfect example of what
Unknown was all about.

"The Roaring Trumpet" was the title of that first collaboration featuring the very un-heroic Harold Shea,

6

UNKNOWN
MAY 1940
M. ISIP

Meet Harold Shea, a very
unlikely hero, brought
to you by L. Sprague de
Camp and Fletcher Pratt.

STREET & SMITH'S

UNKNOWN

FANTASY FICTION

20c

MAY·1940

THE ROARING TRUMPET

by L. SPRAGUE DE CAMP
and FLETCHER PRATT

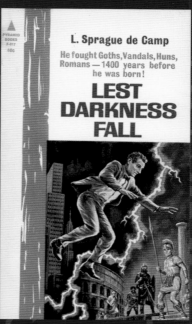

PYRAMID
BOOKS
X-817
40c

L. Sprague de Camp

He fought Goths, Vandals, Huns,
Romans — 1400 years before
he was born!

LEST DARKNESS FALL

7

LEST DARKNESS FALL
L. SPRAGUE DE CAMP
1939 (1963 EXPANDED REPRINT)
EMSH

A paperback edition of de
Camp's time travel fantasy
from *Unknown*.

PYRAMID
BOOKS
F-723
40c

Two scientists explore a world where magic works!

"Delightful fantasy"—GALAXY

L. Sprague de Camp
and Fletcher Pratt THE
INCOMPLETE
ENCHANTER

8

THE INCOMPLETE ENCHANTER
L. SPRAGUE DE CAMP AND FLETCHER PRATT
1940 (1962 REVISED REPRINT)
EMSH

A portrait of our man of many worlds, Harold Shea.

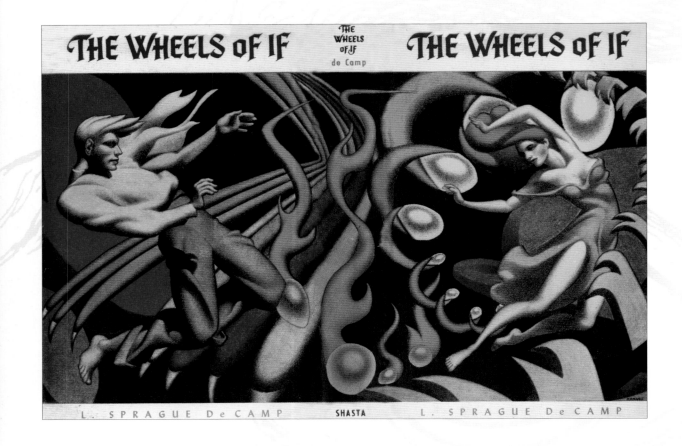

THE WHEELS OF IF
L. SPRAGUE DE CAMP
1948
HANNES BOK

A collection of fantasy and science fiction stories from *Unknown* and *Astounding*.

THE RETURN OF CONAN
BJORN NYBERG AND L. SPRAGUE DE CAMP
1957
WALLACE WOOD

A collaborative novel continuing the adventures of Conan, with comic artist Wood providing the cover.

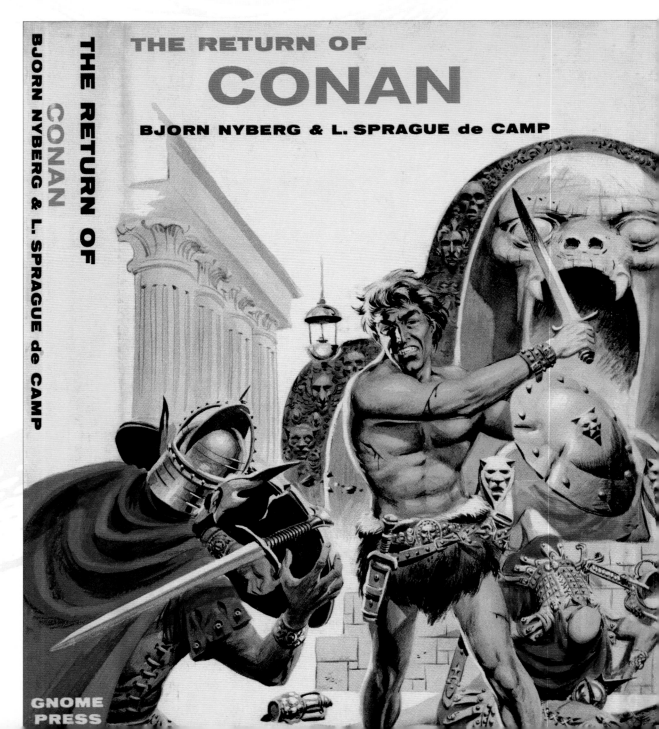

a psychologist who, through experimentation found himself projected into a world of Scandanavian myth and sagas. It was an engaging fantasy, further complemented by a nice M. Isip cover painting featuring an encounter with a dragon, and some beautiful interior art by Edd Cartier. Cartier produced some impressive covers for *Unknown,* but his black and white illustrations are a delight to the eye, perfect for the type of fantasy material that *Unknown* was publishing. His gremlins, dwarves, gnomes, and other fanciful creatures were all executed with a certain sense of personality, and he created a wonderful mood and atmosphere with his compositions.

Harold Shea was back in the August 1940 issue for more experimentation. In "The Mathematics of Magic" he transported himself into the world of Edmund Spenser's *The Faerie Queene* (1590 – 1609). Readers were taken with these offbeat adventures and so de Camp and Pratt obliged them with a novel, *The Castle of Iron,* published in the April 1941 issue of *Unknown.*

Pratt, the older of the two, was a science fiction writer who at one time had worked for A. Merritt back in the Hearst newspaper days. De Camp wrote many fine fantasy and science fiction stories and novels on his own, but their collaborations are literary treats. They also teamed up for such non-Harold Shea novels as *The Land of Unreason* (1941), in which a mortal finds himself in Oberon and Titania's faerie realm, and *The Carnelian Cube* (1948). There were also two more additional Shea stories published in other magazines during the 1950s.

The first two Harold Shea stories were subsequently combined in hardcover as *The Incomplete Enchanter* (1941). *Castle of Iron* (1950) was also published in hardcover with a dust jacket illustration by Hannes

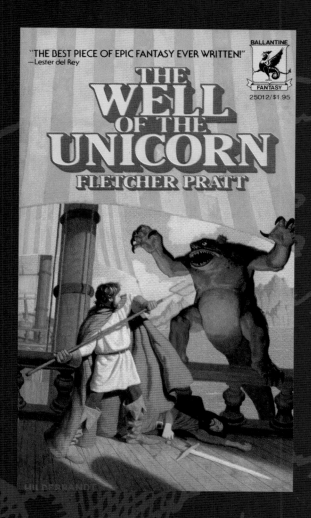

THE BEST PIECE OF EPIC FANTASY EVER WRITTEN!"
—Lester del Rey

THE WELL OF THE UNICORN
FLETCHER PRATT

BALLANTINE FANTASY
25012/$1.95

THE WELL OF THE UNICORN
FLETCHER PRATT
1948 (1976 REPRINT)
THE BROTHERS HILDEBRANDT

Pratt didn't care for the Conan type of story; he preferred classical heroic sagas to muscle-bound barbarians.

Bok. Pratt later wrote two other fantasy novels on his own: *The Well of the Unicorn* (1948) reflected the influence of earlier fantasists Lord Dunsany, William Morris, and E. R. Eddison. It was followed by *The Blue Star* in 1952.

Pratt died in 1956, but de Camp's popular brand of fantasy continued. Pratt had introduced him to the Conan stories when Robert E. Howard's fiction was being reprinted by Gnome Press in the 1950s. De Camp subsequently became involved in editing and collaborating on some of Howard's unfinished manuscripts. He would also go on to play an important part in the revival of the author's work during the 1960s.

Meanwhile, other writers for *Unknown* who were equally at home writing horror, science fiction, and fantasy included Fredric Brown, Theodore Sturgeon, Robert Bloch, Henry Kuttner, Jack Williamson, and Robert A. Heinlein.

FROM
UNKNOWN WORLDS

An Anthology of Modern Fantasy for Grownups

1948
25 CEN
30 CENTS
IN CANA

EDD CARTIER

17

FANTASTIC ADVENTURES
MARCH 1949
ARNOLD KOHN

How about a world deep below the sea, ruled by giant mermaids? That might be one of the more plausible stories from *Fantastic Adventures!*

18

FANTASTIC ADVENTURES
JULY 1942
J. ALLEN ST. JOHN

This issue featured "The Weird Doom of Floyd Scrilch", one of Robert Bloch's zany Lefty Feep stories.

16

THE UNKNOWN
EDITED BY D. R. BENSEN
1963
JOHN SCHOENHERR

Unknown's stories were also ripe for paperback pickings in two editions.

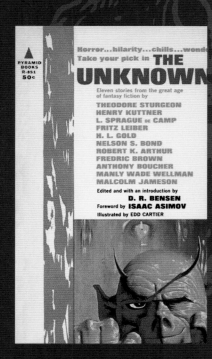

19

IMAGINATION
JUNE 1951
HANNES BOK

During the 1950s, Robert Bloch wrote many humor and pun-filled fantasies.

ROM *UNKNOWN WORLDS*
948
DD CARTIER

n anthology of reprints
rom *Unknown*, illustrated
y the talented Cartier.

Many pulps suffered from the paper shortage during the war years, and *Unknown Worlds* was no exception. October 1943 would be the last edition. In its thirty-nine issue life span it published a staggering array of extraordinary fantasy fiction by an outstanding group of talented individuals. Following Campbell's guidelines, Leiber, Pratt and de Camp, Hubbard, Williamson, and others contributed to the influential effect the magazine still has on the fantasy field today.

Five years after it folded, an oversize issue called *From Unknown Worlds* presented a selection of reprint stories from the magazine with a final cover painting by *Unknown*'s resident da Vinci, Edd Cartier, whose illustrations also graced two paperback reprint anthologies, *The Unknown* (1963) and *The Unknown Five* (1964), both edited by D. R. Bensen.

Another pulp magazine that delved into the fantastic, often with humorous results, was the aptly titled *Fantastic Adventures*. Edited by Raymond Palmer and also debuting in 1939, it was conceived as a fantasy version of *Amazing Stories*, the science fiction field's first and longest-running pulp. It published a mix of the two genres, with work by the usual suspects—Fritz Leiber, Theodore Sturgeon, Robert Bloch, etc.—as well as a good run of Edgar Rice Burroughs' interplanetary adventures, usually packaged with stunning covers by Burroughs' interpreter in oils, J. Allen St. John. *Fantastic Adventures* enjoyed a healthier run than most pulps of the period, lasting until 1953.

Despite his better-known horror output, Robert Bloch was also a master of plot twists and puns and developed his own brand of humorous fantasy stories during the 1940s and 1950s. His whimsical Lefty Feep episodes are perhaps best exemplified by one of my favorite titles, "Time Wounds All Heels" (1942). Need I say more?

In the best of his comic fantasies, Bloch was obviously influenced by American humorist Thorne Smith, whose own earlier style somewhat typified *Unknown*'s. Smith wrote *Topper: An Improbable Adventure* (1926), the misadventures of a man and a ghostly couple who really knew how to "live" it up! It spawned a sequel, movies, and even a television series.

Another of Smith's novels, *Turnabout* (1931), also filmed, involved a couple who magically switched identities, a concept since used numerous times with slight variations. The premise hearkens back to perhaps the original switcheroo tale *Vice Versa, or A Lesson to Fathers* (1882), by British writer and humorist Thomas Anstey Guthrie who, as "F. Anstey", wrote several comedic fantasies. In this particular one, a Victorian father and son switch places with comical results and appropriate lessons learned on both sides. Anstey's *The Brass Bottle* (1900) contained a genie who, upon release, created all sorts of complications for its new master. Both novels were later filmed, and *The Brass Bottle* served as the probable inspiration for the popular television series *I Dream of Jeannie* (1965–70).

Another Thorne Smith fantasy, *The Night Life of the Gods* (1931), brought classical Greco-Roman statues to life for a night on the town in New York and was made into a film in 1935. *The Passionate Witch* (1941), finished after Smith's death by Norman H. Matson, was filmed as *I Married a Witch* in 1942 and, like Anstey's *The Brass Bottle,* was possibly influential in the conception of another popular television series, *Bewitched* (1964–72).

IMAGINATIVE TALES NO. 4
MARCH 1955
HAROLD MCCAULEY

Not just another "fish story"; the mermaid tale is given the Bloch touch.

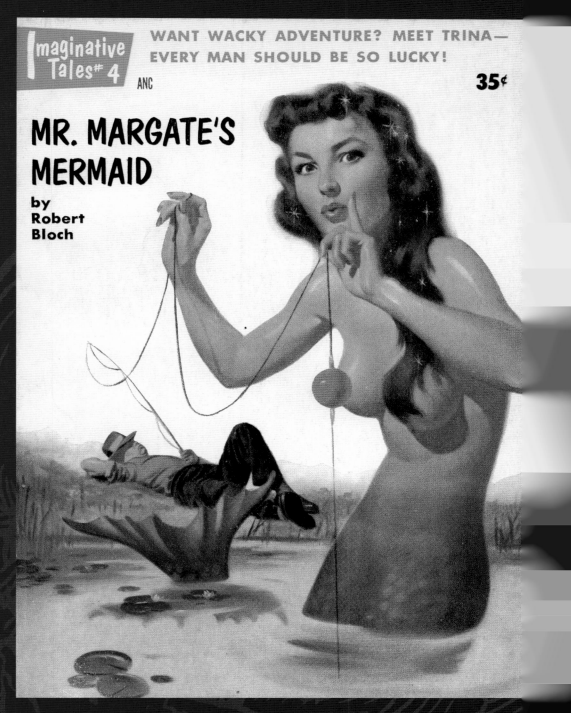

IMAGINATIVE TALES NO. 3
JANUARY 1955
HAROLD MCCAULEY

Robert Bloch, the man who wrote *Psycho*, also wrote a great deal more.

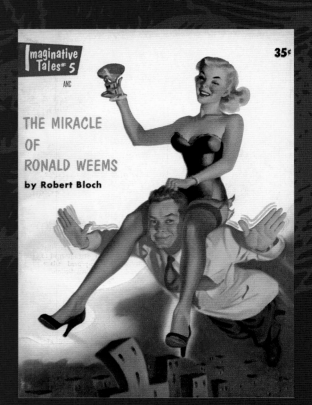

IMAGINATIVE TALES NO. 5
MAY 1955
HAROLD MCCAULEY

Robert Bloch had the heart of a small boy and the boundless imagination to match!

24

THE FANTASY WORLDS OF PETER BEAGLE
PETER BEAGLE
1978
DARREL K. SWEET

This omnibus volume collects four of Beagle's novels.

23

THE INNOCENT EVE
ROBERT NATHAN
1951
RICHARD M. POWERS

Nathan is known for his romantic fantasies.

25

THE CIRCUS OF DR. LAO
CHARLES G. FINNEY
1935 (1948 REPRINT)
GORDON NOEL FISH

A British reprint edition of Finney's novel with wonderfully bizarre illustrations by G. N. Fish.

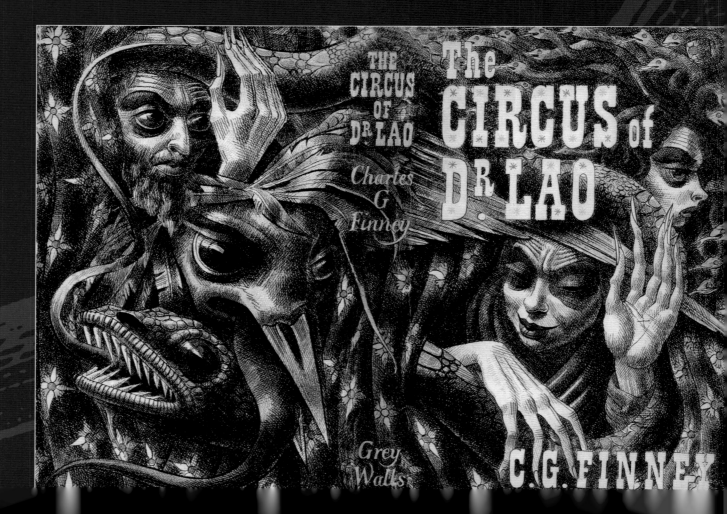

During and after the World War II years, Hollywood produced many uplifting fantasies, either comedic or romantic in tone, sometimes both.

Robert Nathan was the author of many fantasy novels of a more sentimental and thought-provoking nature although, thanks to Hollywood, his two best-known are *Portrait of Jennie* (1940), a haunting love story of an artist and his inspiration, and *The Bishop's Wife* (1928), wherein the Archangel Michael becomes enamored with the title character after coming to Earth to aid her husband in the construction of a new cathedral.

Nathan died in 1985, but he continued to write well into the 1970s. His brand of storytelling was acknowledged by author Peter S. Beagle as being a particular influence on his own work, especially his first novel, *A Fine and Private Place* (1960). It is set in a Bronx cemetery where a recluse, a talking raven and a courting couple (who just happen to be ghosts), discover some things about themselves and about life.

Other works that have solidified Beagle's place as one of the field's finest writers are *The Last Unicorn* (1968), *Lila the Werewolf* (1969), and *The Folk of the Air* (1986). More recently, he has authored *The Innkeeper's Song* (1993), a quest fantasy, plus two collections: *Giant Bones* (1997) and *The Rhinoceros Who Quoted Nietzsche and Other Odd Acquaintances* (1997).

Award-winning science fiction writer Ray Bradbury, whose early pulp stories had a distinct horror bent, incorporated fantasy into much of his work during the later part of *Weird Tales'* run. Two books in particular fall into this area: *Dandelion Wine* (1957), in which a young boy's experiences during a long summer of change are fueled by the gift of his own imagination; and, on a somewhat darker note,

Something Wicked This Way Comes (1962), with its "Dark Carnival" that attracts two young boys with tempting promises that carry a terrible price. Bradbury wrote the screenplay for a Disney film version of the latter in 1983.

Charles G. Finney wrote of the wonders to be found in *The Circus of Dr. Lao* (1935), a magical big top, whose influence is evident in some of Bradbury's and Beagle's work. It was filmed as *Seven Faces of Dr. Lao* in 1964.

Award-winning writer and editor Harlan Ellison, known for his outstanding works of imaginative fiction, created memorable fantasies in short stories such as "Jefty is Five" (1977). The collections *Shatterday* (1980) and *The Essential Ellison* (1987) contain some of his finest stories.

Like Bradbury, Richard Matheson also had his early work published in *Weird Tales*. He too became successful, working in a variety of genres—suspense, science fiction, fantasy, historical westerns—in addition to screenwriting, adapting not only his own work but that of others. His novel, *Bid Time Return* (1975), a beautiful romantic fantasy about two people in love a century apart, won a World Fantasy Award and was filmed (from his screenplay) as *Somewhere in Time* (1980). He followed it with *What Dreams May Come* (1978), another romance, this time of a love that transcends this life through Heaven and Hell. It was also filmed, in 1998, but much of this moving novel was lost in the transition to the screen.

Bradbury and Matheson had their roots in the pulps and are still writing today. Fritz Leiber's adventures were most influential in the formation of the modern sword and sorcery story. These writers, along with de Camp and Pratt, with their exploits of

CHAPTER 5
A GOOD STORY
IS WORTH REPRINTING

"This magazine is the answer to the thousands of requests that we have received over a period of years, demanding a second look at famous fantasies which, since their original publication, have become accepted classics. Our choice has been dictated by your requests and our firm belief that these are the aces of imaginative fiction."— The Editors. With those words to inaugurate its contents page and define its parameters, the first issue of *Famous Fantastic Mysteries* found its place on the stands among the pulps and magazines of late 1939. Considering the competition, it didn't exactly leap out at the potential buyer with a colorful eye-catching cover as you might have expected. It *was* eye-catching, in its lack of artwork, listing the writers and the stories framed within a

❶
FAMOUS FANTASTIC MYSTERIES
SEPTEMBER–OCTOBER
1939
You can't judge a book by its cover, especially this first issue.

circle, accompanied by the appropriate adjectives of course—*Amazing!, Thrilling!, Strange!, Weird!*. It was published by the Frank A. Munsey Company; Munsey was responsible for the first pulp magazine, *The Argosy*, back in 1896, as well as *The All-Story Magazine* and *The Cavalier*. A wide variety of fiction was to be found in the pages of these magazines, from the latest Edgar Rice Burroughs story to the westerns of Zane Gray, and by the late 1930s, pulp magazines reflecting an extensive range of genres really became popular. Science fiction and fantasy were especially prevalent.

Into this flourishing market *Famous Fantastic Mysteries* was born; maybe reborn would be a better description, so far as the stories were concerned.

Since Munsey had already published a large amount of fantasy and science fiction in *Argosy* and other magazines, including quality material from authors like Burroughs and A. Merritt, why not a new pulp to showcase some classic fiction already in the archives? After all, there was a younger generation of genre fans who had missed many of these stories the first time around, and Munsey still owned the magazine publication rights in most cases, so costs could be kept down.

Most of the stories published were lost race adventures, planetary and scientific romances, and an interesting variety of short fantasies. While other pulps were printing a stronger brew of science fiction or horror, the stories in *Famous Fantastic Mysteries* were more in the high adventure vein, full of that special "fantastic" quality.

By the late 1930s, Abraham Merritt was considered one of the finest writers of fantasy fiction, and Munsey had already published his brilliant adventure stories. For the first issue of the "new" magazine, Merritt headed the line-up with his novella "The Moon Pool" (1918). There wasn't much in the way of illustration outside of a few minor interior drawings, but in time this would change significantly.

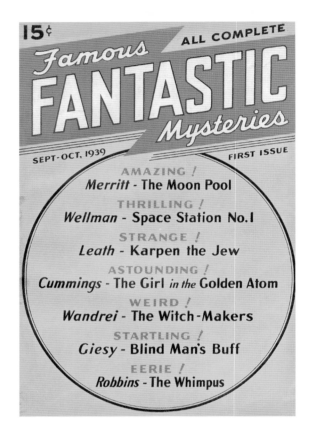

Merritt's 1919 sequel, "Conquest of the Moon Pool", was published in serial form over the next six issues to keep readers coming back for more, which they did. The idea of running several short stories and one continuing novel was a concept employed to great effect by editor Mary Gnaedinger, as the magazine went monthly with its second issue. Original stories were also sometimes used as the magazine tested the pulp waters to see what worked and what didn't. Of course the fans were always ready to add their two cents worth—or rather their fifteen cents (the price of each issue). The letters printed in "The Reader's Viewpoint" column were full of praise for the pulp and made interesting reading in themselves. Most of the suggestions for story material ended up being published sooner or later. One fan confessed to not reading the first issue because he had already read the stories, but he would continue

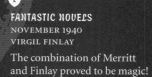

2

FANTASTIC NOVELS
NOVEMBER 1940
VIRGIL FINLAY

The combination of Merritt and Finlay proved to be magic!

3

FAMOUS FANTASTIC MYSTERIES
MARCH 1940
VIRGIL FINLAY

Artwork comes to the covers of this excellent reprint pulp.

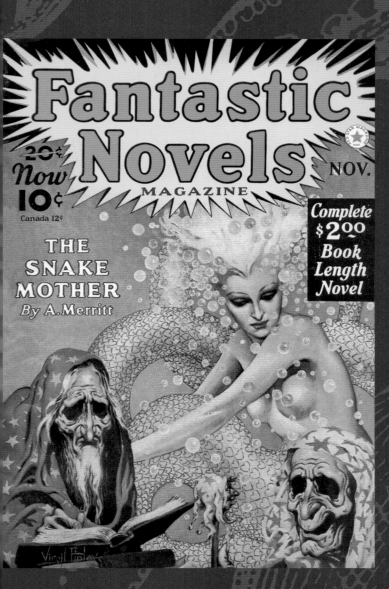

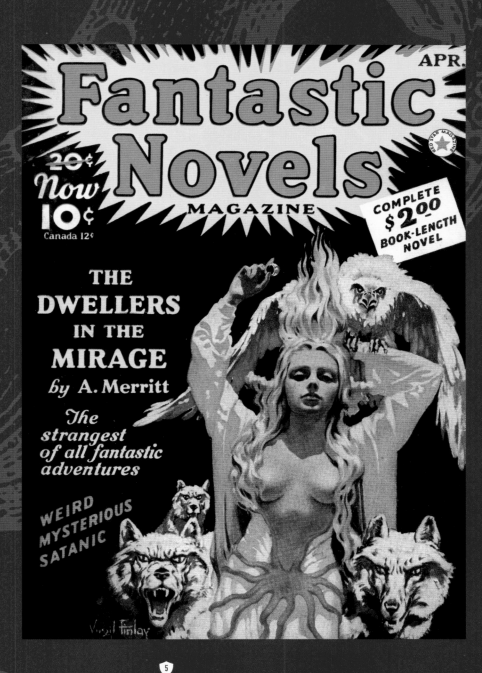

4

FAMOUS FANTASTIC MYSTERIES
MAY–JUNE 1940
FRANK R. PAUL

Celebrated science fiction pulp artist Paul did a few early covers.

5

FANTASTIC NOVELS
APRIL 1941
VIRGIL FINLAY

This was the first time that A. Merritt's original preferred text ending was published. It was another beautiful cover and the "final" issue of the pulp—at least for a while.

6

FAMOUS FANTASTIC MYSTERIES
APRIL 1941
VIRGIL FINLAY

In addition to providing countless interior illustrations for the pulps, Finlay could paint with the best of them.

7

FAMOUS FANTASTIC MYSTERIES
AUGUST 1941
VIRGIL FINLAY

Now combined with *Fantastic Novels*, the pulp gave readers what they wanted, including more Merritt and Finlay.

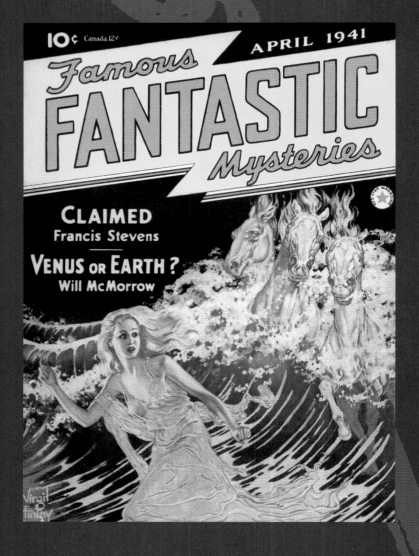

8

FAMOUS FANTASTIC MYSTERIES
APRIL 1942
VIRGIL FINLAY

Other favorite reprints included work by Ralph Milne Farley.

9

FAMOUS FANTASTIC MYSTERIES
FEBRUARY 1942
VIRGIL FINLAY

Francis Stevens was at one time believed to be a pseudonym of A. Merritt.

to buy every issue as he was a *collector!* One reader liked the plain text cover style, another wanted the cover illustrated, and one particular letter writer had a brilliant idea that would contribute to making the magazine collectible for more than just the stories—"Get Virgil Finlay for one of your artists".

Virgil Finlay started providing interior art for the second issue and was hired to do all of the illustrations for the Merritt serial, continuing a happy association between artist and author that had started when Merritt, as editor, had hired Finlay to work for him at *The American Weekly* in 1938. Many of the artist's finest works are his Merritt interpretations.

By the March 1940 issue there was cover art, and it was by Finlay. He and famed pulp science fiction artist Frank R. Paul were already responsible for most of the interiors by this time.

The May/June issue of that year carried an announcement that couldn't have pleased the fans more. A new magazine, *Fantastic Novels,* was to appear in July. Each issue would see a novel in its entirety. The new title was to be published bi-monthly, like *Famous Fantastic Mysteries* which, from then on would no longer include serials. As the two magazines were published on alternate months, all reader requests coming in for novel-length stories could be met and at a much quicker rate than previously.

More letters poured in, with more requests.

One was from a young writer named Ray Bradbury, asking *Famous Fantastic Mysteries* to acquire the services of his artist friend, Hannes Bok. The request was granted.

Bok, a major talent, produced striking interiors for both magazines but, unfortunately, no covers.

Finlay, however, was on a roll, providing some beautiful paintings throughout the early 1940s that raised the standards of pulp art to another level entirely.

FAMOUS FANTASTIC MYSTERIES
DECEMBER 1942
VIRGIL FINLAY

Readers continued to send requests for stories and this pulp was only too happy to oblige them.

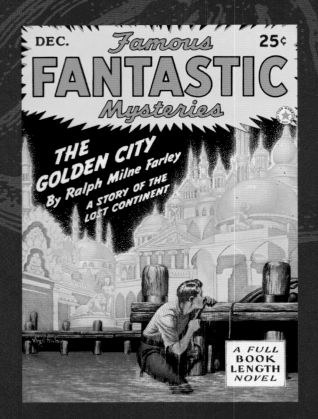

FAMOUS FANTASTIC MYSTERIES
JUNE 1944
LAWRENCE STERNE STEVENS

Artist Lawrence steps up to the batter's box and knocks one out of the park.

FAMOUS FANTASTIC MYSTERIES
DECEMBER 1944
LAWRENCE STERNE STEVENS

In addition to his cover work, Lawrence, like Finlay, supplied excellent interior art.

FAMOUS FANTASTIC MYSTERIES
JUNE 1945
LAWRENCE STERNE STEVENS

William Hope Hodgson and other "imports" start getting attention from the magazine.

FAMOUS FANTASTIC MYSTERIES
APRIL 1947
LAWRENCE STERNE STEVENS

One of H. Rider Haggard's novels gets thawed out for this revival.

FAMOUS FANTASTIC MYSTERIES
JUNE 1948
VIRGIL FINLAY

Maybe I should just shut up. After all, one picture is worth a thousand words.

FAMOUS FANTASTIC MYSTERIES
FEBRUARY 1947
VIRGIL FINLAY

Jack London's novel of racial memory.

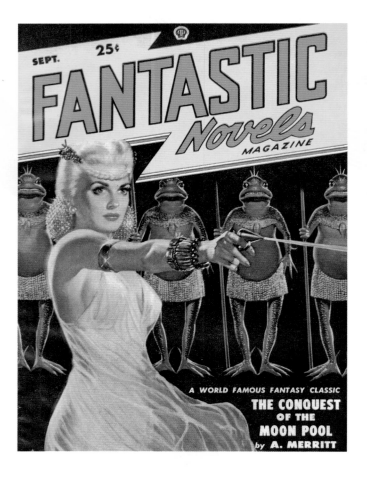

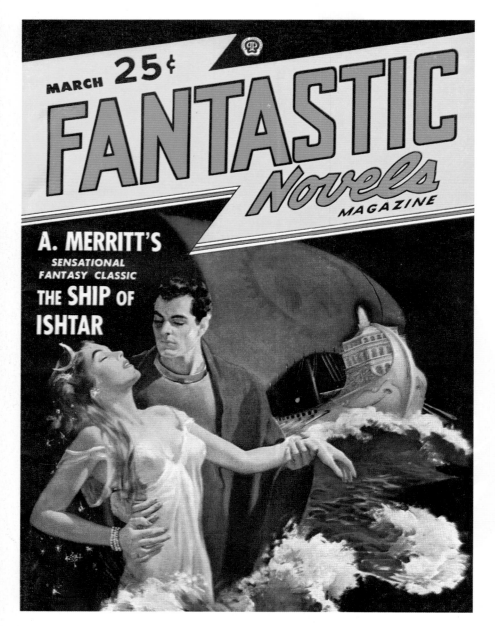

FANTASTIC NOVELS
SEPTEMBER 1948
LAWRENCE STERNE STEVENS
Representatives of
Merritt's Frog Guard
pose for Lawrence for
an inspired cover.

The cover price fluctuated during these early years, up or down a nickel, before finally jumping to twenty-five cents by June of 1942. A veritable cornucopia of classics was to be found in each bi-monthly issue, including Ralph Milne Farley's *Radio Beasts* and *The Golden City; The Citadel of Fear, Serapion* and *Claimed* by Francis Stevens; *The Blind Spot* by Austin Hall and Homer Eon Flint; and *Polaris of the Snows* by Charles B. Stilson. Of course, the ever-popular A. Merritt tales were present, receiving the lavish (by pulp standards) Finlay treatment.

World War II was taking its toll in Europe, and the developing paper shortage and shrinking overseas market was forcing cutbacks stateside. The April 1941 *Fantastic Novels* was the fifth and final issue. The title was combined with *Famous Fantastic Mysteries,* which kept its bi-monthly schedule until mid-1942, when it reverted to a monthly, but still delivered the classic stories for which it was *Famous.*

There were other problems. In an effort to boost sales, the Munsey Company re-designed the look of its major pulp, *Argosy,* but the new image was not acceptable to the Postmaster General, forcing Munsey to take serious stock of a situation where the magazine could no longer be distributed through the mail. In the end, *Argosy* and several other titles, including *Famous Fantastic Mysteries* and its counterpart *Fantastic Novels,* were sold to Popular Publications.

Popular Publications lived up to its name, cornering the weird menace market in the 1930s and later on with hero pulps like *G-8 and his Battle Aces* and *The Spider.* It prided itself on publishing magazines with new stories or ones that had "never appeared before in a magazine". Yet now they were publishing a magazine that had specialized in reprints and had a large following because of that. So, to keep

FANTASTIC NOVELS
MARCH 1948
LAWRENCE STERNE STEVENS
Lawrence takes on Merritt and
proves to be worthy competition
for Finlay.

21

FANTASTIC NOVELS
JANUARY 1949
LAWRENCE STERNE STEVENS

Lawrence did several covers
as well as interiors for Merritt.
This is one of those great
moments in pulp art.

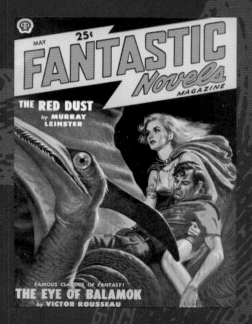

22

FANTASTIC NOVELS
MAY 1949
LAWRENCE STERNE STEVENS

Both *Fantastic Novels* and
Famous Fantastic Mysteries
published excellent stories
accompanied by excellent art.

23

FANTASTIC NOVELS
NOVEMBER 1949
VIRGIL FINLAY

Finlay lets Lawrence
take a break and
steps in with this
fine fantasy piece.

24

FANTASTIC NOVELS
SEPTEMBER 1949
LAWRENCE STERNE STEVENS

Finlay had previously done
a cover for *Dwellers in the
Mirage*, and now Lawrence
turned in his own brilliant
heroic piece for the novel.

FANTASTIC NOVELS
SEPTEMBER 1950
NORMAN SAUNDERS

Prolific pulp artist Saunders contributed
some covers during the later period of
both magazines.

26

A. MERRITT'S FANTASY MAGAZINE
DECEMBER 1949
LAWRENCE STERNE STEVENS

The first issue of this short-lived pulp.

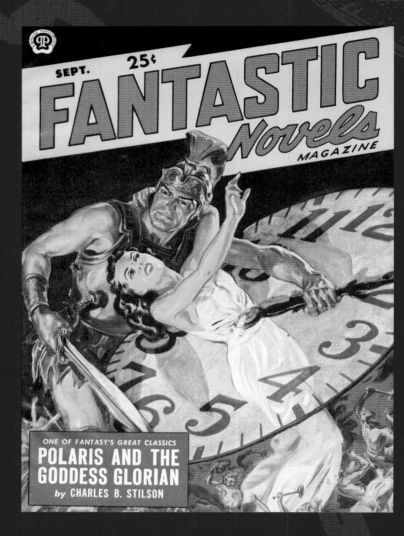

**AVON FANTASY READER
NO. 1**
FEBRUARY 1947
ARTIST UNKNOWN

More reprints, usually
from *Weird Tales*, in this
digest edited by Donald
A. Wollheim.

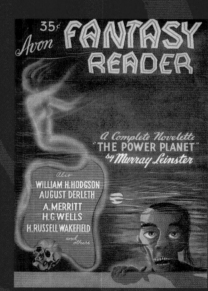

AVON FANTASY READER NO. 2
1947
ARTIST UNKNOWN

Whoever painted this cover was familiar
with the work of illustrator Harry Clarke
and pulp artist Rudolph Belarski, as it
borrows elements of their previously
executed images!

readers happy and provide a larger variety of material, a slight adjustment was made to this policy. It was decided that *Famous Fantastic Mysteries* would reprint fantasy stories that had never appeared in *American* magazines—and this opened up a whole range of classic works by William Hope Hodgson, H. Rider Haggard, Arthur Machen, Lord Dunsany, Algernon Blackwood, and others. The magazine even included original stories and reader response was quite favorable.

Virgil Finlay had meanwhile been inducted into the armed services, but another fine-line artist, Lawrence Sterne Stevens, stepped into the breach and provided outstanding interiors and, later on, covers to match.

By 1948 sales were going so well that *Fantastic Novels* was revived as a separate bi-monthly again, publishing the longer-length reprints, while *Famous Fantastic Mysteries* handled the shorter fiction. This time it was not limited to reprints of a particular type. Finlay was back, too, and along with Lawrence and Bok, created countless mini-masterpieces. Ronald Clyne also added some wonderfully moody illustrations, and even pulp great Norman Saunders contributed several beautiful paintings in the early 1950s.

Unfortunately, publishing costs were growing, as was the popularity of paperback books, and by June 1951 it was finally over for *Fantastic Novels*. Two years later *Famous Fantastic Mysteries* would follow suit. After briefly flirting with a format change to digest in 1951, the magazine returned to its standard pulp size in time for a proper burial.

Virgil Finlay pulled out all the stops in this last issue of *Famous Fantastic Mysteries* in his illustration for Robert E. Howard's novella "Worms of the

CONQUEST OF THE MOON POOL
A. MERRITT
VIRGIL FINLAY

From the September 1948 issue of *Fantastic Novels* comes this example of the artist's intricately detailed black and white work, and he did hundreds like it!

THE DEVIL'S SPOON
1948
LAWRENCE STERNE STEVENS

One of the very fine interiors by Lawrence from *Famous Fantastic Mysteries* which was included in one of the portfolios of his work available through the magazine.

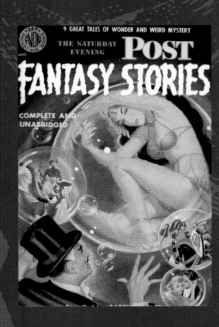

**THE SATURDAY EVENING POST
FANTASY STORIES**
COMPILED BY BERTHOLD FLES
1951
WILLIAM RANDALL

A collection of stories published by
The Saturday Evening Post magazine.

Earth". The artwork was such a selling point over the years that portfolios of Finlay and Lawrence were published and available through the magazines. "Literary" fiction such as Ayn Rand's *Anthem* and Franz Kafka's "Metamorphosis" shared the spotlight with Howard and Ray Bradbury, making it quite a farewell.

Another companion magazine was *A. Merritt's Fantasy Magazine* (possibly the only instance when an author's name has been part of a pulp's title). It reprinted Merritt's own *Creep, Shadow!*, *The Face in the Abyss*, and "Three Lines of Old French", among other stories, and Finlay, Lawrence, and Saunders came up with more visual gems. But the magazine was short lived, lasting only five issues (1949-50).

Continuing the fashion for reprints but in a non-illustrated digest size was *Avon Fantasy Reader*. The first issue was published in 1947 and editor Donald A. Wollheim selected from among the finest; A. Merritt, Robert E. Howard, H. G. Wells, William Hope Hodgson, Clark Ashton Smith, and Lord Dunsany were all present, and the stories were mainly chosen from *Weird Tales*. Wollheim was himself a writer and had a history in the field dating back to his fan days when he corresponded with H. P. Lovecraft. From 1935 he had edited an amateur magazine of fantasy and supernatural fiction called *The Phantagraph*, which published Howard, Lovecraft, Robert Bloch, and Merritt, as well as many young upcoming writers. In the 1940s he became a professional editor, and in 1946 he joined Avon Books, a company already gaining quite a reputation as a paperback publisher. It was out of this collaboration that *Avon*

AVON FANTASY READER NO. 8
1948
ARTIST UNKNOWN

Lasting just eighteen issues, it nevertheless published much fine material. Here Robert E. Howard's Conan gets the cover spot.

THE MOON POOL
A. MERRITT
1918-19
(1951 REPRINT)
ARTIST UNKNOWN

Lakla, handmaiden to The Silent Ones, cuts a pin-up figure on this early Avon paperback.

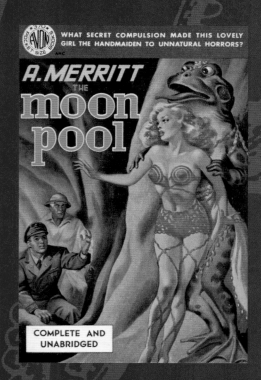

WHAT SECRET COMPULSION MADE THIS LOVELY GIRL THE HANDMAIDEN TO UNNATURAL HORRORS?

A. MERRITT
THE
moon pool

COMPLETE AND UNABRIDGED

A. MERRITT
The Metal Monster

"ONE OF MERRITT'S BEST FANTASIES—IT RANKS WITH THE *MOON POOL* FOR COLOR, IMAGINATION AND SHEER EXCITING ADVENTURE"
—D. A. Wollheim, Editor of FANTASY READER

Fantasy Reader emerged. It was an excellent reprint anthology series and paved the way for a field of digests, but by 1952 it too had run its course after just eighteen issues. Paperback books were the next new wave, and Wollheim was already there to ride it.

Among other work for Avon, he compiled in 1949 the first all-original anthology of fantasy and science fiction, *The Girl with the Hungry Eyes and Other Stories.* Then, in the 1950s, Wollheim created a series of back-to-back double novels for Ace Books; in the 1960s he issued an unauthorized edition of *The Lord of the Rings* by J. R. R. Tolkien. In 1972 he launched his own imprint, DAW Books, publishing fantasy novels by such authors as Lin Carter, Tanith Lee, Michael Moorcock and Andre Norton. Under the capable hand of his daughter Betsy, DAW Books is still going strong today.

For now, though, during the early 1950s, the days of the pulp magazine were coming to an end. The paperback or pocket book was the "new kid on the block", but it was titles like *Famous Fantastic Mysteries* and *Fantastic Novels,* by reprinting classics for a younger generation, which had paved the way for this new format and anticipated the fantasy anthologies which were to come.

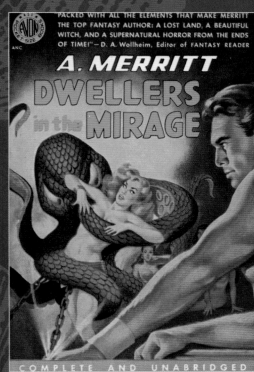

"PACKED WITH ALL THE ELEMENTS THAT MAKE MERRITT THE TOP FANTASY AUTHOR: A LOST LAND, A BEAUTIFUL WITCH, AND A SUPERNATURAL HORROR FROM THE ENDS OF TIME!"—D. A. Wollheim, Editor of FANTASY READER

A. MERRITT
DWELLERS in the MIRAGE

COMPLETE AND UNABRIDGED

34
THE METAL MONSTER
A. MERRITT
1920 (1951 REPRINT)
ARTIST UNKNOWN

Fantasy 1950s paperback style and Merritt is there.

35
DWELLERS IN THE MIRAGE
A. MERRITT
1932 (1952 REPRINT)
ARTIST UNKNOWN

In the early 1950s, Avon Paperbacks had covers that were pure pulp.

Death came, as it does to all things, to the pulp magazines. Those unlucky enough not to be squirreled away by the protective collector-owner, hermetically sealed and lovingly stored, suffered the most. Pages painfully chipped and turned brown; spines sunned and cracked, unable to support their brittle interiors. Insects fed and some, bloated from their meal, expired among the very pages that had nourished them. The graveyard rats came and chewed. They seemed particularly fond of corners. Quack physicians, trying to prolong their patients' lives for their own selfish enjoyment, applied Scotch tape—in most cases a little too liberally. But it was too late. The pulps were gone. It was the end of an era.

WITH THIS
RING...

CHAPTER 6

FANTASY MAGAZINE
MARCH 1953
HANNES BOK

The first issue contained a Robert E. Howard Conan story edited by L. Sprague de Camp. The digest had taken over from the pulp.

Digest magazines and paperbacks were primarily pushing science fiction, horror, and mysteries. Fantasy got in a few licks here and there, mainly with reprints, but where were the new ranks of craftsmen?

The 1950s definitely belonged to science fiction.

Even the movies reflected this, with UFOs, alien invasions and mutated monsters—direct results of A-bomb testing—venting their collective spleens, in every city and every town throughout the world where God-fearing, tax-paying citizens could still be found dead with "enough formic acid in their bodies to kill twenty men". The Government gave us just three words: DO NOT PANIC!

Fantasy wasn't dead, though: it was sleeping out the Cold War and rebuilding its strength. So when it came back, it did so in a big way. Actually, like a seasoned prizefighter, it returned with a one-two punch backed by a lot of muscle.

That first punch was thrown in October 1954, but it didn't actually connect until 1965. The man behind that fantastic left jab was indeed a lord of the ring.

John Ronald Reuel Tolkien was an Oxford professor specializing in Olde and Middle English. In addition, he was skilled in northern languages and writing, particularly in the myths and legends of the Scandanavian and Nordic countries. A husband and father, he would tell his children fairy stories about a world he had created called Middle Earth, the names of its inhabitants and its geography loosely based upon Norse mythology. Tolkien toyed with the idea of writing a book from these stories, and the first fruits of his labors appeared in 1937.

The Hobbit, or There and Back Again contained illustrations and maps of this new realm, drawn by Tolkien himself. Being a children's book, it was written in a simple, storytelling style: Hobbits were a small human-like race, somewhat cherubic, whose outstanding feature was their rather big, hairy feet. The land they dwelled in was The Shire (after the manner of the English countryside). They lived in Hobbit-Holes—houses built into the ground—and they enjoyed the finer things in life like eating and making merry. The Hobbit of the title, one Bilbo Baggins, had this enjoyable life interrupted when he received an unusual visitor, who in turn set him on an adventurous quest. The visitor, the wizard Gandalf, together with thirteen dwarves, convinced Bilbo to join them in regaining the dwarves' treasure from a dragon's lair. The beast was called Smaug and, in true dragon style, it guarded its booty well by lounging on top of it. The game was afoot (especially when Hobbits are involved) and along the way they encountered hungry trolls and goblins. Bilbo, at one stage lost and on his own, found a ring with a power of its own, misplaced by a slimy creature called Gollum. The wearer of the ring became invisible, enabling Bilbo to escape Gollum and the goblins and be reunited with his friends. They had plenty of other encounters before arriving at their destination where, through Bilbo's trickery, Smaug was ultimately destroyed. At the end of the story, a content Bilbo returned to his home.

The book was published in the United States in 1938 and won an award as the best children's book of the year.

A colleague of Tolkien's at Oxford was C. S. (Clive Staples) Lewis. Lewis was an accomplished writer himself and had a seven-volume series published during the 1950s. *The Chronicles of Narnia* (1950—56), although children's books, were wonderfully written and could also be enjoyed by adults. Like the best fantasy fiction, they were filled with wonderful characters, and the world of Narnia joined the most memorable of the enchanted kingdoms of literature.

The two men formed a group of other writers and scholars with similar interests and called themselves The Inklings. They gathered each Thursday evening in Lewis' rooms to try out new literary material and use each other as sounding boards. During these get-togethers, Tolkien began reading from what the others referred to as his "new Hobbit book".

It took him more than ten years to finish this new project, which turned out, at close to 500,000 words, to be one of the longest novels ever written. Titled *The Lord of the Rings* and published in 1954–55, it was made up of three parts. The first part, *The Fellowship of the Ring* (1954), revealed the true nature of the ring found by Bilbo. It was the One Ring of power, once owned by the evil Lord Sauron, who had risen again in search of it. The ring had to be destroyed in

the volcanic fires that forged it but, unfortunately, they were located in Dark Mordor, the very realm of Sauron himself. This set up the quest plot of the three books, completed in *The Two Towers* (also 1954) and *The Return of the King* (1955) wherein Frodo, Bilbo's cousin and the new possessor of the ring, journeyed to the fire, accompanied by a heroic group, in order to destroy its power.

Reaction was good. Tolkien's friend C. S. Lewis sang the book's praises in a review of his own. The epic heroic fantasy, recalling the days of William Morris and E. R. Edison, was back. Sales, however, were initially slow.

Tolkien's "trilogy" presented his new world like a detailed tapestry—intricate and colorful, its people and places woven on a grand scale. Middle Earth was embraced and became a phenomenal bestseller when that first punch finally landed in America in 1965.

THE HOBBIT
J. R. R. TOLKIEN
1937 (1998 REPRINT)
J. R. R. TOLKIEN

The beginning of the Tolkien legacy started out as a story told to his children.

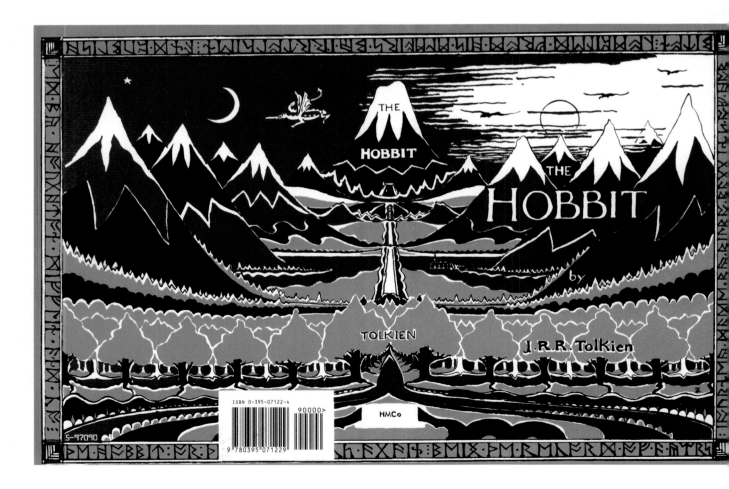

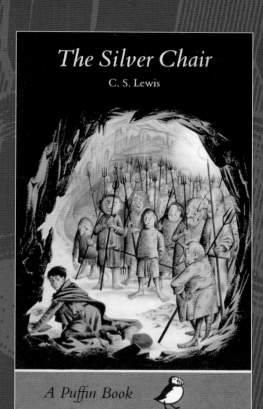

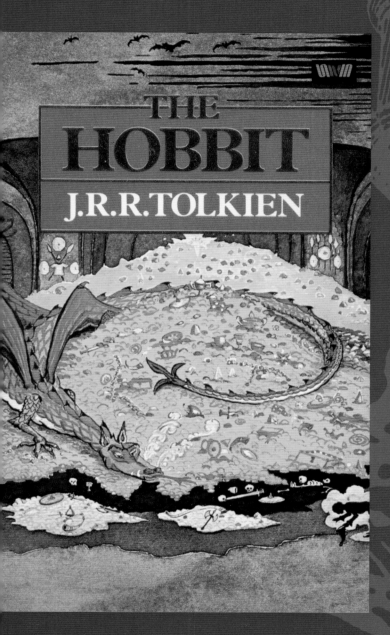

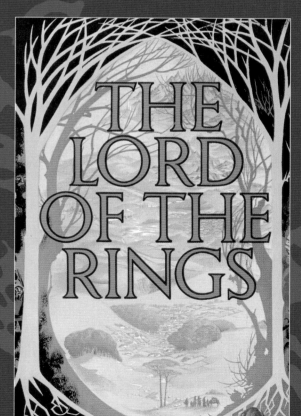

 THE SILVER CHAIR
C. S. LEWIS
1953 (1973 REPRINT)
PAULINE BAYNES

One of the books in Lewis'
'Narnia' series.

 THE LORD OF THE RINGS
J. R. R. TOLKIEN
1954–55 (1973 REPRINT)
PAULINE BAYNES

The most influential
fantasy ever written, in
one hefty volume.

 **THE HOBBIT**
J. R. R. TOLKIEN
1937 (1983 REPRINT)
J. R. R. TOLKIEN

A paperback edition with a
cover illustration by Tolkien.

7

THE FELLOWSHIP OF THE RING
J. R. R. TOLKIEN
1954 (1965 REPRINT)
ARTIST UNKNOWN

And in this corner, wearing blue, weighing slightly *over* eight and one-half ounces, is the opponent, the authorized Ballantine edition, and soon to be the heavyweight champ.

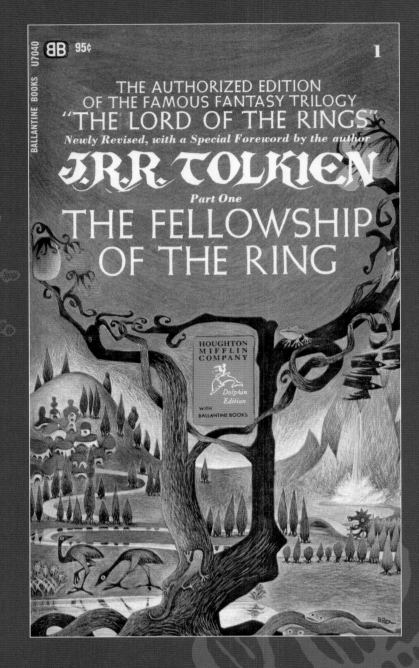

1

BALLANTINE BOOKS U7040   95¢

THE AUTHORIZED EDITION
OF THE FAMOUS FANTASY TRILOGY
"THE LORD OF THE RINGS"
Newly Revised, with a Special Foreword by the author
J.R.R. TOLKIEN
Part One
THE FELLOWSHIP
OF THE RING

HOUGHTON MIFFLIN COMPANY
Dolphin Edition
WITH BALLANTINE BOOKS

ace
SCIENCE FICTION CLASSIC
A-4
75¢

J.R.R. TOLKIEN
WINNER of the INTERNATIONAL FANTASY AWARD
The Fellowship of the Ring

"Superb—one of the major achievements of epic imagination in our lifetimes, and your life is the poorer if you have failed to read it."
—ANTHONY BOUCHER

Complete & Unabridged

6

THE FELLOWSHIP OF THE RING
J. R. R. TOLKIEN
1954 (1965 REPRINT)
JACK GAUGHAN

In this corner, wearing the red wraps and weighing eight and one-half ounces, the Ace unauthorized fantasy champion of the world.

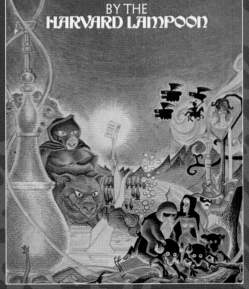

A SIGNET BOOK · N4002 · $1.00

A PARODY OF J.R.R. TOLKIEN'S
"THE LORD OF THE RINGS"
BORED OF THE RINGS
BY THE
HARVARD LAMPOON

8

BORED OF THE RINGS
HENRY N. BEARD AND
DOUGLAS C. KENNEY
1969
MICHAEL K. FRITH

The adventures of Dildo Bugger and Frito!

THE LORD OF THE RINGS

J. R. R. TOLKIEN
1954–55 (1991 REPRINT)
ALAN LEE

The profusely illustrated hardcover Tolkien centenary (1892–1992) edition.

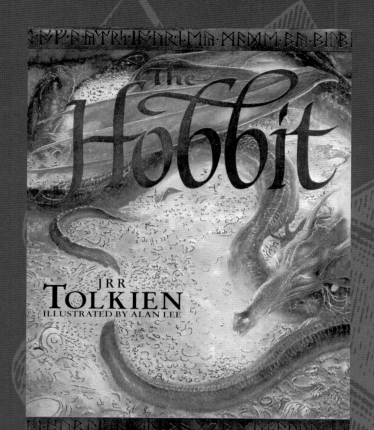

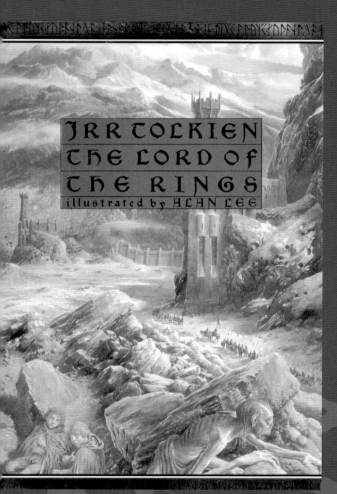

THE HOBBIT

J. R. R. TOLKIEN
1937 (1997 REPRINT)
ALAN LEE

Lee produced a staggering amount of lovely watercolors for the trilogy and *The Hobbit.*

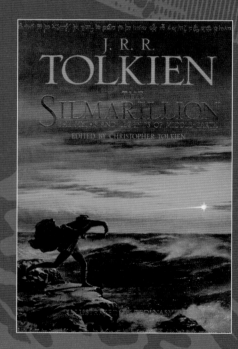

THE SILMARILLION

J. R. R. TOLKIEN
1977 (1998 REPRINT)
TED NASMITH

The posthumously published prequel to *The Lord of the Rings.*

THE 1994 J. R. R. TOLKIEN CALENDAR

1993
MICHAEL KALUTA

Comic artist Kaluta's detailed illustrations made a nice addition to the yearly calendars.

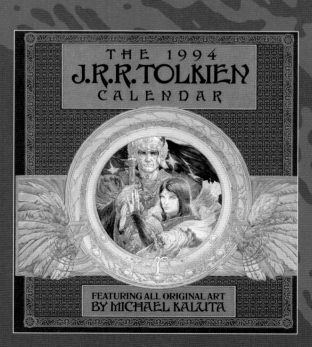

1978 J. R. R. TOLKIEN CALENDAR

1977
THE BROTHERS HILDEBRANDT

Many artists have interpreted Tolkien's trilogy for calendars and books.

14

THE SWORD OF SHANNARA
TERRY BROOKS
1977 (1991 REPRINT)
THE BROTHERS
HILDEBRANDT

Book One of the best-selling fantasy series, in the Tolkien tradition.

Ace Books and Ballantine Books were both interested in publishing the works in paperback. With Tolkien's consent, Ballantine issued the books under contract, but Ace, believing the titles were in the public domain in the U.S., published without authorization and beat the Ballantine editions to the shelves. They eventually settled with Tolkien. Sales went through the roof with figures in the millions. The books were incredibly successful and enormously popular, particularly with students of academe. "Frodo Lives!" buttons and bumperstickers were a common sight. There was even a lampoon in 1969 titled *Bored of the Rings*. Whether readers liked it or not, Tolkien was not going away and fantasy was back, alive and kicking.

Tolkien wrote other books involving Middle Earth as well as several unrelated pieces for both adults and children, often providing his own illustrations.

Greg and Tim Hildebrandt, a twin brothers artist team, produced many paintings for *The Lord of the Rings* in their unique style which recalled the work of earlier American illustrators N. C. Wyeth and Maxfield Parrish and became associated with this type of fantasy art. Initially featuring the artwork of Tolkien himself and artist Tim Kirk, a series of Tolkien calendars have remained popular to this day, featuring interpretations by a wide variety of artists, including the Hildebrandts.

Perhaps the most recognizable of the more recent illustrators of Tolkien is British artist Alan Lee. Earlier in his career he collaborated with fellow artist Brian Froud on the innovative and hugely successful art book *Faeries* (1978). Their work is a throwback to the school of English book illustrators of the early twentieth century and the delicate watercolorists Arthur Rackham, Edmund Dulac, and W. Russell Flint. Lee went off on his own to create more of his

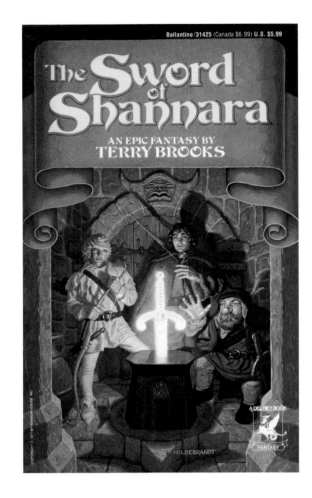

evocative watercolors and in 1991 he illustrated a new hardcover edition of *The Lord of the Rings* with a staggering fifty paintings. He followed that with a giftbook version of *The Hobbit* (1997) containing over twenty-five watercolors and many exquisite pencil drawings.

The Lord of the Rings and Tolkien's other works continue to inspire a wealth of illustrated material, and there are no signs of diminishing interest. Considered by many to be the best and most influential fantasy, and certainly one of the most popular and bestselling books in the world, *The Lord of the Rings* has entertained millions of readers and inspired numerous writers.

It was inspirational in other areas as well. In 1973 Tactical Studies Rules (TSR) run by Gary Gygax and Donald Kaye, created a game that became a phenomenon. It was called *Dungeons & Dragons* (or *D&D*) and became the ultimate fantasy role-playing game.

A NATIONAL BESTSELLER

The Chronicles of Thomas
Covenant the Unbeliever
BOOK ONE

A DEL REY BOOK
FANTASY

LORD FOUL'S BANE

STEPHEN R. DONALDSON

15

LORD FOUL'S BANE
STEPHEN R. DONALDSON
1977 (1982 REPRINT)
DARRELL K. SWEET

Another epic fantasy trilogy
that soon begat other trilogies.

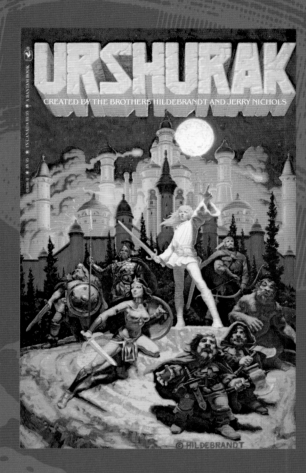

16

URSHURAK
THE BROTHERS
HILDEBRANDT AND
JERRY NICHOLS
1979
THE BROTHERS
HILDEBRANDT

Greg and Tim
Hildebrandt produced
sixteen paintings
and over eighty black
and white drawings
for their co-created
heroic fantasy.

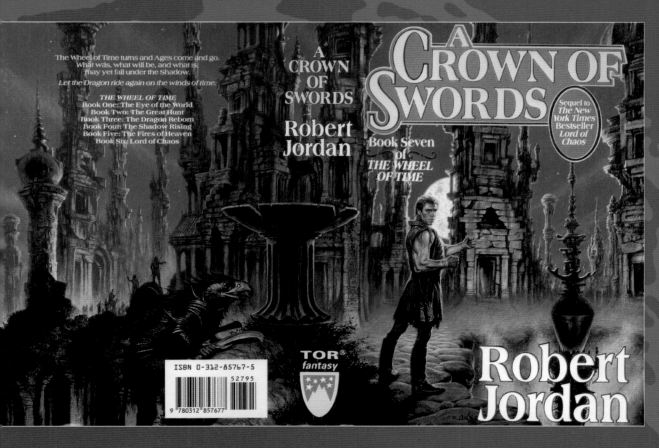

17

A CROWN OF SWORDS
ROBERT JORDAN
1996
DARREL K. SWEET

"The Wheel of Time" is a
phenomenal bestselling
series by Jordan.

THE RUBY KNIGHT
DAVID EDDINGS
1991
KEITH PARKINSON

Eddings, with his wife Leigh, has written several heroic fantasy sequences.

THE HAND OF CHAOS
MARGARET WEIS AND TRACY HICKMAN
1993
KEITH PARKINSON

Volume Five in their ambitious 'Death Gate' cycle.

THE DARK TIDE
DENNIS L. MCKIERNAN
1984 (1985 REPRINT)
ALAN LEE

Another trilogy in the Tolkien mold.

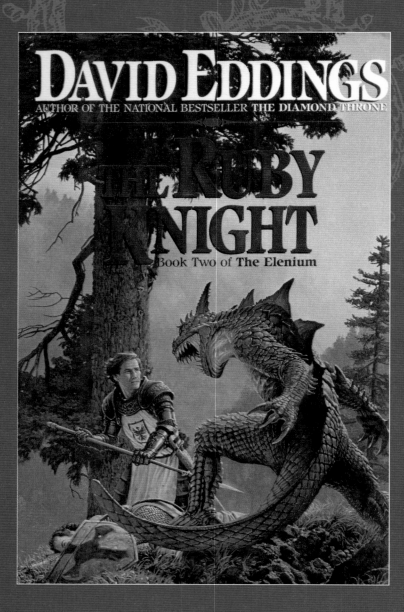

THE FIRE DRAGON
KATHARINE KERR
2000
GEOFF TAYLOR

The final volume in Kerr's 'Dragon Mage' series. They do seem to be popular creatures.

In 1977 *The Silmarillion* was published posthumously. This was Tolkien's long-labored "prequel" to *The Lord of the Rings* and was edited by his son, Christopher Tolkien. That same year, Tolkien's literary legacy became apparent with the publication of works by two new authors, both of which went on to become worldwide bestsellers.

The Sword of Shannara by Terry Brooks inaugurated the Ballantine Del Rey imprint (named after editor Lester Del Rey) and put Brooks on the *New York Times* bestseller list, where no contemporary fantasy writer had featured before. It was the first in a series that would extend over seven volumes into the 1990s. Closely patterned after Tolkien, there was a Hobbit-like central character, a wizard, and a dangerous quest. Brooks has written other light fantasy series since as well as delving into the darker side of fantasy in his more recent work. The Shannara books were given cover treatments by the Hildebrandt brothers, in their best Tolkien tradition, as well as by another talented artist, Darrell K. Sweet, who has produced a remarkable amount of fantasy art for a variety of authors including Tolkien.

The second newcomer was Stephen R. (Reeder) Donaldson, who presented a more unique approach to this type of fantasy with the impressive *Chronicles of Thomas Covenant the Unbeliever,* a trilogy beginning with *Lord Foul's Bane.* The protagonist was a leper, called upon to save an alternate world from the ravages perpetrated by Lord Foul, The Despiser. This series also contained elements similar to Tolkien's epic. The story continued through *The Second Chronicles of Thomas Covenant* sequel trilogy, written by Donaldson in the early 1980s.

Donaldson and Brooks were just two of the writers who burst onto the scene with fantasy blockbusters in the wake of Tolkien; now they are considered seasoned veterans among today's genre talents.

The fantasy field seemed to have a winner on its hands with this heroic quest-type of story. Both publishers and writers alike understood the equation that more fantasy plus more pages (three or even four books) equaled more money.

It was the time of the trilogy, the season of the series. Even Tim and Greg Hildebrandt, who had painted enough of this material for other writers to know what to look for, decided to eliminate the middle man by illustrating and writing their own epic, *Urshurak* (1979) with Jerry Nichols.

A great deal of fine writing came out of this period, but some authors preferred to let J. R. R. do all the "Tolkien" by following his books a little too closely in their own epics.

This type of heroic fantasy, which turned into such a commercial enterprise during the 1970s and 1980s, is probably what the average reader today considers the fantasy genre to be all about. There is still a tremendous amount of Tolkienesque writing being produced, and it remains extremely popular. Many are series creations, running over numerous volumes, making the concept of the trilogy seem old hat. Among the innumerable writers entertaining readers with tales of their own Middle Earths is Robert Jordan, who contributed several novels about Robert E. Howard's character Conan in the 1980s and who later turned to his own epic series, 'The Wheel of Time', in the 1990s. With a gift for storytelling, Jordan has produced a bestselling saga of immense proportions, containing all the elements of the classic fantasy quest.

David Eddings, with his now openly credited wife Leigh, has also amassed both a large body of work and

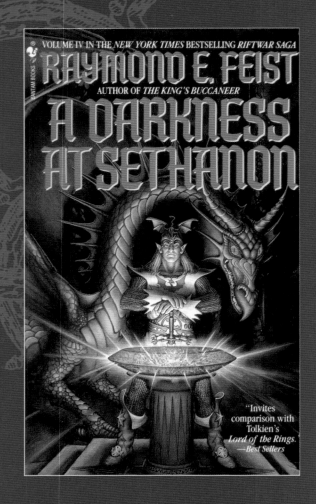

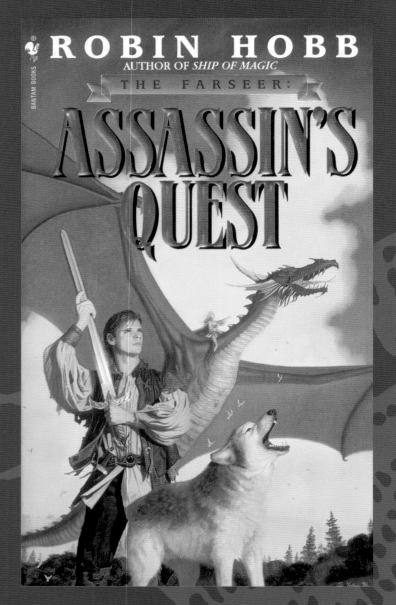

22
A DARKNESS AT SETHANON
RAYMOND E. FEIST
1986 (1993 REPRINT)
DON MAITZ

Feist's 'Rift War' saga draws
to a conclusion and, as
evidenced in other covers,
artist Maitz knows his way
around a dragon.

an equally large following with the 'Belgariad' (1982–
95), 'Malloreaon' (1987–91), 'Elenium' (1989–91),
and 'Tamuli' (1992–94) sequences.

The team of Margaret Weiss and Tracy Hickman is
also extremely popular. Initially a games designer for
TSR, Hickman joined forces with Weiss when TSR
ventured into publishing to produce *The DragonLance
Chronicles* (1984–94) for a ready-made audience. They
have gone on to develop other successful fantasy projects such as the 'Darksword' (1988) and 'Rose of the
Prophet' (1989) trilogies and the longer 'Death Gate
Cycle' sequence (1990–94).

Both Katharine Kerr and Katherine Kurtz work in
the somewhat similar modes of Celtic-influenced
fantasy, Kurtz being the veteran writer of the two with
her long-running 'Deryni' series which began in 1970.

Canadian author Guy Gavriel Kay assisted
Christopher Tolkien with *The Silmarillion* and also
found time to produce his own epic fantasy series,
'The Fionavar Tapestry' (1985–86).

Janny Wurts, wife of fantasy artist Don Maitz and
an artist herself, has contributed 'The Cycle of Fire'
trilogy (1984–88) among others; she teamed up with
another bestselling fantasist, Raymond E. Feist, to
produce the 'Byzantine Empire' trilogy (1987–92).
Feist himself, who also did design work on role-playing games early in his career, set down 'The Riftwar
Saga' (1982–92) and the ongoing 'Serpent Wars' series
(1994–). *Faerie Tale* (1988), a separate novel, was an
effective dark fantasy extending the realm of faerie
uncomfortably close to the contemporary world.

Robin Hobb developed the interesting otherworld
fantasy, 'Farseer Trilogy' (1995–97) and earlier, under her real name of Megan Lindholm, wrote the
Windsingers trilogy (1983–84) and a stand-alone
novel, *The Wizard of the Pigeons* (1996), an urban

23
ASSASSIN'S QUEST
ROBIN HOBB
1997 (1998 REPRINT)
STEVEN YOULL

Another series comes to a close, this time 'The Farseer Trilogy'
by Hobb, the pseudonym of writer Megan Lindholm.

WIZARD OF THE PIGEONS
MEGAN LINDHOLM
1986
ROBERT GOULD

The "wizard" is a Vietnam veteran with magical abilities living in the streets of Seattle in this breakthrough novel.

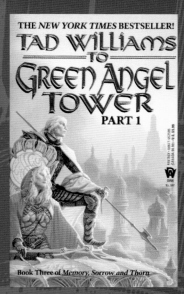

THE *NEW YORK TIMES* BESTSELLER!
TAD WILLIAMS
TO
GREEN ANGEL
TOWER
Part 1

Book Three of *Memory, Sorrow and Thorn*

TO GREEN ANGEL TOWER
TAD WILLIAMS
1993 (1994 REPRINT)
MICHAEL WHELAN

Book Three of the 'Memory, Sorrow and Thorn' high fantasy trilogy.

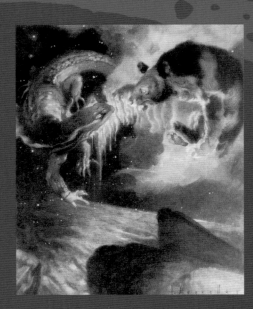

HE NEVER ASKED TO BE A WIZARD.
BUT WHEN EVIL STRIKES, YOU MUST FIGHT—OR DIE...
MEGAN LINDHOLM
WIZARD OF THE PIGEONS

WIZARD'S FIRST RULE

"A phenomenal fantasy, endlessly inventive, that surely marks the commencement of one of the major careers in the genre." —Piers Anthony

A *Sword of Truth* Novel

NEW YORK TIMES
Bestselling Author

"A wonderfully creative, seamless, and stirring epic fantasy debut."
—Kirkus Reviews

TERRY GOODKIND

FAMOUS DREAMS IV—KING ARTHUR'S VISION OF THE BEAR AND THE DRAGON
THE ILLUSTRATED LONDON NEWS CHRISTMAS 1932
JOSÉ SEGRELLES

An interpretation of Arthur's dream of a battle between the dragon (himself) and the bear (the Emperor of Rome) as told by Geoffrey of Monmouth.

WIZARD'S FIRST RULE
TERRY GOODKIND
1994
DOUG BEEKMAN

An impressive debut from Goodkind.

MALORY'S LE MORTE D'ARTHUR

KEITH BAINES
1962
DILLON

A newer rendition by Keith Baines of the most famous book of Arthurian legend.

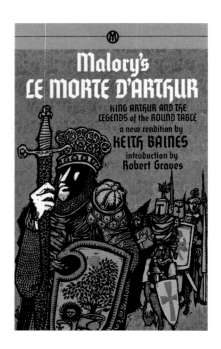

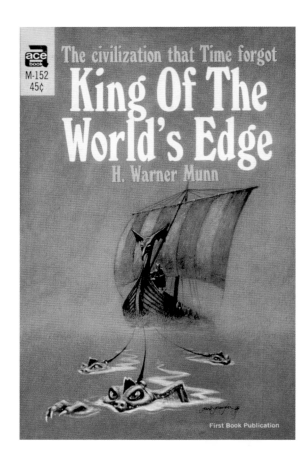

KING OF THE WORLD'S EDGE

H. WARNER MUNN
1939 (1966 REPRINT)
JACK GAUGHAN

Munn's Arthurian adventure fantasy originally appeared in *Weird Tales*.

LE MORTE DARTHUR

SIR THOMAS MABRY
1910–11
W. RUSSELL FLINT

One of 48 stunning watercolors by Flint for the four-volume set and by far the best illustrated version of Malory's text.

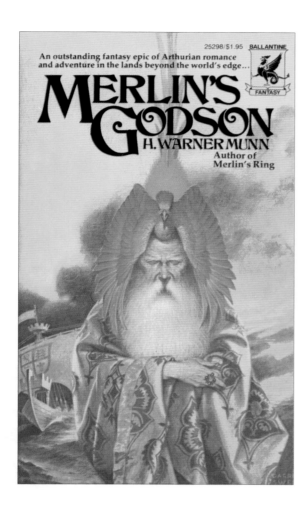

fantasy about a Vietnam veteran with magical abilities living among Seattle's homeless.

Mickey Zucker Reichert (a.k.a. Miriam S. Zucker Reichert) has enjoyed commercial success with the 'Bifrost Guardians' (1988–91) and 'Renshai' (1992–93) sequences as well as other fantasy novels playing upon themes of Norse mythology.

Melanie Rawn created two trilogies, the 'Dragon Prince' (1988–90) and 'Dragonstar' (1990–93) series, that put a different spin on the dragon, a fantasy staple. Veteran writer Anne McCaffrey did the same and has won numerous awards including the British Fantasy Society's Karl Edward Wagner Special Award for her long-running 'Dragons of Pern' books (1968–), although these are usually considered science fiction because of their interplanetary setting.

Tad Williams' main contribution in the high fantasy arena is the 'Memory, Sorrow and Thorn' trilogy

(1988–93), an intelligently written and ambitious fantasy series.

Terry Goodkind is one of the newer writers to achieve bestseller status with the quest fantasy in his 'Sword of Truth' series in the mid-1990s. Although in the Tolkien vein, the fantasy elements in these books are considerably darker than most.

Before revealing the right hook that accompanied that left jab fantasy delivered in the 1960s, another theme that fits into the heading of heroic or quest literature is the Arthurian fantasy.

The first written appearance of the story of Arthur was in *Historia Regum Britanniae*, a history of the kings of Britain, circa 1140 by Geoffrey of Monmouth. Arthur is mentioned along with Guinevere, the wizard Merlin, and the traitor Mordred. Other early French and German contributions to the legend added the concept of the Round Table, Sir Lancelot, the quest for the Holy Grail, and the idea of the sword in the stone. The Germanic tales of Tristan and Parsifal elaborated the legend further.

Le Morte Darthur by Sir Thomas Malory in the late fifteenth century assembled several of those earlier bits and pieces to form what is probably the most famous book in the English language on the subject.

During the 1800s, the theme inspired several epic poems, including *Idylls of the King* (1859) by Alfred, Lord Tennyson. Mark Twain took a humorous shot at the story with his classic *A Connecticut Yankee in King Arthur's Court* (1889). Howard Pyle, American illustrator and teacher and founding father of the Brandywine School (that counted Maxfield Parrish, N. C. Wyeth, Jessie Wilcox Smith and Frank Schoonover among its students), wrote and illustrated his own version of the story, lavishly produced over four volumes between 1903 and

MERLIN'S GODSON
H. WARNER MUNN
1976
DARREL K. SWEET
A combined publication of two Munn novels, with a great cover by Sweet.

**THE ONCE AND
FUTURE KING**
T. H. WHITE
1938–58 (1987 REPRINT)
FREDERICK MARVIN

Four novels make up
this acclaimed version
of Arthur's story.

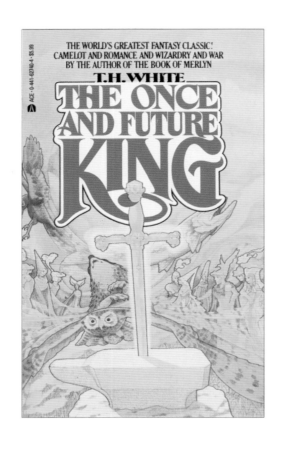

THE CRYSTAL CAVE
MARY STEWART
1970
ARTIST UNKNOWN

The first book in
Stewart's bestselling
Merlin trilogy, exploring
the Arthur story as
seen through the eyes
of the wizard.

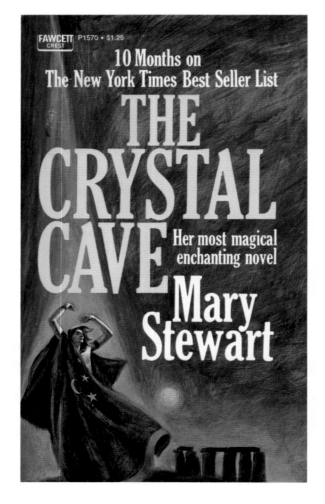

1910. Beginning with *The Story of King Arthur and his Knights,* originally serialized in *St. Nicholas Magazine,* Pyle went on to complete three other volumes: *The Story of the Champions of the Round Table* (1905), *The Story of Sir Lancelot and His Companions* (1907), and *The Story of the Grail and the Passing of Arthur* (1910). It was a success both as a literary and an artistic venture, containing some of Pyle's most ambitious pen-and-ink work, which he completed shortly before his death in 1911.

The subject of Arthurian legend was popular with many illustrators during the so-called Golden Age of Illustration. Sir W. Russell Flint produced what may be the most beautifully illustrated version of *Le Morte Darthur* in 1910–11 from Phillip Lee Warner of London, with forty-eight of his spectacular watercolors spread over four volumes. Much earlier, in 1894, Aubrey Beardsley, master of pen-and-ink decadence, delivered his interpretation of Malory's book with some inspired drawings.

H. (Harold) Warner Munn, the pulp writer famous for his *Werewolf of Ponkert* (1925–28) stories in *Weird Tales,* wrote an Arthurian fantasy called *King of the World's Edge* for the pulp magazine in 1939. It went into paperback in 1966 and the following year a sequel appeared, *The Ship from Atlantis.* The two were combined as *Merlin's Godson* in 1976. Munn also mixed Arthur and Atlantis in *Merlin's Ring* in 1974.

In 1958 one of the most celebrated versions of the Arthurian legend was published. *The Once and Future King,* written by T. H. (Terence Hanbury) White, combined four linked novels to follow the tale of Arthur from his early days as Merlyn's student through his adulthood and the tragedies that followed. White displayed an acute sense of realism, whether describing fantasy moments—as in young

The magical saga of the women behind King Arthur's throne...

THE MISTS OF AVALON

"A monumental reimagining of the Arthurian legends...
reading it is a deeply moving and at times uncanny experience..."
An impressive achievement."
The New York Times Book Review

MARION ZIMMER BRADLEY

THE MISTS OF AVALON
MARION ZIMMER BRADLEY
1982 (1984 REPRINT)
BRALDT BRALDS

For her Celtic fantasy
bestseller, Bradley sees
the Arthur legend from
Morgan Le Fay's point
of view.

EXCALIBUR
SANDERS ANNE
LAUBENTHAL
1973
GERVASIO GALLARDO

A quite different type of
tale about the sword of
Arthur Pendragon.

SWORD AND SORCERESS I
EDITED BY MARION
ZIMMER BRADLEY
1984
VICTORIA POYSER

A long-running anthology
of heroic fantasies of
courageous women
featuring stories by
Emma Bull and Jennifer
Roberson among others.

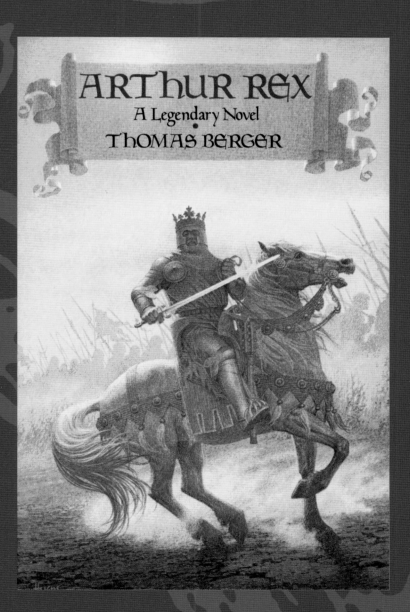

ARTHUR REX
THOMAS BERGER
1978
JEAN-LOUIS HUENS

Arthur's story from the
author of *Little Big Man*.

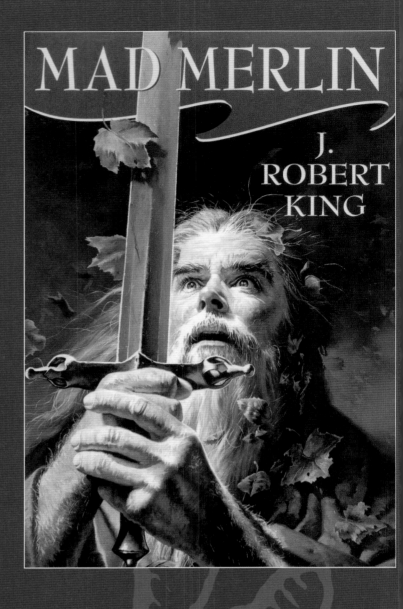

MAD MERLIN

J. ROBERT KING

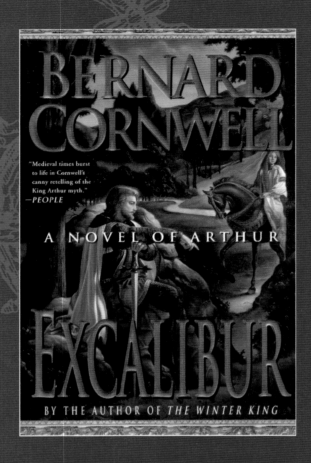

EXCALIBUR
BERNARD CORNWELL
1997 (1999 REPRINT)
DAVID BOWERS

Volume Three of
Cornwell's 'War Lord
Chronicles' that began
with *The Winter King*.

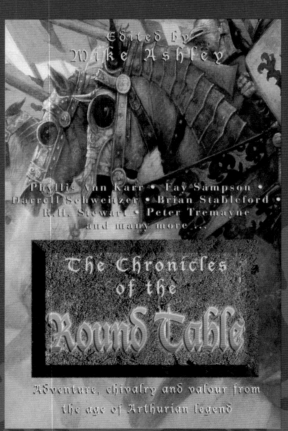

**THE CHRONICLES OF THE
ROUND TABLE**
EDITED BY MIKE ASHLEY
1997
JULEK HELLER

An anthology of
Arthurian tales by
some of today's fantasy
practitioners.

Arthur's transformations into various animals by
Merlyn—or everyday mediaeval period trappings.
The narrative is told with a good deal of humor,
making it a charming and imaginative work of literature. The first three parts of the book were published
separately and then revised when the fourth section
was added and they were combined into a single volume. Not only a bestseller, *The Once and Future King*
was the basis for Lerner and Loewe's 1961 Broadway
musical *Camelot*, as well as several films including
Disney's animated *The Sword in the Stone* (1963).
Fantasy writer and editor Lin Carter described the
book as "The single finest fantasy novel written in
our time, or for that matter, ever written". High praise
indeed, coming from someone who would play a
large part in the revival of fantasy literature during
the 1960s and 1970s and bring an awareness of its
early practitioners to a modern reading public.

MAD MERLIN
J. ROBERT KING
2000
GARY RUDDELL

An original tale from an author whose previous work included novels based around TSR, Inc.'s role-playing games.

In 1970, British writer Mary Stewart's very successful 'Merlin Trilogy', beginning with *The Crystal Cave*, was the Arthur legend as told from Merlin's point of view. She later added other books of Arthur's saga to the series as well as writing other fantasies for children and adults.

Another British author and founder of the U.K. Tolkien Society, Vera Chapman, told of the events from a female perspective, starting with *The Green Knight* (1975) and continuing through *The King's Damosels* (1976) and *King Arthur's Daughter* (1976) combined into an omnibus edition, *The Three Damosels*, in 1976. This was followed by *The Enchantress*, telling the stories of Ygraine's daughters, Arthur's half-sisters Morgause, Vivian, and Morgan. It was published in 1998, two years after Chapman's death at the age of ninety-eight. Chapman clearly anticipated the feminist slant used by Marion Zimmer Bradley in the bestseller *The Mists of Avalon* (1982) in which Arthur's story is perceived by Morgan Le Fay.

Bradley also wrote the borderline science fiction/ fantasy 'Darkover' series (1958–1994) in addition to some sword and sorcery and contributions to the 'Thieve's World' (1979–89) shared world series. *Sword and Sorceress* was a long-running annual anthology concept of hers, and in 1988 the fantasy magazine bearing her name was first published. It continued to appear until 2000, the year after Bradley's death. Her ashes were scattered on Glastonbury Tor in England.

Among the other innumerable novels which cover Arthurian territory are *Parsival; or a Knight's Tale* (1977), *The Grail War* (1979), *The Final Quest* (1980), and *Blood and Dreams* (1985) all by Richard Monaco; *Arthur Rex* (1978) by Thomas Berger; David Drake's 1979 novel *The Dragon Lord;* Parke Godwin's trilogy

Firelord (1980), *Beloved Exile* (1984) and *The Last Rainbow* (1985); and the *Daughter of Tintagel* series (1989–92) by Fay Sampson. British writer Haydn Middleton's 'Mordred Cycle', starting with *The King's Evil* (1995), went for a decidedly darker look at the legend and Stephen Lawhead's *Pendragon* series, which stretched over five novels during the 1980s and 1990s, was followed by his *Avalon: Return of King Arthur* (1999).

Arthur and Camelot continue to hold a great fascination for fantasy writers, as does the concept of the enchanted object as featured in Tolkien's epic and other fantasies and fairy tales. These and similar concepts are often used as major ingredients in a wide range of heroic high fantasy.

The popularity of Tolkien's books and the mythical Excalibur and its owner has not been lost on Hollywood either. *The Lord of the Rings,* or at least a part of it, received a disappointing animated treatment by Ralph Bakshi in 1978. There is also a long-anticipated live action presentation in three parts, due in 2001 from New Zealand director Peter Jackson.

Arthur has run the gamut from the sublime to the ridiculous, with portrayals ranging from Sean Connery to Graham Chapman of Monty Python. Malory's version of the legend received a beautiful treatment by director John Boorman as *Excalibur* (1981).

By the latter part of the 1960s, heroic fantasy, like one of its own protagonists, seemed unbeatable. But this was just the first part of that combination punch. Unsuspecting readers had no idea that a strong right hook was about to be delivered or that its impact would be so great—especially when the writer who would soon "knock 'em dead" had been dead himself for almost thirty years.

CHAPTER 7

HAVE SWORD, WILL TRAVEL

At the top of the paperback the title stood out in bold white letters against a black background—*Swords & Sorcery*. Listed below in bright yellow was quite an impressive array of names, most of them recognizable from the pulps: H. P. Lovecraft, Robert E. Howard, Henry Kuttner, Clark Ashton Smith, C. L. Moore, even Lord Dunsany. There was also a Fritz Leiber 'Fafhrd and the Gray Mouser' story from *Fantastic* from 1960, but it mostly included older material. The artwork below depicted a warrior-knight with raised sword confronting a sorceress with three demon-like figures within swirling flames. It even looked

1

SWORDS & SORCERY
EDITED BY L. SPRAGUE
DE CAMP
1963
VIRGIL FINLAY

De Camp brings 'em back
alive and kicking from the
pulps and puts together a
first-class anthology.

2

THE SPELL OF SEVEN
EDITED BY L. SPRAGUE
DE CAMP
1965
VIRGIL FINLAY

Another de Camp
anthology contributing
to the heroic fantasy
revival.

like a pulp. With good reason, as the artist was Virgil Finlay, who had cut his artistic teeth during the pulp heyday and provided countless interior illustrations for *Weird Tales* and *Famous Fantastic Mysteries* among many other titles, as well as numerous beautiful cover paintings. Some of those old interior drawings were reprinted inside this paperback.

It was edited and introduced by L. Sprague de Camp, no stranger to the field himself. Published by Pyramid Books in 1963, it sold for the princely sum of fifty cents. What a bargain! It also marked a turning point in the revival of heroic fantasy literature.

In his introduction, de Camp provided a brief history of the genre and encouraged the interested reader to seek out more of the same.

In 1965 he followed it with another anthology for Pyramid. *The Spell of Seven* was the title; it showcased another original Virgil Finlay cover, even more pulp-like than the previous one. Repeating the formula for success, it again contained classics by Howard, Smith, and Dunsany. There were also more recent stories, notably another 'Fafhrd and the Gray Mouser' tale by Fritz Leiber, again reprinted from *Fantastic*. Also included was a story by a young British writer, Michael Moorcock, reprinted from its first appearance in 1962 in *Science Fantasy*, a U.K. digest magazine. Entitled "Kings In Darkness", it was a story of Elric, Prince of Melniboné. What distinguished Elric immediately from the usual run-of-the-mill swordsman was his physical appearance: he was a scarlet-eyed, white-maned, weak-looking albino whose strength lay in his runic sword, Stormbringer, which sucked the souls of those it slayed. The only problem was that once drawn from its scabbard, Stormbringer had to feed, sometimes on the innocent as well as the evil.

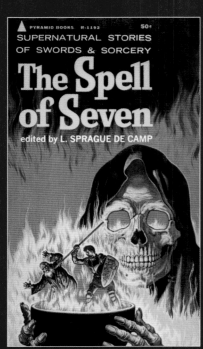

LANCER BOOKS 78751-125 $1.25

The Stealer of Souls

★ MEET THE INCREDIBLE ELRIC ★
★ FIVE MAGNIFICENT STORIES ★
★ FANTASY ADVENTURE AT ITS BEST ★

Michael Moorcock

3

THE STEALER OF SOULS
MICHAEL MOORCOCK
1961–62 (1973 REPRINT)
JEFF JONES

More of Elric's saga, reprinted and revised from the British digest *Science Fantasy*.

LANCER BOOKS 73-879 60¢

STORMBRINGER

ELRIC, THE HAUNTED WARRIOR-KING, FIGHTS A TITANIC DUEL AGAINST THE FORCES OF CHAOS. "POWERFUL AND SUSTAINED IMAGINATION" —J. G. BALLARD

MICHAEL MOORCOCK
AUTHOR OF THE STEALER OF SOULS

4

STORMBRINGER
MICHAEL MOORCOCK
1965 (1967 REPRINT)
JACK GAUGHAN

Enter Elric, albino prince of Melniboné, and not your typical heroic figure.

127

6

**THE SAILOR ON THE
SEAS OF FATE**
MICHAEL MOORCOCK
1976
MICHAEL WHELAN

One of Whelan's
atmospheric covers
for the Elric series.

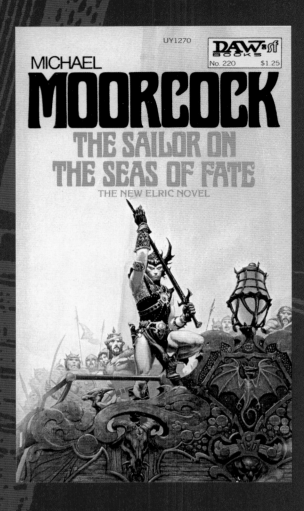

UY1270

DAW sf
BOOKS
No. 220 $1.25

MICHAEL
MOORCOCK
**THE SAILOR ON
THE SEAS OF FATE**
THE NEW ELRIC NOVEL

UW1335

DAW sf
BOOKS
No. 264 $1.50

MICHAEL
MOORCOCK
STORMBRINGER

5

STORMBRINGER
MICHAEL MOORCOCK
1965 (1977 REPRINT)
MICHAEL WHELAN

A striking and dramatic portrait of Elric
from one of the series published by Donald
A. Wollheim's DAW books.

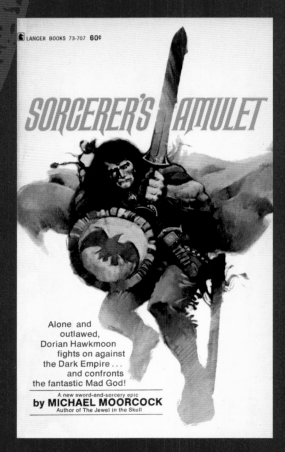

LANCER BOOKS 73-707 60¢

SORCERER'S AMULET

Alone and
outlawed,
Dorian Hawkmoon
fights on against
the Dark Empire . . .
and confronts
the fantastic Mad God!

A new sword-and-sorcery epic
by **MICHAEL MOORCOCK**
Author of The Jewel in the Skull

7

SORCERER'S AMULET
MICHAEL MOORCOCK
1968
JEFF JONES

Another of Moorcock's unique heroes, Dorian
Hawkmoon, and an early fantasy cover by Jones.

8

THE ELRIC SAGA PART I
MICHAEL MOORCOCK
1984
ROBERT GOULD

A hardcover collection of three of the
books in the series about Moorcock's
celebrated thin, white prince.

The Elric stories were originally published in *Science Fantasy* between 1961–1964 and later assembled in collections in both the U.K. and United States. Each collection went through numerous printings as Moorcock proved to be one of the most successful writers in the field. He went on to create several series characters, all of which would be written in his unique style, and many of whom would form the concept of "The Eternal Champion", tying together different volumes with the idea of alternate realities or the "multiverse", as Moorcock called it. Some of these characters included Prince Corum of the Silver Hand; Dorian Hawkmoon, who had a living black jewel embedded in his forehead; and Erekose, who remembered other lives he lived as an embodiment of the Eternal Champion. These and other heroes interrelated in over a dozen books.

Michael Moorcock, who would become a major talent, writing and editing in many fields, also contributed a superior fantasy with *Gloriana, or the Unfulfilled Queen* (1978), set in an alternate Elizabethan England reminiscent of Mervyn Peake's *Gormenghast* sequence (1946–59). It won the World Fantasy Award for Best Novel in 1979.

The Elric series from DAW Books, the Donald A. Wollheim imprint, was published with beautiful covers by award-winning artist Michael Whelan.

Another story of note in *The Spell of Seven* was "Mazirian the Magician" by Jack Vance. Vance was an important science fiction writer, but he wrote a series of linked stories called *The Dying Earth* in 1950 in which a distant future earth, lit by a dying sun, is populated by all manner of magicians and monsters. It was pure fantasy and recalled the otherworldly beauty of Clark Ashton Smith in both language and the use of imagery.

THE DYING EARTH
JACK VANCE
1950 (1976 REPRINT)
GEORGE BARR

This landmark fantasy gets a beautiful illustrated hardcover treatment from
Underwood-Miller, who went on to do the same for many of Vance's books.

THE EYES OF THE OVERWORLD
JACK VANCE
1966
JACK GAUGHAN

More adventures of the Dying
Earth and Cugel the Clever.

Vance would later follow up with *The Eyes of the Overworld* in 1966, introducing Cugel the Clever and his adventures in trying to gain the upper hand over wizards and demons. He usually managed to do so but invariably paid more of a price than he bargained for, being a bit too clever for his own good.

In the 1970s Vance gave permission to Michael Shea to write a sequel to *The Eyes of the Overworld, A Quest for Simbilis* (1974), which engagingly continued Cugel's story in Vance's style. Shea returned to similar country with *Nifft the Lean* (1982) for which he won a World Fantasy Award the following year. Vance himself continued the *Dying Earth* sequence with *Cugel's Saga* in 1983, followed by a number of other stories. Then came the trilogy, *Lyonesse* (1983–89), set in a time a few generations before that of King Arthur, in the "Elder Isles" (west of France and the English Channel) that are now, like Atlantis, sunken lands. Full-blown fantastic elements included faeries, giants, and changelings, as well as the beauty of magic and landscape that he displayed so well in the *Dying Earth* series. The last part of the trilogy, *Madouc,* was the winner of the World Fantasy Award for Best Novel in 1990; Vance justifiably received the World Fantasy Award for Lifetime Achievement in 1984.

There was a nugget of information in *The Spell of Seven* that would soon prove to have quite an effect on the genre.

At the end of his introduction to the last story in the collection, Robert E. Howard's Conan piece "Shadows in Zamboula", de Camp wrote: "Plans are on foot to reprint the entire Conan saga in paperback form."

In 1964, Ace Paperbacks had published Howard's interplanetary fantasy, *Almuric,* with a cover by

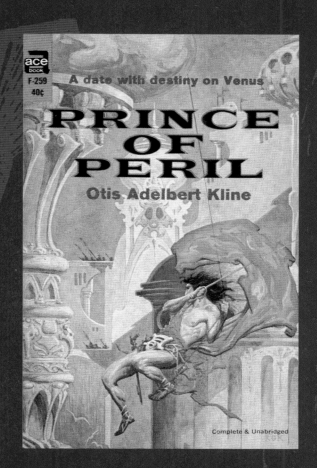

A date with destiny on Venus

ace book

F-259
40¢

PRINCE OF PERIL

Otis Adelbert Kline

Complete & Unabridged

Alone on an uncharted planet.

ace book

F-305
40¢

ALMURIC
ROBERT E. HOWARD

First Book Publication

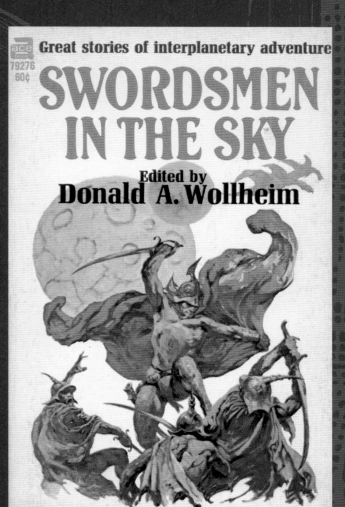

Great stories of interplanetary adventure

ace book

79276
60¢

SWORDSMEN IN THE SKY

Edited by Donald A. Wollheim

CONAN THE CONQUEROR
ROBERT E. HOWARD
1950 (1967 REPRINT)
FRANK FRAZETTA

The only Conan novel by Howard.
If you close your eyes you can
almost hear the clash of steel and
the screams, but then you wouldn't
see that beautiful cover.

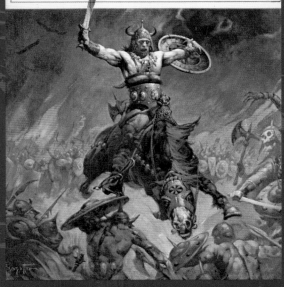

LANCER BOOKS 73-572 60¢ • VOLUME THREE OF THE COMPLETE CONAN

ROBERT E. HOWARD edited by L. SPRAGUE DE CAMP

"HOWARD'S ONLY BOOK-LENGTH NOVEL. WORTHY
TO STAND BESIDE SUCH HEROIC FANTASY AS
E. R. EDDISON AND J. R. R. TOLKIEN." ☐ ☐ ☐

CONAN
THE CONQUEROR

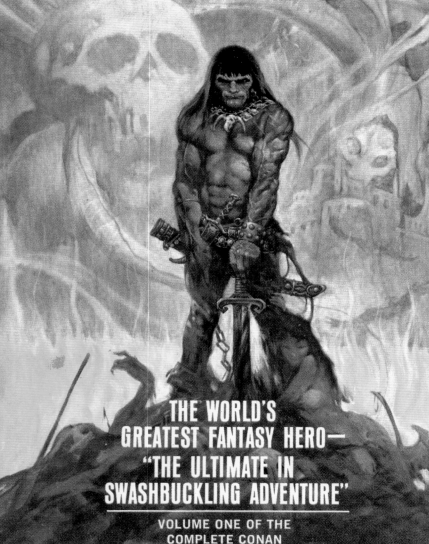

LANCER ✦ BOOKS   73-526   60

CONAN
THE ADVENTURER

THE WORLD'S
GREATEST FANTASY HERO—
"THE ULTIMATE IN
SWASHBUCKLING ADVENTURE"

VOLUME ONE OF THE
COMPLETE CONAN
ROBERT E. HOWARD and L. SPRAGUE DE CAMP

LANCER ✦ BOOKS 73-599 60¢ • VOLUME FOUR OF THE COMPLETE CONAN

ROBERT E. HOWARD and L. SPRAGUE DE CAMP
SWORDSMEN AND SORCERERS, DEMONS AND DOOMS—
GREAT TALES OF THE MIGHTIEST ADVENTURER...

CONAN
THE USURPER

CONAN THE ADVENTURER
ROBERT E. HOWARD AND
L. SPRAGUE DE CAMP
1966
FRANK FRAZETTA

A fantasy publishing
milestone. The winning
combination of Howard
and Frazetta was a bonus!

CONAN THE USURPER
ROBERT E. HOWARD AND
L. SPRAGUE DE CAMP
1967
FRANK FRAZETTA

Times change and so
do snakes on covers for
Howard stories. This
one is impressive to say
the least.

LANCER ■ BOOKS 73-685 60¢ • VOLUME FIVE OF THE COMPLETE CONAN

ROBERT E. HOWARD, L. SPRAGUE DE CAMP
and **LIN CARTER**
THE EARLIEST, MOST SAVAGE BATTLES OF
FANTASY-ADVENTURE'S MIGHTIEST HERO

CONAN

science fantasy artist Jack Gaughan. Under the editorship of Donald Wollheim (who had previously worked for Avon on anthologies including *Avon Fantasy Reader*), Ace had been reprinting the pulp work of Otis Adelbert Kline and Edgar Rice Burroughs in paperback. These boasted beautiful color cover paintings by Roy Krenkel and Frank Frazetta, artists whose work went back to the EC Comics of the 1950s and who were themselves influenced by J. Allen St. John and others. These reprints proved to be extremely popular.

Apart from *Almuric*, the last time a Howard novel had seen major paperback publication was also with Ace, in 1953, when *Conan the Conqueror* was brought out as half of an Ace Double. Ace Doubles were two-for-one book bargains: two novels published back-to-back in one paperback with different covers on the front and back. The Conan cover was by pulp great Norman Saunders, whose Conan looked a little like a Roman centurion. Now, twelve years later, here was news of plans to bring the whole series back. The wait was not long.

The following year, 1966, Lancer Books published the first volume of the complete Conan. Originally set to appear in chronological order in eight volumes, this first title would actually be number four in sequence upon completion. It was edited by de Camp, who was also completing fragments or writing new stories based upon outlines discovered after Howard's tragic death in 1936.

Conan the Adventurer introduced a whole new audience to Robert E. Howard as well as giving old fans a reason to rejoice. The cover painting was by Frank Frazetta, with grateful acknowledgement to advisor Roy Krenkel. And what a painting it was! There stood Conan, every inch the muscular, battle-

CONAN
ROBERT E. HOWARD,
L. SPRAGUE DE CAMP,
AND LIN CARTER
1967
FRANK FRAZETTA

Howard gets literary company and Conan gets Thak, courtesy of Frazetta, who painted eight covers for the barbarian's exploits.

THE RETURN OF CONAN
BJORN NYBERG AND L. SPRAGUE DE CAMP
1951 (1971 REPRINT)
ICHIRO MOTO

Howard was gone but you can't keep a good barbarian down, in this illustrated Japanese reprint of the Gnome Press book.

THE FANTASTIC SWORDSMEN
EDITED BY L. SPRAGUE
DE CAMP
1967
JACK GAUGHAN

The third in de Camp's Swords and Sorceries anthologies.

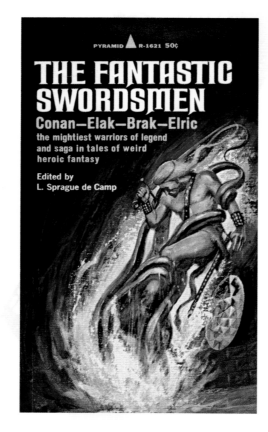

scarred, brooding barbarian, atop a pile of human detritus; a naked woman clinging to one leg, his sword in front of him thrust point down into the mound below; behind him flames and vague, threatening, shadowy images in the sky. This *was* Conan. Frazetta had done something special.

In his too-short lifetime, Robert E. Howard had only seen the somewhat ordinary interpretation of his barbarian as depicted on a few covers of *Weird Tales* by Margaret Brundage, certainly nothing as striking or dramatic as Frazetta's version—and one can't help but think he would have loved it.

Obviously, quite a few people did. The Lancer editions sold over a million copies during the first few years of publication. It was a milestone in fantasy publishing and a perfect marriage of author and artist. In 1966 Frank Frazetta won the Hugo award—science fiction's most prestigious honor, named after publisher Hugo Gernsback—for Best Professional Artist.

Other volumes in the series soon followed, written by Howard, edited or completed by de Camp. As J. Allen St. John's art was associated with Burroughs, so Frazetta's would be with Howard. De Camp continued to put together new collections along with Bjorn Nyberg (a Swedish fan) and Lin Carter, later writing original stories himself to fit in to the overall sequence of Conan tales. Even outlines designed by Howard with other characters in mind were transformed into Conan stories by these later "contributors" to the saga.

Conan has become one of the most enduring characters in fantasy literature, and long after his death, Robert E. Howard has left behind a great legacy and is recognized the world over for it. The Conan stories have been reprinted many times throughout the years, as has Howard's other work, and many writers have had their "try" at the character. But there is only one.

In 1967, Pyramid Books published the third anthology edited by de Camp to keep swords and sorcery firmly in the public eye. *The Fantastic Swordsmen* was the title, but this time the names on the cover were not the authors but their characters: Conan-Elak-Brak-Elric (sounding more like something Michael Rennie's character Klatuu meant as a message for his robot Gort in the film *The Day The Earth Stood Still*). What it really said was simple: we *know* these characters. This time around there were more of the usual suspects—Lord Dunsany, Henry Kuttner, Howard, de Camp, Moorcock, Lovecraft. The only missing element was the Finlay cover and interiors, but Jack Gaughan capably stepped into the spotlight.

One newer writer who was featured was John Jakes, with his story "The Girl in the Gem". Jakes had been writing science fiction and fantasy and had a series of sword and sorcery stories published in *Fantastic* in the mid-1960s about Brak the Barbarian. Brak's was a parallel world to ours but with the same problems faced by many a Barbarian: i.e., the minions of evil gods, namely one Yob-Haggoth, who sounded suspiciously like a distant relative of a certain H. P. Lovecraft elder deity.

Jakes, best known for his *American Bicentennial* series of historical novels (1974–1980) and the Civil War novel *North and South* (1982), had his Brak novels collected and published in paperback in a series of five books (1968–80). Some of his writing was more along the lines of planetary romance, such as *Master of the Dark Gate* (1970) and *Witch of the Dark Gate* (1972). Another of his heroic fantasies was *The Last Magicians* (1969), and he cleverly lampooned the field in the 1972 spoof, *Mention My Name in*

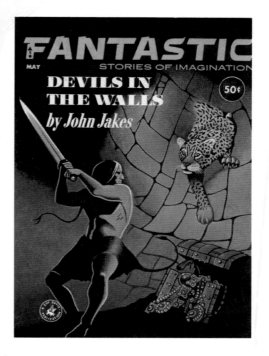

20

FANTASTIC
MAY 1963
VERNON KRAMER

Fantastic published much memorable fantasy. This time around, John Jakes' Brak the Barbarian gets the cover spot.

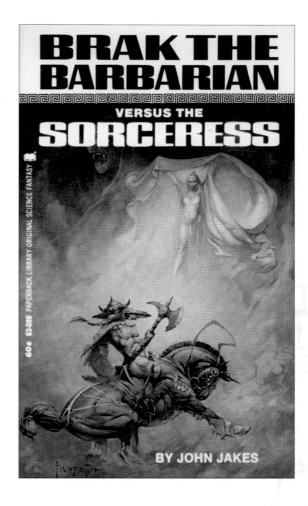

21

BRAK THE BARBARIAN VERSUS THE SORCERESS
JOHN JAKES
1969
FRANK FRAZETTA

There were several Brak novels, and this one had a great Frazetta cover.

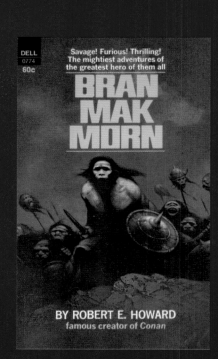

Superb fantasy by the creator of CONAN
ROBERT E. HOWARD
Witches,
warlocks,
and demons!

WOLFSHEAD

LANCER BOOKS 73-721 60¢

LANCER BOOKS 73-650 **60¢**

KING KULL

ROBERT E. HOWARD and **LIN CARTER**

A MIGHTY HERO OF WEIRD FANTASY AND
HIGH ADVENTURE BY THE CREATOR OF **CONAN**

DELL
0774
60c

Savage! Furious! Thrilling!
The mightiest adventures of
the greatest hero of them all

**BRAN
MAK
MORN**

BY ROBERT E. HOWARD
famous creator of *Conan*

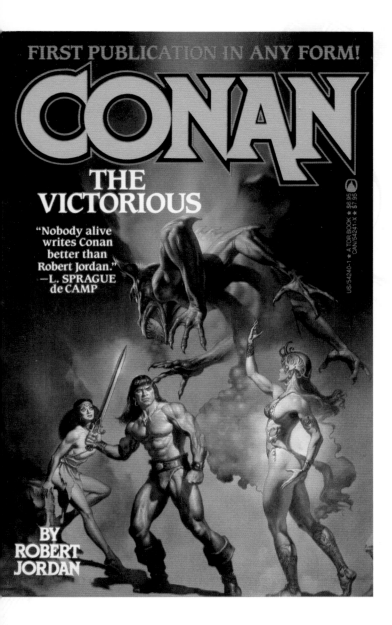

Atlantis. Several of his books had the additional advantage of cover paintings by Frazetta "in the Conan tradition"—a phrase that was cropping up more and more on book covers of the period. Conan was selling, and it didn't take much to figure out that if you wanted to sell like Conan, you had to look like Conan.

Meanwhile, over at Lancer Books, 1967 saw a new collection of Robert E. Howard stories—not Conan, this time, although his name was featured prominently on the cover.

King Kull was the title of the book and the name of its central character, "by the creator of Conan". Kull, an Atlantean exile, captured the throne of Valusia for himself, battling a shape-shifting serpent race along the way. It was edited by Glenn Lord, who was administrator of the Howard estate, while Lin Carter wrote some of the stories from unfinished pieces by the author. It collected the Kull stories from *Weird Tales* and presented them all in a neat package, further enhanced with a stunning cover painting by Roy Krenkel. As Frazetta had done with the first Conan book, Krenkel pulled off a similar feat of magic for Kull.

The following year Lancer published *Wolfshead,* a mix of horror and fantasy by Howard from the pulps, with another brilliant Frazetta painting on the cover. Obviously Howard was selling very well, especially the heroic fantasy material. Before long Dell published *Bran Mak Morn* (1969), a collection of stories from *Weird Tales* dealing with the exploits of the King of the Picts. The stories were pure Howard, and Frazetta added another cover to his output.

Solomon Kane, yet another of Howard's pulp characters, would soon be reprinted, and more Conan books and pastiches by diverse writers would continue to be published over the following decades.

CONAN THE VICTORIOUS
ROBERT JORDAN
1984
BORIS VALLEJO

Just one of the many Conan adventures written by acclaimed writer Jordan.

26

FANTASTIC
FEBRUARY 1964
EMSH

More adventures of
Fafhrd and the Gray
Mouser from the man
who put the sword and
sorcery into Sword and
Sorcery, Fritz Leiber.

27

SWORDS AND DEVILTRY
FRITZ LEIBER
1970
JEFF JONES

One of the 'Swords' books
from Ace, for which artist
Jones created some memo-
rable covers.

Authors who contributed to the series included Poul
Anderson, Andrew J. Offutt, Karl Edward Wagner,
and Robert Jordan.

Many other sword swingers were now finding their
exploits collected in book form. Some were reprinted from the pulps for a new audience eager for more
adventures. Others were either original characters,
following the tried-and-true formula of the past or
new stories by old masters who were finding their
work very much in demand again. One of the best in
the latter category was Fritz Leiber.

Back in the late 1930s Leiber had written of those
two mismatched adventurers, Fafhrd and the Gray
Mouser. More new adventures of the two were published in *Fantastic* during the 1960s. Their stories
were eventually collected in paperback forming the
'Swords' series, first published in five volumes by Ace
Books (1968–70). These and subsequent books in
the series stand among the finest works of heroic
fantastic fiction and have recently gone through new
hardcover and paperback editions in both Britain
and America. The humor, colorful locations, bizarre
denizens of the cities both above ground and below,
and the gods who play their games with our heroes
make for unforgettable reading. Leiber is credited
with having created the phrase "Sword and Sorcery",
and he certainly knew how to write it.

When Ace originally packaged the series, the covers
were painted by Jeff Jones. Jones had provided artwork for various fanzines before going to New York
in the late 1960s to find professional work. During
the next decade he painted more than a hundred
covers for a wide range of paperback publishers. His
technique was obviously inspired by Frazetta but
soon developed into his own unique style, changing
over the years and showing the influence of N. C.

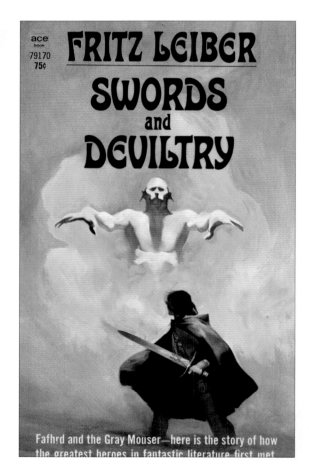

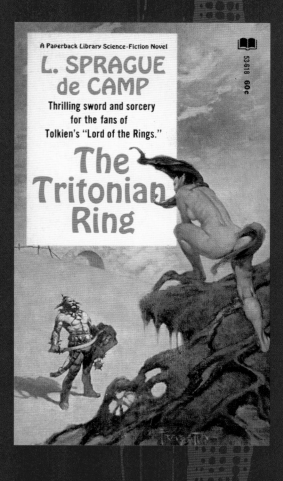

29

THE TRITONIAN RING
L. SPRAGUE DE CAMP
1951 (1968 REPRINT)
FRANK FRAZETTA

It's Prince Vakar against the gods in this reprint of de Camp's adventure tale.

28

FANTASTIC
MAY 1964
EMSH

Ningauble of the Seven Eyes, Fafhrd's sorcerous mentor, nicely rendered by Emsh. Note our heroes in the bubble.

30

SWORDS & ICE MAGIC
FRITZ LEIBER
1977
MICHAEL WHELAN

The Leiber magic continues and Whelan does a nice portrait of the boys.

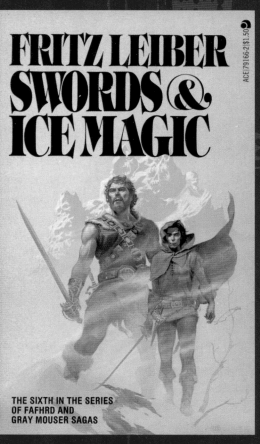

Thongor must battle his way out of the land of death with but a single weapon—the mysterious Sword of Light!

32

THONGOR AT THE END OF TIME
LIN CARTER
1968
JEFF JONES

Thongor takes time out from his swordplay to pose for one of several Jones covers.

50¢ 52-586 A Paperback Library Science-Fiction Novel

THONGOR
AGAINST THE GODS

Exciting science, sword and sorcery in the tradition of Robert E. Howard and A. Merritt
LIN CARTER

31

THONGOR AGAINST THE GODS
LIN CARTER
1967
FRANK FRAZETTA

Another one of so many brilliant paintings Frazetta did for book covers in the 1960s and 1970s.

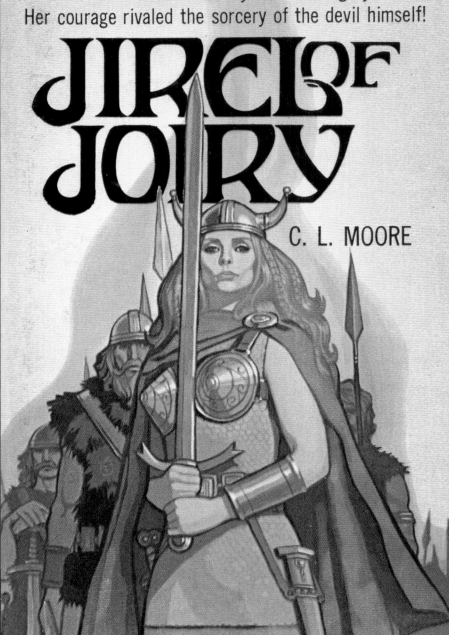

63-166 PAPERBACK LIBRARY SCIENCE FANTASY **60¢**

Her sword matched any man's savagery.
Her courage rivaled the sorcery of the devil himself!

JIREL OF JOIRY

C. L. MOORE

33

JIREL OF JOIRY
C. L. MOORE
1969
ARTIST UNKNOWN

A reprint of the exploits of the first female sword and sorcery heroine from *Weird Tales*.

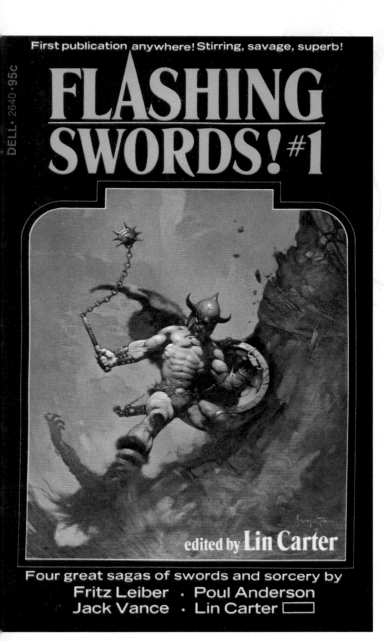

First publication anywhere! Stirring, savage, superb!

FLASHING SWORDS! #1

DELL · 2640 · 95c

edited by **Lin Carter**

Four great sagas of swords and sorcery by
Fritz Leiber · Poul Anderson
Jack Vance · Lin Carter

Wyeth, Gustav Klimt, and even evidence of the later Pre-Raphaelite painters, most notably J. W. Waterhouse. There was a romantic, painterly quality to his work, and he created a unique showcase for the Leiber books.

The sixth book in the series, *Swords & Ice Magic* (1977) collected the later stories from 1973–1977. Michael Whelan painted a dramatic portrait of Fafhrd and the Gray Mouser, which really hadn't been attempted before. Whelan is one of the most successful artists in the science fiction and fantasy fields. He won the Hugo award for Best Professional Artist every year from 1980–1986 as well as in 1988, 1989, 1991, 1992, and 2000.

Although L. Sprague de Camp and Lin Carter became linked with the works of Robert E. Howard over the years by editing and writing stories continuing the exploits of Conan, they also had more of their own adventures of the sword-slinging variety published. De Camp had written several pieces featured in *Unknown* magazine and in 1953 several were collected in *The Tritonian Ring,* including the novel-length title story.

Sword and sorcery fantasy was at an all-time high, and many older stories were being given a fresh coat of paint, often by Frazetta. *The Tritonian Ring* received just such a treatment. Billed as "A Paperback Library Science Fiction Novel", it was described as "Thrilling sword and sorcery for the fans of Tolkien's *Lord of the Rings*". However you describe it, it is de Camp at his best. The author's other stories for *Unknown* had also been reprinted in paperback including *Lest Darkness Fall* (1941) and *The Land of Unreason* (1942). De Camp continued to turn out fantasy as well as non-fiction, including major biographies of H. P. Lovecraft and Robert E. Howard.

 34

FLASHING SWORDS! #1
EDITED BY LIN CARTER
1973
FRANK FRAZETTA
Carter, like de Camp, edited many anthologies promoting sword and sorcery and the fantasy genre.

35 THE DARK WORLD
HENRY KUTTNER
1946 (1965 REPRINT)
GRAY MORROW

Kuttner's pulp otherworld fantasy, like many other older classics, was brought back in paperback.

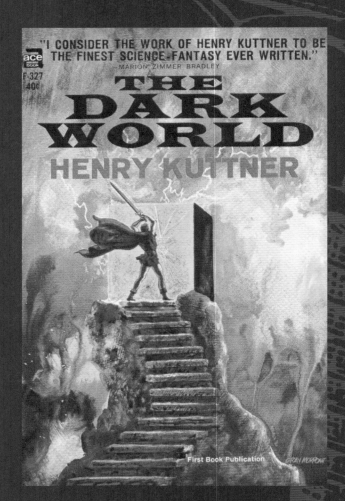

"I CONSIDER THE WORK OF HENRY KUTTNER TO BE THE FINEST SCIENCE-FANTASY EVER WRITTEN."
—MARION ZIMMER BRADLEY

ace
F-327
40¢

THE DARK WORLD
HENRY KUTTNER

First Book Publication

GRAY MORROW

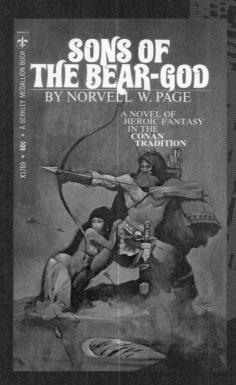

SONS OF
THE BEAR-GOD
BY NORVELL W. PAGE

A NOVEL OF
HEROIC FANTASY
IN THE
CONAN
TRADITION

X1769 • 60¢ • A BERKLEY MEDALLION BOOK

AVON / S229 / 60¢

From the Fantastic Worlds

A. MERRITT

THE SHIP OF ISHTAR

The American adventurer was pitch[ed] out of his own time and into a weird world of incredible and enticing marv[els]

36 SONS OF THE BEAR-GOD
NORVELL W. PAGE
1939 (1969 REPRINT)
JEFF JONES

Thirty years earlier, the pulp magazine *Unknown* published this adventure which was now described as being "in the Conan tradition".

38 THE SHIP OF ISHTAR
A. MERRITT
1924 (1966 REPRINT)
DOUG ROSA

Merritt's popular novels continued to go through many printings over the years.

142

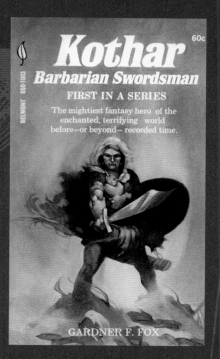

Kothar
Barbarian Swordsman
60¢
FIRST IN A SERIES
The mightiest fantasy hero of the enchanted, terrifying world before—or beyond—recorded time.

GARDNER F. FOX

39

KOTHAR BARBARIAN SWORDSMAN
GARDNER F. FOX
1969
JEFF JONES

Armed with his enchanted sword, Frostfire, Kothar is off to a good start.

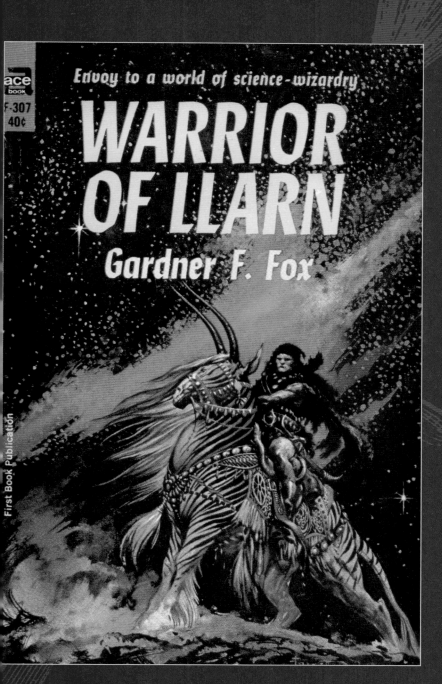

Envoy to a world of science-wizardry

WARRIOR OF LLARN
Gardner F. Fox

39

WARRIOR OF LLARN
GARDNER F. FOX
1964
FRANK FRAZETTA

Fox wrote comics, barbarian sword and sorceries, and Burroughs-styled planetary adventures like this one.

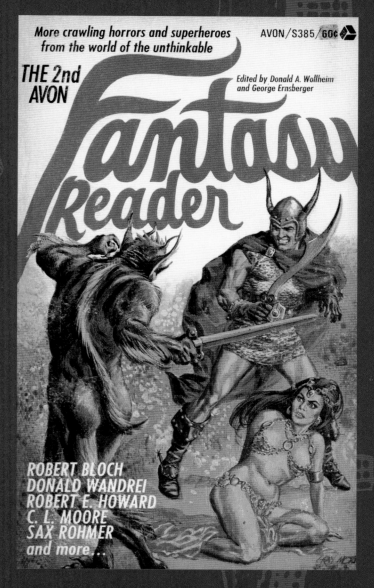

More crawling horrors and superheroes from the world of the unthinkable

AVON/S385/60¢

THE 2nd AVON

Edited by Donald A. Wollheim and George Ernsberger

Fantasy Reader

ROBERT BLOCH
DONALD WANDREI
ROBERT E. HOWARD
C. L. MOORE
SAX ROHMER
and more...

 40

THE 2ND AVON FANTASY READER
EDITED BY DONALD A. WOLLHEIM AND
GEORGE ERNSBERGER
1969
GRAY MORROW

These paperback editions offered more great stories courtesy of Donald A. Wollheim's *Avon Fantasy Reader*, which in turn had reprinted them from the pulps.

41
KYRIK: WARLOCK WARRIOR
GARDNER F. FOX
1975
KEN BARR

The mighty sword in this case is called Blue Fang and as every barbarian knows, you can always trust steel.

42
NINE PRINCES IN AMBER
ROGER ZELAZNY
1970 (1972 REPRINT)
JEFF JONES

The beginning of Zelazny's well-crafted 'Chronicles of Amber' series.

43
WITCH WORLD
ANDRE NORTON
1963 (1983 REPRINT)
JOHN POUND

Norton's *Witch World* series drew more on fantasy elements than science fiction as the series progressed.

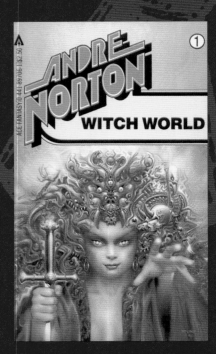

44
TARNSMAN OF GOR
JOHN NORMAN
1966
ROBERT FOSTER

The start of a long-running planetary fantasy adventure series that spawned two films, neither of which was as good as this cover.

Lin Carter went on to edit the Adult Fantasy line for Ballantine Books (1969–1974). His love for the genre and the writers who helped shape it from its earliest days is evident in his anthologies and various books written about the field. He also had several running series of his own, influenced by Burroughs and Howard, the Thongor stories being the most well-known. Originally published by Ace in the mid-1960s, the series soon developed and was repackaged and expanded. His first fantasy novel, *The Wizard of Lemuria* (1965), introduced the adventures of Thongor the Barbarian and his battle against a serpent race determined to—dare I say it—rule the world. It would later be revised for Berkley Books, along with *Thongor of Lemuria* (1966), and new titles would be added to the series. Jeff Jones produced some fine cover paintings for the books and Frazetta did the same for *Thongor Against the Gods* (1967) and *Thongor in the City of the Magicians* (1968). Carter's 'Green Star Rises' (1972–83), 'Callisto' (1972–78) and 'Zanthodon' (1979–82) series were heavily influenced by Burroughs and eventually totaled twenty books. All of them are obviously written with relish and a love for the pulps that inspired them.

However, it was as an editor that Carter was at the top of his game. Five volumes of the *Flashing Swords!* (1973–81) anthologies and six of *The Year's Best Fantasy Stories* (1975–80) did their share of spreading the gospel of the wizard and warrior, and the field lost one of its true champions with his death in 1988.

C. L. Moore's flame-haired female fighter Jirel of Joiry found her pulp adventures from *Weird Tales* collected by Paperback Library in 1969. Henry Kuttner's tales of Elak of Atlantis, also from *Weird Tales,* were finally revived (in 1985), as were his other science fiction and fantasy classics *Valley of the Flame* (1964) and *The Dark World* (1965). *Flame Winds* (1965) and *Sons of the Bear-God* (1969) by Norvell W. Page also received a resurrection from the pulps, both bearing striking Jeff Jones covers.

Gardner F. Fox, author and comic book writer for DC and later Marvel Comics, started to write fantasy in the 1940s. His planetary swordplays, *Warrior of Llarn* and *Thief of Llarn,* were published by Ace in 1964 and 1966 respectively. He also wrote novels about Kothar and Kyrik, barbarian heroes more in the tradition of you-know-who. Kothar successfully slashed away against wizards and witches through five books (1969–70), while Kyrik did the same in just four (1975–76), with cover art provided by Jones and Ken Barr.

Award-winning science fiction writer Roger Zelazny also dabbled in planetary romance fantasy. He is probably best known for the 'Chronicles of Amber' sequences, beginning with *Nine Princes in Amber* (1970). The world of Amber, of which our Earth is just a shadow, and the exploits of its inhabitants and their struggles for the throne, ran in two linked series (1970–78 and 1985–91). Meanwhile his *Dilvish, the Damned* stories, first published in *Fantastic* during the 1960s, are more vengeance-driven sword and sorcery.

Other planetary adventures with major swordplay elements at their heart also had successful runs. Andre Norton, who began writing in the 1930s, turned to science fiction in the 1950s but by the 1960s was leaning more toward fantasy adventures. Her *Witch World* series (1963–) gradually steered away from its sci-fi beginnings toward more fantastic trappings. The planet Witch World has since become a shared world, with Norton either editing

books in the series or working with other writers on
stories. She has produced a large body of work over
the years and won many awards.

Leigh Brackett who, like C. L. Moore, made her
name in the pulps, created Erik John Stark whose
adventures on Mars were published in *Planet Stories*
during the 1940s. More of Stark's adventures were
published in the 1970s but set on a different, distant
world. Her books have influenced many writers, including Lin Carter and Michael Moorcock.

John Norman wrote the long-running 'Gor' series
of planetary swash and buckle which, unfortunately,
became more sexist and degrading to women as the
series progressed. It proved to be popular though,
and starting with *Tarnsman of Gor* (1966) carried on
for more than two dozen books until 1988.

More and more sword and sorcery collections were
also appearing.

Hans Stefan Santesson edited two anthologies for
Lancer, which by now was publishing quite a selection of this material. *The Mighty Barbarians* (1969)
and *The Mighty Swordsmen* (1970) were both in the
L. Sprague de Camp mould. Stories by Howard,
Moorcock, Carter, Leiber, Kuttner and de Camp were
featured, with eye-catching cover paintings by comics
artist pioneer and a pulp fan himself, Jim Steranko.

De Camp himself compiled a fourth major anthology, *Warlocks and Warriors* (1970), returning to the
pulps for over half of the collection. Howard,
Kuttner, Smith, and C. L. Moore were back with
more brilliant gems, as was Steranko on the cover.

As the market grew larger for this type of story,
more and more anthologies were published, many
featuring new material. *Swords Against Darkness* ran
through five volumes (1977–1979) and was edited by
Andrew J. Offutt, who had written several Howard

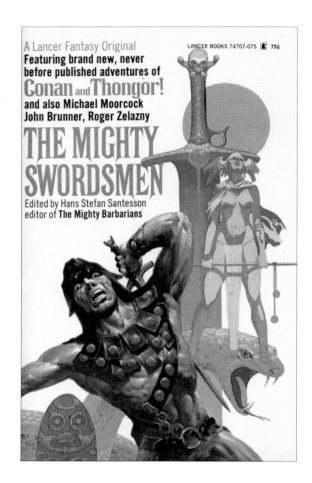

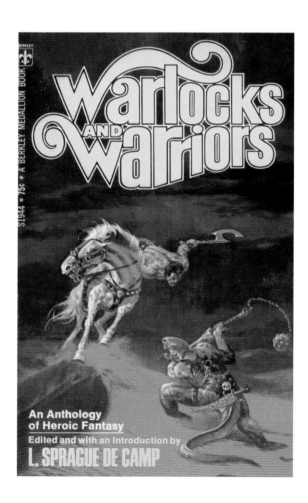

LANCER BOOKS 74-556   75¢

THE MIGHTY BARBARIANS

GREAT SWORD AND SORCERY HEROES

Edited by Hans Stefan Santesson

CONAN
ELAK · THONGOR
SUAR PEIAL
THE GRAY MOUSER

STERANKO

47
THE MIGHTY BARBARIANS
EDITED BY HANS STEFAN
SANTESSON
1969
STERANKO
Are there any other kind?
By this time barbarians
were enjoying their pop-
ularity and getting good
press in anthologies like
this one.

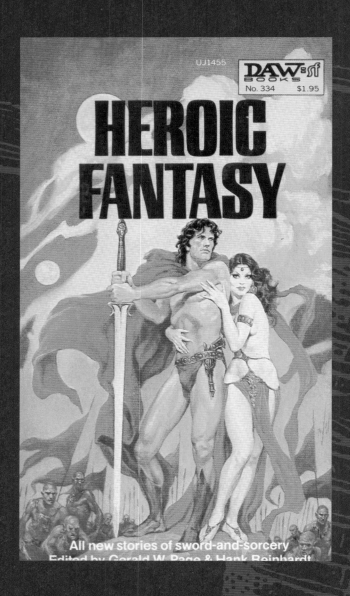

HEROIC FANTASY

UJ1455

DAWsf
BOOKS
No. 334 $1.95

All new stories of sword-and-sorcery
Edited by Gerald W. Page & Hank Reinhardt

DARKNESS
WEAVES

KARL
EDWARD
WAGNER

Kane leads the avenging forces of a sorceress linked with the devils of the deep

WARNER BOOKS

88-598 $1.95

KARL EDWARD WAGNER

DARK CRUSADE

WARNER BOOKS 88-154 $1.50

Kane commands an army against
the power of primeval black sorcery.

48

HEROIC FANTASY
EDITED BY GERALD W. PAGE
AND HANK REINHARDT
1979
JAD

A girl, a boy, and his sword,
plus all-new tales of warriors
and wizardry.

49

DARKNESS WEAVES
KARL EDWARD WAGNER
1978
FRANK FRAZETTA

Originally published
in 1970 in a quite
altered form, this
edition presents the
first written novel of
Kane, the tall, dark,
and intelligent swords-
man, the way Wagner
intended it to be.

50

DARK CRUSADE
KARL EDWARD WAGNER
1976
FRANK FRAZETTA

Another book in a brilliant
and unfortunately too-brief
series that boasted some
beautiful Frazetta covers.

pastiches of his own. DAW published *Heroic Fantasy* in 1979 and Ace had *Heroic Visions* in 1983. Female fighters got their chance in *Amazons!* (1979) and *Amazons II* (1982), both edited by Jessica Amanda Salmonson, who won the 1980 World Fantasy Award for the first volume.

At one time readers had to scour used bookstores for collections or reprints, but now barbarians were flexing their literary muscles everywhere. However a lot of them weren't as tough or as good as they looked on the surface. The field was getting flabby.

If anyone could be said to have given the sword and sorcery subgenre a shot in the overdeveloped bicep, it would have to be Karl Edward Wagner.

His first novel, *Darkness Weaves with Many Shades* (1970), introduced the immortal Kane, influenced by Howard's Conan, but much more than that. *Death Angel's Shadow* (1973), *Bloodstone* (1975), and *Dark Crusade* (1976) took Kane through more intelligently written adventures, along with the stories collected in *Nightwinds* (1978). Frank Frazetta produced another inspired series of covers as he had earlier for Conan.

As a writer and editor, Wagner also made major contributions to the series of often formulaic pastiches of Howard books. For Zebra Books he contributed the novel *Legion from the Shadows* (1976), a brilliant entry in the series, concerning itself with Bran Mak Morn rather than Conan. Utilizing elements from Howard's Bran stories, in particular "Worms of the Earth", Wagner put together a classic homage in his own unique fashion. Jeff Jones painted an attractive wraparound cover, as he had done for several of the Howard series.

Berkley Medallion published three books of Conan stories, edited by Wagner, as authorized editions.

51

THE HOUR OF THE DRAGON
ROBERT E. HOWARD
1935–36 (1977 REPRINT)
KEN KELLY

Part of editor Karl Edward Wagner's short-lived series of authorized editions of Conan, utilizing Howard's original, unaltered texts.

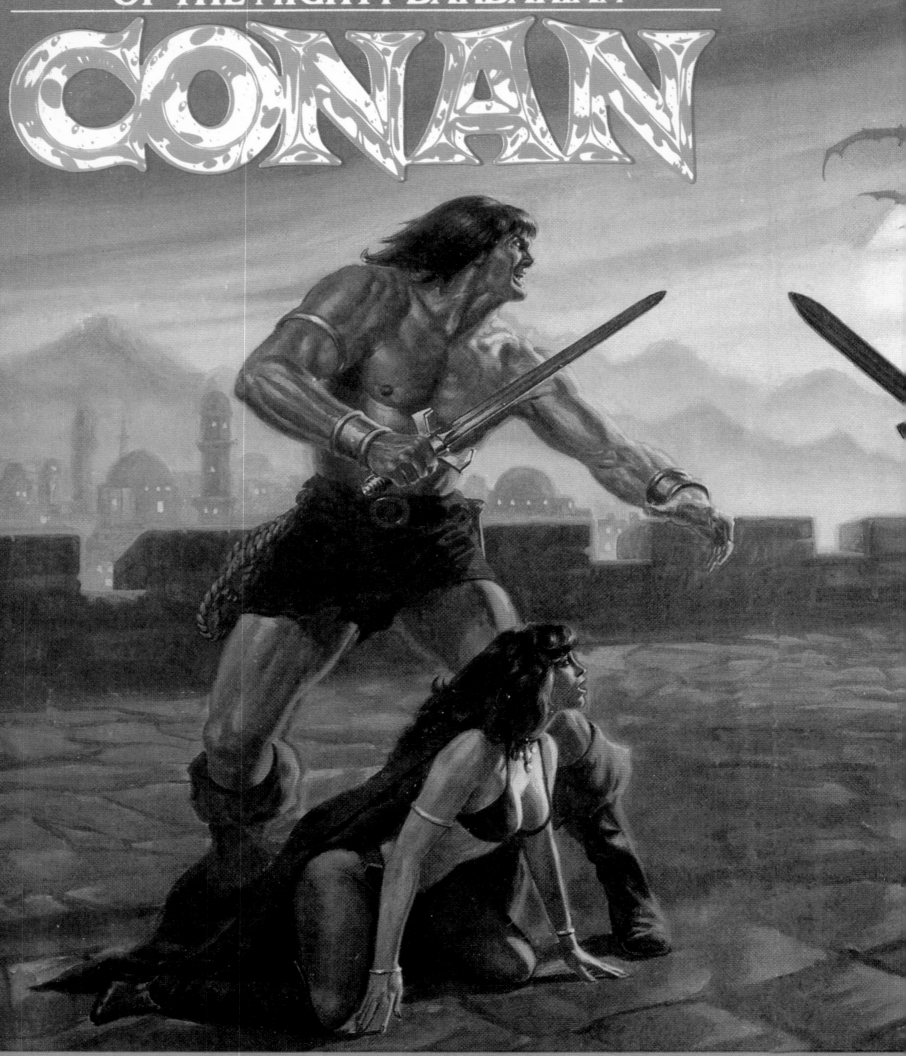

A SENSATIONAL SAGA OF THE MIGHTY BARBARIAN

CONAN

THE ROAD OF KINGS
BY KARL EDWARD WAGNER

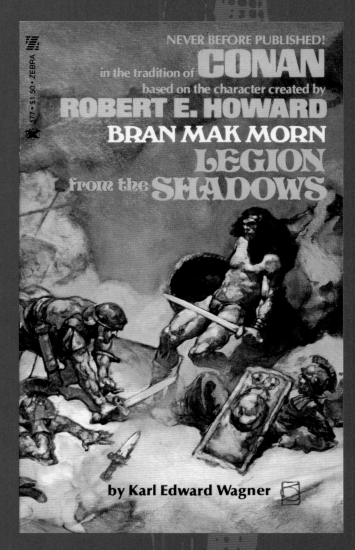

NEVER BEFORE PUBLISHED!
in the tradition of **CONAN**
based on the character created by
ROBERT E. HOWARD
BRAN MAK MORN
LEGION
from the **SHADOWS**

by **Karl Edward Wagner**

53

LEGION FROM THE SHADOWS
KARL EDWARD WAGNER
1976
JEFF JONES

Wagner's novel of Robert E. Howard's character Bran Mak Morn, and one of his best.

52

THE ROAD OF KINGS
KARL EDWARD WAGNER
1979
BOB LARKIN

The cream of the crop among the multitude of Conan pastiches.

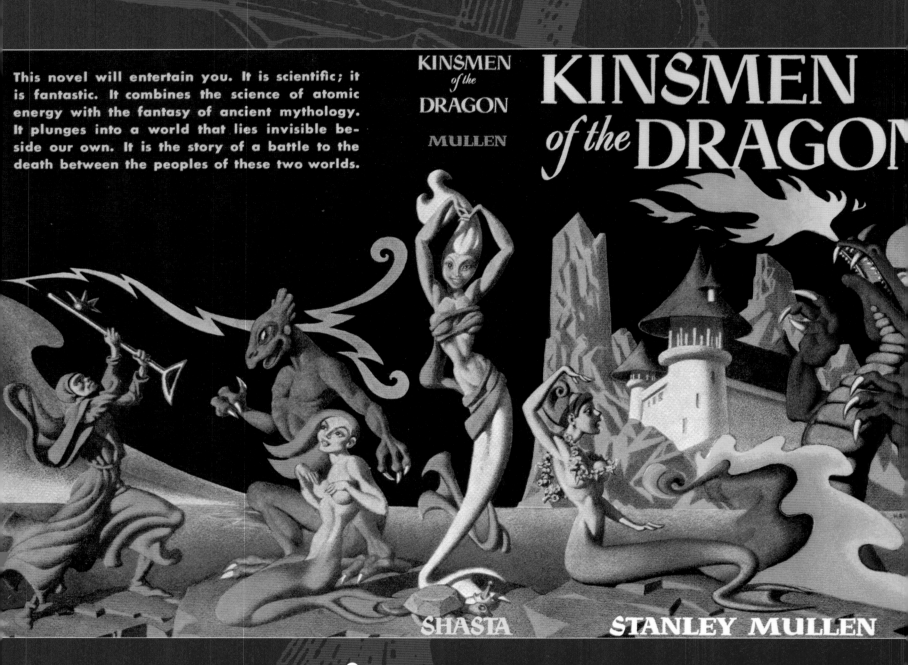

This novel will entertain you. It is scientific; it is fantastic. It combines the science of atomic energy with the fantasy of ancient mythology. It plunges into a world that lies invisible beside our own. It is the story of a battle to the death between the peoples of these two worlds.

KINSMEN
of the
DRAGON

MULLEN

KINSMEN
of the DRAGON

SHASTA

STANLEY MULLEN

54

KINSMEN OF THE DRAGON
STANLEY MULLEN
1950
HANNES BOK

An A. Merritt-styled fantasy from Shasta Books, a small press publisher.

Beginning with the novel *The Hour of the Dragon* (1977), Robert E. Howard's text was used as written and unaltered. Elsewhere, Conan had been reduced by too many watered-down adventures to the literary equivalent of the later Abbott and Costello movies. Who would he meet and where would he go next?

For Bantam books in 1979, Wagner took him down *The Road of Kings,* a high adventure in the style he had been accustomed to, battling sorcery and a living army of stone warriors. Wagner also edited three volumes of *Echoes of Valor* (1987–91), reprinting classic pulp sword and sorceries.

Also known for his own excellent horror stories, Karl Wagner went on to edit fifteen volumes of *The Year's Best Horror Stories* series for DAW Books (1980–94) and major hardcover collections of pulp stories by Manly Wade Wellman, E. Hoffman Price, and Hugh B. Cave for the Carcosa imprint in which he was a partner. An award-winning writer and editor and champion of the small press (from which he found much of the talent for his anthologies), Wagner died in 1994 and his presence is still sorely missed today.

Fantastic was steadily publishing more stories by Leiber, Carter, and others. In the 1970s, it changed its sub-heading from "Science-Fiction and Fantasy" to "Sword and Sorcery and Fantasy". Leiber had a column reviewing fantasy books, and de Camp wrote a series on literary swordsmen and sorcerers that would later be published in hardcover by Arkham House, the small press imprint that had its beginnings publishing H. P. Lovecraft's collection, *The Outsider and Others* back in 1939.

The concept of the small or private press had been around for quite some time. William Morris established the Kelmscott Press in 1891 and produced beautiful illustrated books, starting with his own

55

FANTASTIC
AUGUST 1972
JEFF JONES
Swords against sorcery showed up frequently in *Fantastic* during this period.

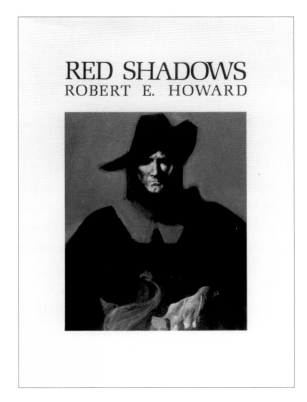

56

RED SHADOWS
ROBERT E. HOWARD
1968
JEFF JONES
Donald M. Grant published much of Howard's writing in deluxe illustrated editions.

fantasy *The Story of the Glittering Plain.* Throughout the years many small presses published fantasy, among them Gnome Press (which published Howard's Conan stories in the 1950s), Prime Press, Shasta, and Fantasy Press.

Donald M. Grant had a minor involvement in small press publishing in the 1950s; then in 1965 he began issuing the works of Robert E. Howard under his own imprint of Donald M. Grant, Publisher. Occasionally reprinting other material from the pulps, it was with the Howard books that he produced some of his most beautiful volumes. Putting swords between boards, he published an illustrated series of the Conan books in matching design dust jackets, each one illustrated in both color and black and white by a different artist. One of the best was *Red Nails* (1975), illustrated by award-winning artist George Barr. *Red Shadows* (1968) collected the Solomon Kane stories, with art by Jeff Jones, and was susequently reprinted with new work by Jones. The Kull tales were given a lavish treatment by Ned Dameron who also worked on one of the Conan books. Some of Karl Edward Wagner's best work was collected in *The Book of Kane* (1985), again illustrated by Jones.

Another important specialty press house was Underwood-Miller. Partners Tim Underwood and Chuck Miller published many Jack Vance titles, among them *The Dying Earth* (1976), with art by George Barr, and *The Eyes of the Overworld* (1977) to which Stephen E. Fabian contributed the illustrations.

Michael Whelan did some wonderful work for Archival Press' edition of *The Vanishing Tower* (1981) by Michael Moorcock. Elric never looked better.

However, the high water mark was reached in another edition of Howard's Solomon Kane stories.

**BRAN MAK MORN
THE LAST KING**
ROBERT E. HOWARD
2001
GARY GIANNI

Wandering Star repeats its
winning production, this time
around for Bran Mak Morn,
with more art by Gianni.

THE SAVAGE TALES OF SOLOMON KANE
ROBERT E. HOWARD
1998
GARY GIANNI

Howard's Solomon Kane stories get top of the
line treatment in this beautiful example of fine
bookmaking, brilliantly illustrated by Gianni.

BRAN MAK MORN
• THE LAST KING •
ROBERT E. HOWARD

ILLUSTRATED BY
GARY GIANNI

WANDERING STAR
ROBERT E. HOWARD
LIBRARY OF CLASSICS

www.wanderingplanet.com

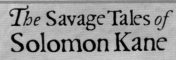

The Savage Tales of
Solomon Kane
ROBERT E. HOWARD

Illustrated by
GARY GIANNI

A one of a kind, never before seen deluxe limited edition book.

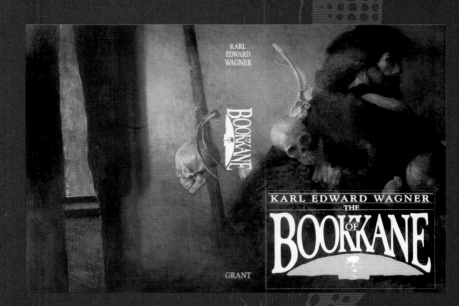

KARL
EDWARD
WAGNER

KARL EDWARD WAGNER
THE
BOOK OF KANE

GRANT

THE BOOK OF KANE
KARL EDWARD WAGNER
1985
JEFFREY JONES

Another Donald M. Grant book with a selection
of Wagner's Kane stories, deservedly put into
hardcover, with paintings by award-winner Jones.

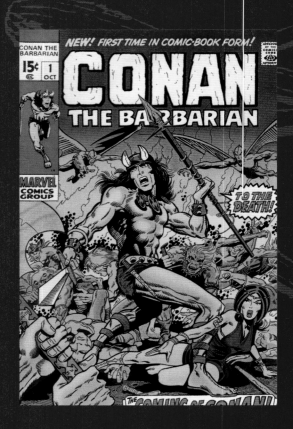

61

CONAN THE BARBARIAN #1
OCTOBER 1970
BARRY SMITH

Howard's Conan proved just as popular with the comics crowd, as did the artist formerly known as Barry Smith.

62

CREEPY NO. 9
JUNE 1966
FRANK FRAZETTA

Although they usually published horror comics in the E.C. tradition, both *Creepy* and *Eerie* caught the barbarian bug at times, and artist Frazetta delivered an early dose of the type of cover for which he became famous.

63

CONAN AND THE DEATH LORD OF THANZA
ROLAND J. GREEN
1997
KEEGAN

The barbarian's occupations have been countless over the years and continue to prove so. He's been a pirate, a pauper, a usurper, a warrior, a pawn, and a king. But that's life.

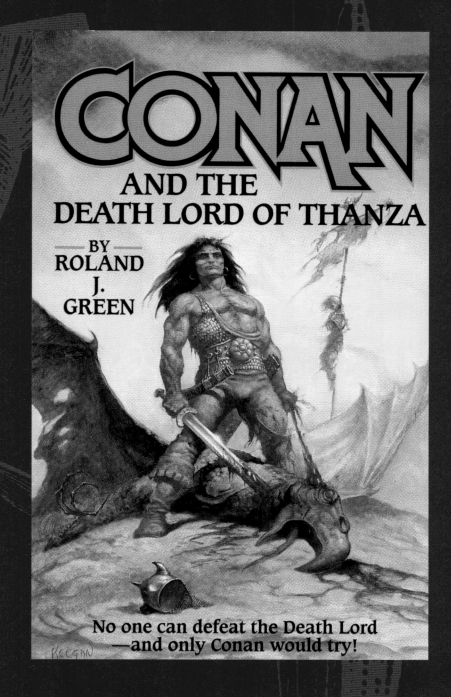

Published in 1998 by Wandering Star of England and illustrated by Gary Gianni, it's a beautiful piece of work. Bringing to mind the illustrated gift books of older days like Scribner's *Treasure Island* (1911) with paintings by N. C. Wyeth, *The Savage Tales of Solomon Kane* is book production at its finest. With color plates and numerous pen and ink pieces *à là* Joseph Clement Coll, the deluxe edition includes an extra suite of the color plates in an envelope and a CD of the verse in the text. Did I mention it is also signed by Gianni and slipcased?

A Frazetta-illuminated Howard collection, *The Ultimate Triumph,* followed from the same publisher in 1999, and Gianni returned for *Bran Mak Morn: The Last King* in 2001.

And then there are the comic book adventures. Marvel Comics published *Conan the Barbarian* in 1970 and the stories are still running today. That first issue was written by Roy Thomas and drawn by Barry Smith. It soon gained both awards and imitators. Howard's barbarian was embraced by a new audience—the comic book enthusiast—and was once again to receive deserved recognition. Thomas and Smith presented new tales as well as adapting many of Howard's classics. Smith's art evolved from his Jack Kirby influence into a more meticulous, detailed style in the later issues. Today he is recognized as a major romantic fantasy artist, but Barry Windsor Smith and Conan still have ties.

King Kull, Bran Mak Morn, and Solomon Kane all got the Marvel treatment, as did Red Sonja, a minor Howard female fighter.

Marvel also adapted John Jakes' Brak the Barbarian and Lin Carter's Thongor in *Savage Tales* (1974) and *Creatures on the Loose* (1973), respectively. DC Comics had their own barbarian entry with *Sword of Sorcery*

(1973) featuring Fritz Leiber's characters Fafhrd and the Gray Mouser, while Michael Moorcock's Corum, Hawkmoon, and Elric found adaptations by Pacific, First, and Dark Horse Comics. Elric even met Conan in one of Marvel's early Smith comics.

Comic books or graphic novel adaptations continued the tradition of Conan, and the mighty barbarian was still king. Paperbacks, digests, hardcovers, and comics were all enjoying a popularity of blades and brawn against wizardry and wild women. But where would it go from there? What do you get the barbarian who has everything? How about a movie deal?

CHAPTER 8
SEEING IS BELIEVING

In December of 1958 for my seventh birthday, I was taken to see a film at the Garrick Theatre, one of the majestic old movie palaces in downtown Chicago. Outside around the marquee were huge cut-out figures. One was a cloven-hoofed, one-eyed horned giant, engaged in a battle with a fire-breathing dragon; another featured an enormous two-headed bird attacking a group of men armed with swords; a third, not as large as the others but no less impressive, featured a man swordfighting with…a *skeleton!* They were the most beautiful things I had ever seen. The movie was *The 7th Voyage of Sinbad* and those miraculous monsters were in actuality small models, brought to life through

THE CINEMA OF
THE FANTASTIC

THE THIEF OF BAGDAD
ACHMED ABDULLAH
1924
Dust jacket for the photo-play novelization of the film by acclaimed illustrator and designer Willy Pogány.

L'ATLANTIDE
METRO (FRANCE) 1921
PRESSBOOK

The first of many versions, based on the *She*-like novel by Pierre Benoit.

These early films were no more than thirty minutes long and relied more upon their visual trickery than any story content to move the action along. Today there are films two hours and longer that still rely on this approach!

As technology progressed and gave moviemakers the ability to create longer films in a timely and cost-effective manner, the story became more of the focal point and the effects were used to fill the gaps.

Brief fantasy sequences turned up in many early silent films. In Europe, Germany in particular, fantasy elements were creeping into the Expressionist school of macabre movies. Off-kilter camera angles, shadows, and forced-perspective sets were used to great effect in *The Cabinet of Dr. Caligari* (1919). *L'Atlantide* (1921) was a French silent film based on the novel by Pierre Benoit, which in turn was inspired by H. Rider Haggard's novel *She* (1886). This tale about an immortal queen of the ruined lost city of Atlantis was filmed several times. Haggard's *She* also received no fewer than four early silent treatments and, like its eponymous character, would continue to be reincarnated down through the years.

The legend of Siegfried was imaginatively presented by Fritz Lang in the *Niebelungen Saga* (1924). This silent heroic fantasy was filmed in two parts: *Siegfried* and *Kriemhild's Revenge*. It features all of the major components: the hero, his quest, the battles and a fearsome beast. The sets are stunning—huge trees dwarf the actors in the atmospheric forest sequences. A giant "animatronic" fire-breathing dragon is fought and killed by Siegfried (Paul Richter) who bathes in its blood to make himself invincible. Many of the scenes reflected the look of illustrations featured in books of the 1900s, anticipating conventions still practiced by fantasy filmmakers today.

The first of many screen treatments of *The Thief of Bagdad* was made in 1924. A seminal fantasy film, Douglas Fairbanks (Sr.) produced, starred in, and co-wrote the screenplay. Raoul Walsh directed it and, at a cost of an unprecedented $2,000,000, it is filled with fantastic sequences and effects. Add to that imaginative set designs by William Cameron Menzies and Anton Grot, not to mention a flying horse, a giant bat, and an undersea spider, and you have a major achievement in early fantasy film. In 1940 Menzies associate-produced (with Zoltan Korda) another *The Thief of Bagdad*. Co-directed by Michael Powell, this vibrant, Technicolor *Thief* featured a great music score by Miklos Rozsa and stand-out performances by Sabu and the so-good-at-being-so-bad Conrad Veidt. In 1960 Steve Reeves (of *Hercules* fame) flexed his way through the role of the thief for a third try at it, but the charm was wearing thin, as a 1978 television version starring Roddy McDowall also confirmed.

In 1925 *The Lost World*, based on the novel by Sir Arthur Conan Doyle, opened to critical acclaim. Willis O'Brien, the effects creator, used stop-motion animation to give dinosaur miniatures the illusion of life. The models were filmed one frame at a time, their position slightly changed between frames. For every twenty-four exposures, one second of film was completed, making it a painstaking and costly process. But when a finished sequence was combined with footage of actors and backgrounds, the illusion was complete. O'Brien had previously experimented with this technique in short films and brought it to its zenith in *King Kong* (1933). The story of the giant ape from Skull Island and the woman he could never have influenced many films but has never been rivaled for sheer excitement, originality and, even by today's standards, stunning special effects. Other

Courtesy of Ronald V. Borst / Hollywood Movie Posters

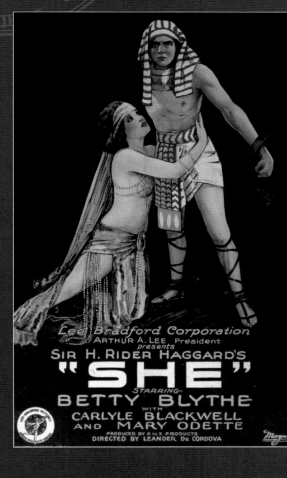

Courtesy of Ronald V. Borst / Hollywood Movie Posters

4
SHE
RECIPROCITY 1926
ONE-SHEET POSTER

A silent version of
H. Rider Haggard's
classic.

5
THE THIEF OF BAGDAD
UNITED ARTISTS 1924
ONE-SHEET POSTER

A beautiful poster
for one of the greatest
fantasy films ever made.

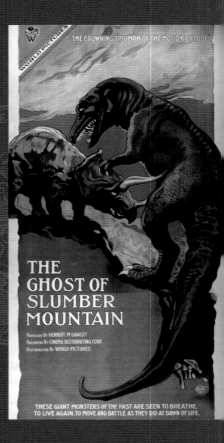

7

THE GHOST OF SLUMBER MOUNTAIN

WORLD PICTURES 1919
THREE-SHEET POSTER

Willis O'Brien's stop-motion dinosaurs proved to be a hit in this early film.

6

KING KONG

RKO RADIO PICTURES 1933
SIX-SHEET POSTER

A cinematic masterpiece and a triumph for Willis O'Brien. "It's money and adventure and fame; it's the thrill of a lifetime and a long sea voyage that starts at six o'clock tomorrow morning!"

8

THE THIEF OF BAGDAD

LONDON FILMS 1940
ONE-SHEET POSTER

The wonderful *Alexander Korda*-produced version in brilliant technicolor.

early silent attempts followed more of a fairytale approach to fantasy, including adaptations of such classics as *Peter Pan* (1924) and *The Wizard of Oz* (1908, 1910 and 1924). Films could show audiences things that couldn't exist and yet...

With the advent of sound in the late 1920s, older films began to be remade. The horror film experienced a golden age during the following decade, especially at Universal Studios. Though audiences loved to be scared, they also wanted to be thrilled and, more importantly, entertained.

Edgar Rice Burroughs' Tarzan, as played by Elmo Lincoln, made his film debut in the 1918 silent film *Tarzan of the Apes.* Former Olympic swimmer Johnny Weismuller assumed the role he would become identified with in *Tarzan the Ape Man* in 1932, and his now-familiar jungle yodel was heard for the first time. Tarzan returned for numerous adventures over the years, receiving a quite respectable retelling in *Greystoke* in 1983 and as an animated musical from Disney in 1999.

1934 movie audiences were shown what would happen when *Death Takes a Holiday.* To complicate matters, the grim reaper—in the guise of Prince Sirki, played by Fredric March—falls in love. It was remade in 1971 as a TV movie and again in 1999 as *Meet Joe Black,* with ladykiller Brad Pitt in the title role.

Fantasy elements were often present in many films of the period, even those that weren't genre films at all. A prime example is *Dante's Inferno* (1935). In the midst of a melodrama about an unscrupulous carny spieler (Spencer Tracy) who finds redemption is an incredible ten-minute sequence of damned souls in Hell (partially taken from an Italian silent movie). His sideshow may be called "Dante's Inferno" but

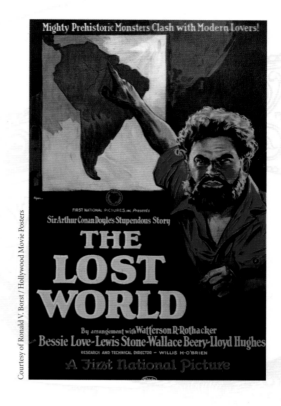

Courtesy of Ronald V. Borst / Hollywood Movie Posters

this scene of naked, writhing figures meeting eternal damnation is right out of Gustave Doré's illustrations for an early edition of the classic book. The sets by Willy Pogány, himself an illustrator who used his designs to great effect in many genre films (including *The Mummy* (1932)), make this segment a standout in an otherwise ordinary potboiler.

A Midsummer Night's Dream from Warner Brothers was released in 1935. It followed the original Shakespeare play fairly well and featured some inspired casting, including James Cagney, Olivia de Havilland, Dick Powell, Victor Jory, Joe E. Brown, and Mickey Rooney as the impish Puck. William Dieterle, who went on to direct Charles Laughton in *The Hunchback of Notre Dame* (1939), co-directed with theatrical producer Max Reinhardt and provided fantasy cinema with some inspired moments. Anton Grot once again designed the stylized sets.

RKO Radio Pictures, for whom *King Kong* was a huge success two years earlier, tried for another hit with *She,* based on H. Rider Haggard's novel. Presented by *King Kong* producer Merian C. Cooper and co-directed by Lancing C. Holden and actor Irving Pichel, the film holds up well despite changes to the book and uneven performances. Nigel Bruce (best known for his later role as Dr. Watson to Basil

Rathbone's Sherlock Holmes), Randolph Scott and Helen Mack all carry the film along and future U.S. Senator Helen Gahagan as "She-Who-Must-Be-Obeyed" is very impressive. Another film version of *She* was made thirty years later by England's Hammer Films. Known primarily for their horrors, Hammer put their two leading men, Peter Cushing and Christopher Lee, along with Andre Morell and John Richardson in the presence of Ayesha, this time played by former James Bond girl Ursula Andress. Stylishly done and very successful, a sequel, *The Vengeance of She,* was to follow in 1967. John Richardson was back, but not Ursula Andress, which might account for the lack of vengeance at the box office.

Roland Young starred as *The Man Who Could Work Miracles* in 1936, based on the H. G. Wells story, and in 1937, Hollywood tried its luck with another Haggard story, *King Solomon's Mines,* also featuring Young. Audiences would flock to see an even more exotic location that year—the lost Tibetan city of Shangri-La. *Lost Horizon,* directed by Frank Capra and based on the book by James Hilton, was an ambitious production, despite changes from the novel to the film. An excellent cast, headed by Ronald Colman and including Edward Everett Horton, Sam Jaffe, and Jane Wyatt, plus breathtaking sets and production values all added up to a first-class production. Originally previewed at 132 minutes, it was cut down to 118 minutes for general release. In the 1980s an almost complete version was released on video, after a long and laborious process of restoration. A 1972 musical remake of *Lost Horizon* should have remained so.

Topper (1937) was based on Thorne Smith's humorous novel about the eponymous banker (Roland Young again) and his misadventures with a ghostly

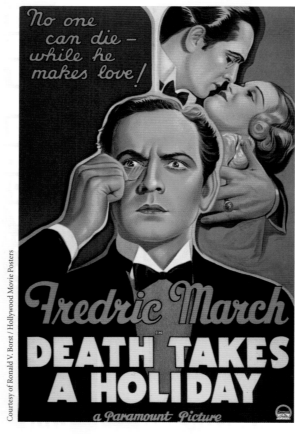

Courtesy of Ronald V. Borst / Hollywood Movie Posters

couple, played by Constance Bennett and Cary
Grant. Young would return as Cosmo Topper for
two sequels, *Topper Takes a Trip* (1939) and *Topper
Returns* (1941), before giving up the ghost(s). The
idea was so popular that it was adapted as a television series in the 1950s starring Leo G. Carroll as
Topper, and remade as a pilot television movie in
1979 featuring Kate Jackson and Andrew Stevens as
the ghostly duo.

Until the mid-1930s animators like Walt Disney
had been producing cartoon shorts, but they then
began to see a future in longer features. In 1937
Disney released *Snow White and the Seven Dwarfs,*
the first feature-length animated movie, to critical
and popular acclaim. To this day the Disney Studio
continues the tradition with animated features cov-
ering fantasy in all its many forms.

In 1939 a film based on a popular children's book
was released. *The Wizard of Oz* was destined to become one of the most famous films of all time. There
had already been several silent versions of L. Frank
Baum's Oz books, as far back as 1910, but nothing
compared to this lavish MGM musical. Filmed in
sepia but switching to dazzling Technicolor for the
sequences set in Oz, the Yellow Brick Road was easily
and happily followed as Judy Garland, Ray Bolger,
Jack Haley and Bert Lahr took moviegoers off to see
the Wizard in this movie milestone.

The Blue Bird with Shirley Temple, based on the
play by Maurice Maeterlinck, was released the following year. It had the misfortune to premiere in the
shadow of *The Wizard of Oz,* where it undeservedly
remained. A 1976 musical remake starring Elizabeth
Taylor, Jane Fonda, and Ava Gardner failed to spread
happiness at the box office.

This brilliant and highly popular story was awarded the Hawthornden Prize in 1934, and the dramatised version of it has several times been broadcast. *Lost Horizon* has now been made the subject of a clever and magnificently staged film, in which Ronald Colman and Jane Wyatt play the leading parts.

The novel deals with a mysterious aeroplane journey to Tibet, and the weird and fantastic adventures there of its kidnapped passengers, " Glory " Conway and his companions.

by JAMES HILTON

THE
STORY
OF
THE
FILM

MACMILLAN

RONALD COLMAN and JANE WYATT
in CAPRA'S GREAT FILM

LOST HORIZON

By

JAMES HILTON

2s

15.
LOST HORIZON
JAMES HILTON
1933 (1936 REPRINT)

Dust jacket for the British movie edition.

"I READ LOST HORIZON

when it was first published and immediately I wanted to do it. I saw in the book one of the most important pieces of literature in the last decade. The story had bigness. It held a mirror up to the thoughts of every human being on earth. It held something of greatness. Any story that reaches into the hearts and minds of all humanity is a story that can be put on the screen successfully as good entertainment."

Frank Capra

A new dimension was added to fantasy films through the use of color. Sabu traded in his magic carpet from *The Thief of Bagdad* for an elephant when he portrayed Rudyard Kipling's Mowgli in the *Jungle Book* (1942). The film was remade twice by Disney, as an animated version in 1967 and in live action in 1994.

With the success of films like *Snow White and the Seven Dwarfs*, *The Wizard of Oz*, *The Thief of Bagdad*, *Pinocchio*, and *Fantasia*—the latter a highly successful attempt by Disney to interpret works of classical music through animation—and other visual extravaganzas, audiences were clamoring for more effects-laden escapist fantasies. However these films cost a great deal of money to make, and with the advent of World War II budgets had to be curtailed. So in the 1940s, subtler and less expensive methods were used to convey the fantastic in live action films, and in many cases the results were even more effective.

Films like *Here Comes Mr. Jordan* (1941), *I Married a Witch* (1942), *Heaven Can Wait* (1943), *Blithe Spirit* (1945), and the horror films of Val Lewton for RKO Radio Pictures, particularly *Curse of the Cat People* (1944), did not rely on effects so much as mood and atmosphere to convey their thrills. These and other titles belonged to the less-is-more school of filmmaking.

Courtesy of Ronald V. Borst / Hollywood Movie Posters

I MARRIED A WITCH
UNITED ARTISTS 1942
ONE-SHEET POSTER

Since she looks like Veronica Lake it's not exactly a shotgun wedding for Fredric March, who seemed susceptible to fantasy film roles.

More direct effects of the war were reflected in such films as *A Matter of Life and Death* (1946; U.S. title: *Stairway to Heaven*), and *A Guy Named Joe* (1943), remade by Steven Spielberg in 1989 as *Always*. There was also a turn towards romantic fantasies in the 1940s, perhaps because people needed to believe in happy endings, whether it was with the living, the dead, or the mythical. *Portrait of Jennie* (1948), based on the novel by Robert Nathan, *The Ghost and Mrs. Muir* (1947), *Miracle on 34th Street* (1947), *Mr. Peabody and the Mermaid* (1948), and the quintessential feelgood movie, Frank Capra's *It's a Wonderful Life* (1946), all used fantasy as a way of enriching their characters' lives.

In 1946 French writer and artist Jean Cocteau directed the definitive film version of a fairytale fantasy. His adaptation of Madame Leprince de Beaumont's fable of Beauty and the Beast, *La Belle et la Bête,* is a grand achievement. Simple yet stylish effects that harked back to the early cinema parlor tricks of Georges Méliès were combined with beautiful sets and photography to create a very real and elegant fairy tale. Cocteau also took the legend of Orpheus and Eurydice for his 1950 film *Orphée* and once again created another memorable fantasy, again starring his beastly leading man from *La Belle et la Bête,* Jean Marais.

On the subject of beasts, another big gorilla, a Mr. Joseph Young of Africa, more commonly known as *Mighty Joe Young,* took his bow in 1949. The father of both Kong and his Son, Willis O'Brien, won the Oscar that year for special effects with a good deal of assistance from a twenty-eight year-old Ray Harryhausen, who was working on his first full-length film with his mentor. Disney remade the film in 1998 with cameo appearances by Harryhausen and original leading actress Terry Moore.

The 1950s, after an interesting start, were claimed by science fiction cinema. Later on, horror was revived, often combined with the "troubled juvenile" genre, an element that guaranteed box office dollars since movie audiences were made up primarily of teenagers. However, before the UFO, post-atomic bomb mutant monster, and various I-was-an-anything-but-normal-teenager movies struck, a handful of lighter, more whimsical fare charmed audiences.

James Stewart found a friend in a six foot, three-inch-tall invisible white rabbit called *Harvey* in 1950. Talking animals are a film genre unto themselves, and there were over half a dozen 'Francis the Talking Mule' films alone throughout the 1950s, starting with *Francis* with Donald O'Connor in 1949 and ending with *Francis in the Haunted House* in 1956.

America's favorite pastime was given a heavenly pitch in the 1951 fantasy *Angels in the Outfield* (remade in 1994), a theme revisited in *Field of Dreams* (1989) in which a farmer (Kevin Costner) cuts down his cornfield to make a baseball diamond so that the ghosts of famous baseball stars can play once more.

THE CURSE OF THE CAT PEOPLE
RKO RADIO PICTURES 1944
ONE-SHEET POSTER

Like most of producer Val Lewton's films it's a horror title, but this is a finely crafted and sensitive fantasy film.

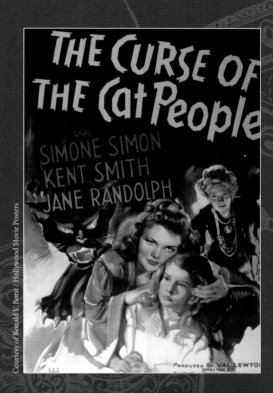

Courtesy of Ronald V. Borst / Hollywood Movie Posters

Courtesy of Ronald V. Borst / Hollywood Movie Posters

20.
THE GHOST AND MRS. MUIR
20TH CENTURY FOX 1947
ONE-SHEET POSTER

Gene Tierney was never lovelier (not that you can tell from this poster). Rex Harrison was the ghostly captain and George Sanders was—what else?—the cad, in this romantic fantasy.

21.
PORTRAIT OF JENNIE
UNITED ARTISTS 1948
ONE-SHEET POSTER

Robert Nathan's novel is given the Hollywood treatment, with customary re-tooling.

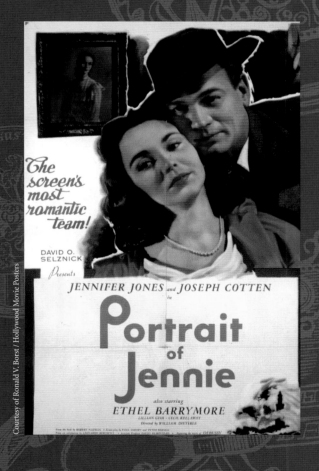

Courtesy of Ronald V. Borst / Hollywood Movie Posters

22.
STAIRWAY TO HEAVEN
(ORIG. A MATTER OF LIFE AND DEATH)
THE ARCHERS 1946
ONE-SHEET POSTER

A brilliant British film from Michael Powell and Emeric Pressburger, appropriately retitled for the U.S. so that Americans could tell what it was about.

171

ANDRÉ PAULVÉ
PRÉSENTE
UN FILM DE
Jean Cocteau
&
JEAN MARAIS
JOSETTE DAY
dans

la BELLE et la BÊTE

HISTOIRE, PAROLES, MISE EN SCÈNE DE **JEAN COCTEAU** D'APRÈS LE CONTE DE MADAME **LEPRINCE DE BEAUMONT**
illustré par
CHRISTIAN BÉRARD
avec
MILA PARELY, NANE GERMON, MICHEL AUCLAIR *et* **MARCEL ANDRÉ**
CONSEILLER TECHNIQUE: R.CLÉMENT   IMAGES DE ALEKAN   MUSIQUE DE GEORGES AURIC   DIRECT. DE PRODUCT. ÉMILE DARBON
UNE SUPERPRODUCTION ANDRÉ PAULVÉ

 23

LA BELLE ET LA BÊTE
(U.S. BEAUTY AND
THE BEAST)
DISCINA (FRANCE) 1946
FRENCH POSTER

Right from the opening
"Once upon a time…"
this is the perfect fairytale
fantasy captured on film.

24

MIGHTY JOE YOUNG
RKO RADIO PICTURES 1949
ONE-SHEET POSTER

Ray Harryhausen got
to work with his mentor,
Willis O'Brien, on the
Academy Award-winning
special effects.

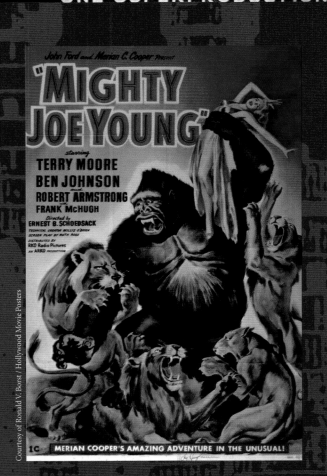

Courtesy of Ronald V. Borst / Hollywood Movie Posters

In *The 5,000 Fingers of Doctor T* (1953), a young
boy's fantasy about his piano teacher and his hated
lessons provided the basis for a very bizarre children's film, co-scripted by Theodore Geisel, a.k.a.
Dr. Seuss.

Brigadoon (1954) gave Gene Kelly a quaint Scottish
village to sing and romance in, the catch being that
the village and its inhabitants only appear once
every hundred years. The romantic fantasy was also
well represented by *Pandora and the Flying
Dutchman* (1950) with James Mason as the supernatural wanderer and Ava Gardner as Pandora, the
rich and beautiful socialite in love with him.

Ulysses (1955), based on Homer's epic and filmed
in Italy with Kirk Douglas, had some effective fantasy sequences and seemed to be the forerunner of the
"sword and sandal" subgenre, although that was truly

launched with the Italian *Hercules* (1957), starring former Mr. Universe Steve Reeves in the title role. Flexing major box office muscle, Reeves returned as *Hercules Unchained* (1959); this was followed by a whole slew of muscle-bound adventurers throughout the 1960s as Hercules, Samson, Ulysses, Machiste, and anyone else who could look good while being badly dubbed took a shot at the title role. A young Arnold Schwarzenegger (billed as Arnold Strong) even got his chance in *Hercules in New York* (1969) while his bodybuilding rival, ex-Incredible Hulk Lou Ferrigno, played Hercules twice in 1983. Both actors looked their best and were dubbed badly.

On a more serious note, Swedish director Ingmar Bergman's *The Seventh Seal* (1956) was somewhat reminiscent of Fritz Lang's 1921 silent film *Destiny*. Max von Sydow played a mediaeval knight engaging Death in a game of chess for the fate of mankind. It remains a thought-provoking piece of work, light-years removed from the average film fantasy.

Special effects were coming back in a big way in the science fiction films of the 1950s, and in the latter part of the decade a number of major fantasy movies would also benefit from an increased effects budget. George Pal's *Tom Thumb* (1958) was a light musical taken from the Brothers Grimm about the vertically challenged boy (played by Russ Tamblyn). It justifiably won an Oscar for its special effects.

After destroying parts of Washington D.C., San Francisco, New York, and Rome in the science fiction films *The Beast from 20,000 Fathoms* (1953), *It Came from Beneath the Sea* (1955), *Earth vs. the Flying Saucers* (1956), and *20 Million Miles to Earth* (1957), Ray Harryhausen eventually switched to an Arabian Nights adventure, chronicling the aforementioned *The 7th Voyage of Sinbad* in 1958. He showed us more

imaginative effects two years later in *The 3 Worlds of Gulliver*. Star Kerwin Mathews was back, trading his Sinbad costume to play Dr. Lemuel Gulliver.

Walt Disney saw the decade out with the entertaining *Darby O'Gill and the Little People* (1959), a leprechaun fantasy starring Sean Connery, and *The Shaggy Dog* (1959), which spawned the runt of the litter with *The Shaggy D.A.* (1976).

The 1960s were far from prosperous for fantasy films but did produce several notable examples. Bert I. Gordon's *The Magic Sword* (1961) might not have been that magical but it was certainly entertaining and an early step in the direction of the sword against sorcerer film. In this case, the sorcerer was Lodac, played by veteran Basil Rathbone. *Jack the Giant Killer* (1961) co-starred Kerwin Mathews and Torin Thatcher, both reunited from *The 7th Voyage of Sinbad*, again as hero and villain, with Jim Danforth's effects patterned after those of Harryhausen, although not nearly as effective. Producer George Pal's *The Wonderful World of the Brothers Grimm* (1962) contained some magical moments in the colorful bio-pic including a superb dragon, constructed by Wah Chang and animated by Jim Danforth. The film was co-written by famed fantasy and science fiction writer Charles Beaumont.

HERCULES
EMBASSY. 1957
SOUNDTRACK SLEEVE
Steve Reeves' Greatest Hit!

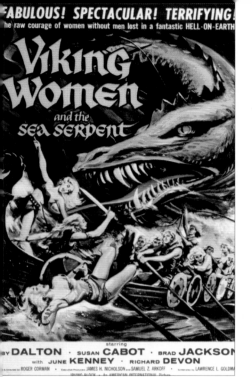

Courtesy of Ronald V. Borst / Hollywood Movie Posters

Courtesy of Ronald V. Borst / Hollywood Movie Posters

VIKING WOMEN AND THE SEA SERPENT
AMERICAN INTERNATIONAL 1957
ONE-SHEET POSTER

The original title "The Saga of the Viking Women and their Voyage to the Waters of the Great Sea Serpent" was longer than the movie.

SWORD AND THE DRAGON
MOSFILM (SOVIET) 1956
ONE-SHEET POSTER

A Russian heroic fantasy epic with some great sequences, relating the tale of Ilya Mourometz.

Ray Harryhausen returned with harpies, a six-headed hydra, and a battle with not just one but a whole army of skeleton warriors for the incredible visuals in *Jason and the Argonauts* (1963). It remains without doubt his finest achievement. Walt Disney produced *The Sword and the Stone* (1963), an animated take on T. H. White's Arthurian fable, and the following year filmgoers got to spend a jolly holiday with *Mary Poppins*. The film was a huge hit, winning five Academy Awards, making Julie Andrews a household name, and surprising U.S. audiences who had never before suspected Dick Van Dyke's cockney heritage.

7 Faces of Dr. Lao (1964) provided actor Tony Randall with the opportunity to play not only the title character but also quite a few members of *The Circus of Dr. Lao,* the novel by Charles G. Finney upon which the film was based. Screenwriter Charles Beaumont incorporated elements of his own work into the script he produced for this George Pal-directed film, and it remains an imaginative example of fantasy cinema. William Tuttle's make-up effects won an Oscar, but Jim Danforth's stop-motion Loch Ness monster, which nearly steals the show, was only nominated. Racquel Welch donned a fur bikini and became an instant 1960s icon while cavorting with Ray Harryhausen's dinosaurs in Hammer Films' *One Million Years B.C.* (1966). There also shouldn't have been cavemen lurking about *When Dinosaurs Ruled the Earth* (1969) but like the earlier Hammer film, if it ain't broke don't fix it.

The decade had its share of expensive flops, including *Doctor Doolittle* (1967), *Chitty Chitty Bang Bang* (1968), and *Finian's Rainbow* (1968), but it also saw some offbeat items like *Bedazzled* (1967), a Faustian comedy starring English duo Peter Cook and Dudley

JACK THE GIANT KILLER
UNITED ARTISTS 1961
ONE-SHEET POSTER

A nice poster for the somewhat *7th Voyage of Sinbad* clone.

Moore (which was recently remade), and *Yellow Submarine* (1968), pitting cartoon versions of The Beatles against the music-hating Blue Meanies.

Ray Harryhausen returned to animating his first love, dinosaurs, in *The Valley of Gwangi* (1969). The story was based on an original concept by Willis O'Brien where cowboys battle prehistoric creatures in a forbidden lost valley.

The 1970s were slim for fantasy films but there were occasional high points. *The Golden Voyage of Sinbad* (1973) was one of them, with Harryhausen returning to territory explored in his earlier Sinbad film, but by the time his *Sinbad and the Eye of the Tiger* appeared in 1977 the material seemed old and rehashed.

Children's musicals didn't fare much better, although *Willy Wonka & the Chocolate Factory* (1971), based on the book by Roald Dahl, raised itself above the fare that included *Bedknobs and Broomsticks*

(1971), *The Little Prince* (1974), and *Pete's Dragon* (1977). Britain's irreverent comedy troupe Monty Python took on the Arthurian legend in *Monty Python and the Holy Grail* (1974), while Python member Terry Gilliam directed *Jabberwocky* (1977), a comic fairy tale of the dragon-slayer variety based on Lewis Carroll's nonsense poem.

Disney fared well with the live-action *Freaky Friday* (1976), in which a mother and daughter "switch" places for the day, and the feature cartoon *The Rescuers* (1977), based on the stories by Margery Sharp about a pair of heroic mice.

A very different kind of animation was used by Ralph Bakshi to adapt underground comic artist Robert Crumb's character *Fritz the Cat* (1971). Bakshi followed it with *Wizards* (1976), a post-holocaust fairy tale that was an impressive little feature and more effective than his much-anticipated but

JACK THE GIANT KILLER
UNITED ARTISTS 1961
Production art featuring
key sequences in the film.

disappointing version of Tolkien's *The Lord of the Rings* (1978). The rotoscope animation was interesting, but the overall film was lackluster and the remaining two parts of the proposed trilogy were never made.

In 1977 *Star Wars* was a runaway blockbuster and imitators quickly jumped on the genre bandwagon. Special effects budgets soon increased to provide the best that money could buy. The style-over-substance brand of filmmaking was gearing up, but all was not yet lost for fantasy fans.

Resurrection (1980) was grounded by Ellen Burstyn's strong perfomance as a woman who gained healing abilities after surviving a near-fatal car crash, and *Somewhere in Time* (1980), scripted by Richard Matheson and based on his romantic time travel novel *Bid Time Return,* helped announce the decade with two of its more quietly elegant moments.

Hawk the Slayer (1980), a low-budget sword and sorcery potboiler, was the first of a number of barbarian heroes to reach the screen. Two years later, Robert E. Howard's favorite son finally got that film contract, and *Conan the Barbarian* allowed Austrian-born body-builder Arnold Schwarzenegger to flex his acting muscles a bit. Although not strictly Howard, it still contained several striking moments and Schwarzenegger returned for *Conan the Destroyer* (1984), a lighter and more pulp-like take on the character. A minor Howard character, *Red Sonja,* got the big screen treatment the following year, but even Schwarzenegger's presence (although not as Conan), couldn't redeem it. Schwarzenegger went on to become a major box office star, although it would appear that his sword-swinging days are behind him now. Howard's King of Valusia got a big screen shot in 1997, with Kevin Sorbo of television's popular

Hercules series (1995–99) in the lead as *Kull the Conqueror.* A final cinematic note on Howard is the excellent *The Whole Wide World,* (1996), based on the 1986 memoir by Novalyne Price Ellis, *One Who Walked Alone.*

The Beastmaster (1982) was added to the sword and sorcery genre and spawned two sequels and a short lived television series in the 1990s. *The Sword and the Sorcerer* (1982) continued in the Conan tradition and was followed by a horde of average or below-standard hokum like the *Ator: The Fighting Eagle* series (1983), *The Barbarians* (1987), *The Warrior and the Sorceress* (1984), *Deathstalker* (1984), and its many sequels, *Barbarian Queen* (1985), and countless others, including *Gor* and *Outlaw of Gor* (both 1987), two minor attempts at filming John Norman's misogynistic interplanetary fantasies.

Other highlights of the early 1980s included *Raiders of the Lost Ark* (1981), the first episode of Steven Spielberg's pulp adventure serial which produced two sequels and a dull television series; Terry Gilliam's quirky *Time Bandits* (1980), a crazed adventure through history with a group of eccentric dwarfs and a young boy, and *Excalibur* (1981), a beautiful treatment of Arthurian legend from director John Boorman, based on Sir Thomas Malory's *Le Morte Darthur.*

Dragonslayer (1981), although not a box office success, remains a brilliant example of fantasy filmmaking. Sadly less impressive was *Clash of the Titans* (1981), which re-teamed Ray Harryhausen with Greek mythology for the animator's cinematic swan song.

The Last Unicorn (1982), although scripted by its original author, Peter S. Beagle (who also co-wrote the 1978 *The Lord of the Rings*), could not approach its source material in this disappointing cartoon

 **JASON AND THE ARGONAUTS**
COLUMBIA 1963
ONE-SHEET POSTER

They don't get much better than this. Harpies, Talos, the Hydra, great music by Bernard Herrmann, one of the best screen Hercules' *and* good acting—and watch out for the children of the Hydra's teeth! —all are here in Ray Harryhausen's finest hour and forty-four minutes.

 7 FACES OF DR. LAO
METRO-GOLDWYN-MAYER 1964
ONE-SHEET POSTER

Eddie Murphy wasn't the first multiple-character actor. Tony Randall plays almost all the attractions in the circus of Dr. Lao, including Lao himself.

version. The same year *The Dark Crystal* created a world of pure fantasy with characters designed by British illustrator Brian Froud and beautifully brought to life by Jim Henson's Creature Shop. The team of Henson and Froud were reunited in 1986 with *Labyrinth,* which included human actors David Bowie as the Goblin King and Jennifer Connelly as a young girl trying to rescue her brother, alongside various puppet creations.

Ray Bradbury expertly adapted his novel *Something Wicked This Way Comes* (1983) for Disney, and Ralph Bakshi collaborated with artist Frank Frazetta for *Fire and Ice* (1984), a barbarian cartoon fantasy patterned after Frazetta's style of art. Effects extravaganzas blossomed in 1984 with *Ghostbusters, Gremlins,* and *The NeverEnding Story,* the latter a visually impressive adaptation of the first half of the bestseller by German author Michael Ende (who had his name removed from the credits). Unfortunately it gave way to two sequels (in 1990 and 1994) which traveled further away from the original book. A decade later, *The Pagemaster* (1994) combined animation and live action to tell a similar tale.

The Company of Wolves (1984), based on the writings of Angela Carter and directed by Neil Jordan (later to direct *Interview with the Vampire* (1994)), was another beautiful-to-look-at piece of work, combining horrific moments with a fantasy elegance. On the lighter side that year was *All of Me,* a reincarnation comedy with Steve Martin, and *Splash* with Tom Hanks and Daryl Hannah as his mermaid love. In 1988 Hanks played a young boy who wished he was *Big* and found his wish granted with unexpected results. Hanks' performances in these two films show why he is such an enduring actor, still moving audiences with his performance as a death row prison guard making the acquaintance of a condemned prisoner with healing powers in *The Green Mile* (1999), based on the serial novel by Stephen King.

Walt Disney attempted to adapt Lloyd Alexander's the Chronicles of Prydain with *The Black Cauldron* (1985), but the animated feature was not entirely successful.

Ladyhawke (1985), with its ill-fated shape-shifting lovers played by Rutger Hauer and Michelle Pfeiffer, fared better, while director Ridley Scott's *Legend* (1985) with Tom Cruise, although breathtaking to look at, did not. The U.S. version was shorter, and Jerry Goldsmith's wonderful music score replaced with one by Tangerine Dream. A future complete DVD release may reveal that the film deserved better.

Return to Oz (1985) put a darker fantasy spin on L. Frank Baum's books and was a counterpoint to such entertaining light vehicles as Woody Allen's *The Purple Rose of Cairo* (1985), *Peggy Sue Got Married* (1986), and *Made in Heaven* (1987). *The Princess Bride* (1987) was scripted by William Goldman and based on his own book; *Beetlejuice* (1988), was an inspired piece of madness from Tim Burton; and *Who Framed Roger Rabbit* (1988) pioneered a combination of computerized animation and live action.

Terry Gilliam was back with *Brazil* in 1985, a brilliantly surreal film which owed much to Kafka and Orwell, which meant of course that he had to go through hell to eventually prove it. Gilliam also filmed *The Adventures of Baron Munchausen* (1989), with John Neville perfect in the title role, and *The Fisher King* (1991), a contemporary delusional fantasy spin on Parsifal and his quest for the Holy Grail.

Highlander (1986), another contemporary fantasy with flashbacks to ages past, told the story of an immortal Scotsman and coined the phrase, "There can

THE LORD OF THE RINGS
UNITED ARTISTS/SAUL ZAENTZ PRODUCTION
COMPANY 1978
ONE-SHEET POSTER

That may be a pretty big sword, but in this case the pen of Tolkien was mightier.

THE GOLDEN VOYAGE OF SINBAD
COLUMBIA 1973
LASER DISC SLEEVE

Harryhausen returns to the Sinbad formula. John Philip Law cuts a dashing figure as the Arabian Nights adventurer, and Tom Baker is excellent as Koura, the evil wizard.

SINBAD AND THE EYE OF THE TIGER
COLUMBIA 1977
POSTER ARTWORK

The poster art was great but by this time the magic was wearing thin.

be only one". It was a huge success that garnered three sequels, three television series, and a cult following. *Willow* (1988) was about a Tolkienesque quest to protect a baby princess from a wicked queen, directed by Ron Howard and starring a young Val Kilmer. From Germany, Wim Wenders' *Wings of Desire* (1987), about an angel in love with a human and who longs to be human himself, was beautifully visualized although the sequel, *Far Away So Close* (1993) was not. *City of Angels* (1998) with Nicolas Cage and Meg Ryan was a moving American take on the first film. *The Navigator: A Medieval Odyssey* (1988) is an intriguing New Zealand fantasy moving between the fourteenth century and today, directed by Vincent Ward.

In 1989 *The Little Mermaid*, based on the story by Hans Christian Andersen, marked a new beginning for Walt Disney and the animated film. The studio followed it up with *Beauty and the Beast* (1991) (the only animated picture to receive an Oscar nomination for Best Picture), *Aladdin* (1992), *The Lion King* (1994), *The Hunchback of Notre Dame* (1996), *Hercules* (1997), *Tarzan* (1999), a new but not necessarily improved *Fantasia 2000,* and *Dinosaur* (2000). The latter broke new ground when it brought to the screen computer-generated realism of form set against actual filmed landscapes. Of course, the dinosaurs spoke, which may give us a moment's reflection on another possible theory as to their extinction.

Ghost (1990) was a huge commercial hit, but a more sensitive and beautiful handling of similar themes was found in *Truly Madly Deeply* (1991) with wonderful performances from Juliet Stevenson and Alan Rickman as her dearly departed.

Jacob's Ladder (1990), scripted by Bruce Joel Rubin (who also wrote *Ghost*), put Tim Robbins in a Vietnam War update of Ambrose Bierce's 1886 story "An Occurrence at Owl Creek Bridge". Tim Burton's beautiful modern fairy tale, *Edward Scissorhands* (1990), is one of the director's finest and the first of several to star Johnny Depp, who has become something of the definitive Burton actor since. *The Witches* (1990) gave Anjelica Huston a chance to have fun as the Grand High Witch at a convention of spellcasters, whose evil schemes are thwarted by a small-boy-turned-mouse in this adaptation of Roald Dahl's children's novel. *Dead Again* (1991) was a fun but silly reincarnation-romance-murder-thriller starring and directed by Kenneth Branagh. *Defending Your Life* (1991) starring, directed and written by Albert Brooks was a clever Heavenly courtroom fantasy. *Hook* (1991), Steven Spielberg's sequel of sorts to J. M. Barrie's *Peter Pan,* needed more hook than it had to succeed, as did Ralph Bakshi's combination of cartoon animation with live action in the uncool *Cool World* (1992).

Groundhog Day (1993) gave Bill Murray the chance to live the same day over and over again, ultimately making him a better person. Arnold Schwarzenegger officially became the *Last Action Hero* in 1993, a film that, despite its financial failings was stylish entertainment. Style was also very evident in *The Nightmare Before Christmas* (1993), a superb stop-motion black-comedy fable from a story by co-producer Tim Burton.

Steven Spielberg had a mega-hit in 1993 with the dinosaur-patrolled *Jurassic Park,* whose incredible saurians were a breakthrough in computer-generated special effects at that time. Striking a very different note, *The City of Lost Children* (1995) was a wildly original French/Spanish fantasy about a sideshow

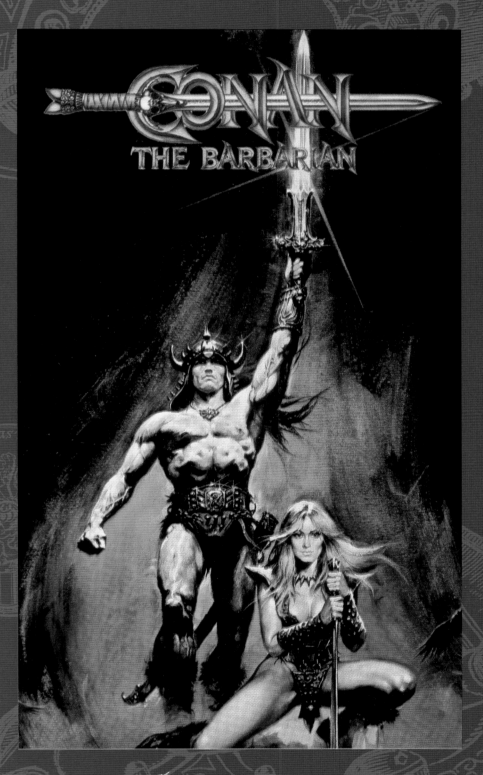

CONAN THE BARBARIAN
UNIVERSAL 1982
MCA HOME VIDEO BOX ART
A star is born! Robert E. Howard's adventurer gets his name up in lights and Arnold Schwarzenegger gets crucified (and not just by the critics).

181

strongman attempting to rescue his adopted little brother from the clutches of a mad genetic engineer who steals the dreams of children as a sideline!

More and more computer-generated images (CGI) were being used to create amazing visuals at the cost of story and characters. Anything you could imagine could be made to look real. In *Jumanji* (1995), based on the book by artist Chris Van Allsburg, hordes of incredible jungle creatures are seen stampeding after Robin Williams and friends. *Toy Story* (1995) was the first feature film animated entirely by computer and is an amazing achievement, while *Dragonheart* (1996) gave Draco, the last dragon in existence, the voice of Sean Connery and a body created by the finest computer-generated imaging money can buy. A direct-to-video follow-up was released in 2000, minus Connery of course.

A double header year for fairies was 1997 with releases of *Fairy Tale: A True Story* and *Photographing Fairies,* two very different approaches to the same real-life incident. Robin Williams starred in *What Dreams May Come* (1998), a visually impressive film but not up to its source material, the novel of the same name by Richard Matheson.

During the past decade, comic book heroes and cartoon characters continued to garner big budget productions with varying results. Science fiction, fantasy, and horror experienced major treatments, laden with expensive special effects, and budgets continued to grow but, unfortunately, much of the time their subjects weren't deserving of the huge sums spent on them.

On the small screen, fantasy has been traditionally played for children or for laughs. Arthur Lubin, who brought the talking mule Francis to the screen, successfully reworked the concept into the television series *Mr. Ed* (1961–65) about a talking horse who gave his owner endless frustration, while Samantha, the nose-wrinkling housewife witch in *Bewitched* (1964–72) provided her husband with the same. *Bewitched* had a very successful run, as did the F. Anstey-inspired *I Dream of Jeannie* (1965–70).

The 1960s also gave us *The Flying Nun* and *The Ghost and Mrs. Muir,* amongst other fluff. Rod Serling's *The Twilight Zone* (1959–64), although predominantly science fiction, had strong fantasy episodes, as did the subsequent series in 1985–89. *Amazing Stories* (1985–87), co-produced by Steven Spielberg, also provided a few fantasy moments, but the series was thankfully short-lived.

Fantasy Island was a fixed location from 1977–82 where Ricardo Montalban was the master of ceremonies. It was briefly revived with Malcolm McDowell in the late 1990s and given a darker edge. *The Hobbit* (1977) received a nice animated treatment, faring a lot better than the theatrical release of *The Lord of the Rings* the following year.

Highway to Heaven (1984–88) was a major start for the help-from-on-high school, perhaps best exemplified by *Touched by an Angel* (1994–) and its spin-off series *The Promised Land* (1996–99). *Teen Angel* visited Earth in 1997–98, while *Teen Angel Returns* was an earlier 1989 series starring Jason Priestly.

Beauty and the Beast (1987–90) co-produced by George R. R. Martin, proved popular in the Phantom of the Opera love story vein, and the 1992–98 series *Highlander,* based on the 1986 film, remained durable as well. However, the spin-off shows *Highlander The Animated Series* (1994) and *Highlander: The Raven* (1998–99) weren't as successful.

Wizards and Warriors (1983) was a short-lived sword and sorcery series set in the mythical king-

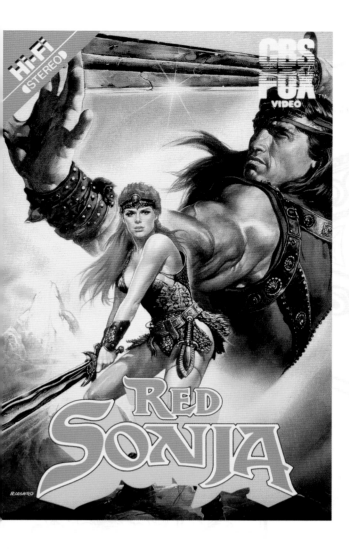

 EXCALIBUR
ORION PICTURES 1981
WARNER HOME VIDEO
BOX ART

John Boorman's very visual take on Arthurian legend is extremely polished—especially the suits of armor on the Knights of the Round Table.

 DRAGONSLAYER
PARAMOUNT 1981
LASER DISC SLEEVE

A poster by artist Jeff Jones for a ground-breaking effects adventure that also has a very good story.

 FIRE AND ICE
PSO/THORN EMI 1984
RCA COLUMBIA PICTURES HOME VIDEO
BOX ART

Fantasy artist Frank Frazetta's visual poetry in animated motion.

DEAR
MR. FANTASY
CHAPTER 9

Whoever said that if you can remember the 1960s, you weren't there, was certainly not a fan of fantasy litera-ture. "Make love, not war", might have been the message of a world youth movement embittered with authority, but those of us with our noses buried in J. R. R. Tolkien or Robert E. Howard books—and you know who you are —had our own slogans: "Frodo Lives" and "Reading Fantasy Can Be Hobbit-Forming". Amid the *sturm und drang* of the Ring Cycle (and I mean Tolkien's of course), and the clash of swords from various barbarians, a champion of fantasy appeared. Those interested and will-ing to learn more about the genre that they were consuming faster than you could say "Crom's Devils!" were given an inexpensive way to feed their habit, without having to resort to sharing books with other addicts.

A dream-dealer came along and, for the price of a paperback, you got a high (fantasy, that is) that would last long after the book was finished and put back on the shelf. Sure, there were some bum trips—you can't please everyone all of the time. I even had a few of them myself. But Mr. Fantasy, like any good dealer, knew his stuff and his clients; and once you were hooked, you kept coming back for more. As it should be in the best of all possible worlds, his supply seemed endless.

His name was Lin Carter and he could take you for a "trip"—to *Imaginary Worlds,* just one of a number of titles he produced under the imprint of the unicorn's head. The logo was the sign of an Original Adult Fantasy brought to you courtesy of Ballantine Books, the folks who published those authorized editions of Tolkien that went through the roof in 1965.

Born Linwood Vrooman Carter in June 1930, he wrote many novels inspired by Edgar Rice Burroughs and Robert E. Howard, but he made a far greater contribution to fantasy with his anthologies, in particular his work as creator and editor of the Ballantine Adult Fantasy series.

With the success of *The Lord of the Rings,* Ballantine displayed an obvious and keen interest in the genre by reprinting earlier fantasy classics, not just turning out imitation Tolkien to feed to Hobbit-hungry readers. After Tolkien, they went to E. R. Eddison and printed the loosely connected three books in the *The Worm Ouroboros* series (1922–41), along with an uncompleted fourth, *The Mezentian Gate* (1958).

Perhaps looking to ignite sales through series fantasy, another trilogy received the Ballantine paperback treatment: *Titus Groan* (1946) was the first of three novels by Mervyn Peake, followed by *Gormenghast* (1950) and *Titus Alone* (1959). Peake, an English writer and artist, created a Gothic fantasy of Dickensian proportions. The trilogy followed Titus, 77th Earl of Groan, from infant to man, but there were myriad characters making up the whole and revolving around the looming structural maze of Gormenghast, the ancient ancestral city-castle where the action takes place.

Casting their literary net a little further back, to 1920 to be exact, Ballantine also resurrected the allegorical novel *A Voyage to Arcturus,* by another British writer, David Lindsay. Although containing elements of science fiction (the voyage of the title being an interplanetary journey in a spaceship of sorts) the book also included many dream-like elements and, like *The Worm Ouroboros,* is recognized for its high fantasy qualities.

Ballantine Books had reprinted more than fifteen titles by 1969, reflecting the imprint's interest in the genre and its desire to bring long-neglected fantasy classics back into circulation in paperback. Someone who was extremely knowledgeable, and who possessed a love and enthusiasm for the field, would be an invaluable asset in this venture. Enter Lin Carter.

Carter was given the green light by publishers Ian and Betty Ballantine for a book he was interested in writing about Tolkien and the *The Lord of the Rings* trilogy. The book was delivered and Carter was called in for a meeting. One of the things Betty Ballantine really liked about the book had nothing to do with Tolkien, at least not directly. *Tolkien: A Look Behind The Lord of the Rings* (1969) was in part a response to those readers who praised Tolkien's work as if it had sprung fully-formed, totally new and original, from its creator, without any precedent or traditional influence. As much as Carter loved

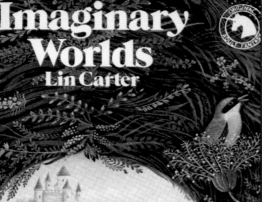

1

IMAGINARY WORLDS
LIN CARTER
1973
GERVASIO GALLARDO

Lin Carter's look behind the field he loved.

2

GORMENGHAST
MERVYN PEAKE
1950 (1968 REPRINT)
BOB PEPPER

Before the Adult Fantasy series began, Ballantine, who had published Tolkien, started publishing fantasy classics like Peake's trilogy.

4

THE WIZARD OF LEMURIA
LIN CARTER
1965
GRAY MORROW

Carter's first fantasy novel.

3

A VOYAGE TO ARCTURUS
DAVID LINDSAY
1920 (1968 REPRINT)
BOB PEPPER

An allegorical fantasy, resurrected by Ballantine.

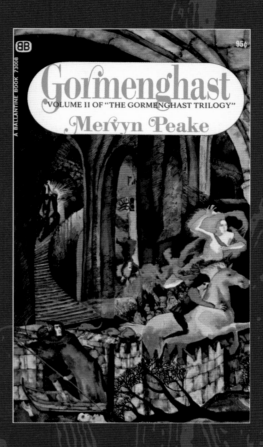

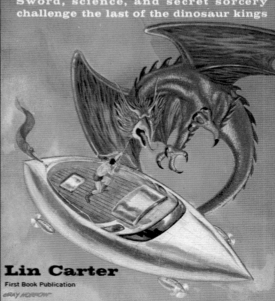

BEYOND THE FIELDS WE KNOW
LORD DUNSANY
1972
GERVASIO GALLARDO

A collection of short stories taken from several of Dunsany's books.

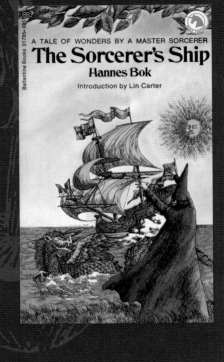

THE SORCERER'S SHIP
HANNES BOK
1942 (1969 REPRINT)
RAY CRUZ

A brilliant artist, Bok was also a gifted storyteller.

BEYOND THE GOLDEN STAIR
HANNES BOK
1948 (1970 RESTORED)
GERVASIO GALLARDO

Cut almost in half for its original pulp publication, "The Blue Flamingo" was restored and retitled here.

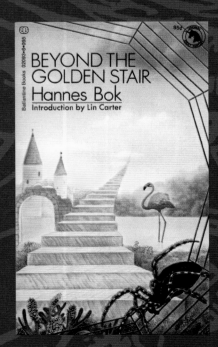

THE SILVER STALLION
JAMES BRANCH CABELL
1926 (1969 REPRINT)
BOB PEPPER

One of Cabell's wonderful fantasies set in imaginary Poictesme.

Carter had the right idea and Ballantine knew it. They offered him the position of consultant on a series of books reprinting fantasy classics. He enthusiastically embraced his new role, and in May 1969 inaugurated the Adult Fantasy series with Fletcher Pratt's *The Blue Star* (1952). Eight more titles followed that year, with material by Lord Dunsany, William Morris, George MacDonald, and Hannes Bok, and two anthologies of short stories edited by Carter himself. The series proved to be extremely popular.

From that first year of paperbacks, all carrying the small iconic image of a unicorn head on the cover, the "Fantasy Seal of Approval", only one writer received double duty.

The Silver Stallion, published in August and *Figures of Earth* in November, were both written by James Branch Cabell in 1926 and 1921 respectively. Cabell became famous, or rather, notorious, with his fantasy *Jurgen: A Comedy of Justice* (1919), which was banned in America in 1920 for the suggested sexual content of its double-entendres and promptly put him firmly in the literary spotlight. It was part of a series of satirically humorous novels about the exploits and lineage of their hero, Manuel, set in the imaginary mediaeval province of Poictesme.

In addition to *Jurgen* and the above-mentioned titles, the series also included *The High Place* (1923) and *Something About Eve* (1927).

Cabell wrote more imaginative fiction outside of this series, and for these works he used the shorter pen name of Branch Cabell. Several of his fantasies were given deluxe hardcover treatments with art by Frank C. Papé. Papé's wonderful full-page black and white drawings and decorations brought the inhabitants of Poictesme to life and were later used by Carter in his Ballantine paperback editions.

THE BLUE STAR
FLETCHER PRATT
1952 (1969 REPRINT)
ARTIST UNKNOWN

The unicorn head, signifying an Adult Fantasy book, makes its first appearance on the cover of this novel of a magical world.

Tolkien, he wanted to set the record straight; in his book, he outlined the history of "imaginary world" fantasy, which was conceived long before Tolkien. For this alone he should be commended.

Many readers will be familiar with some if not most of the material covered here. Some may buy this book as collectors of the series, others might just want to look at the pictures. However, what I'm really hoping for is this: that younger fantasy readers out there, as much as they might be enjoying whatever type of genre series they are into at the moment, might be on the verge of discovering this tremendous literary heritage of which they were hitherto blissfully unaware. My hope is that they will be inspired to seek out and sample the labors of those early pioneers, who helped to shape the face of modern fantasy fiction. To enjoy the present and anticipate the future, we must always acknowledge the past.

Meanwhile, Carter had plunged into the pool of fantasy and surfaced with fourteen titles with which to start the new decade. In addition to Lord Dunsany, Morris, MacDonald, Bok, and Cabell, two of *Weird Tales'* finest writers were represented with *new* collections— *The Dream-Quest of Unknown Kadath* by H. P. Lovecraft and *Zothique* by Clark Ashton Smith joined the line-up of classic fantasy.

Not every title was a reprint of older material.

Number nineteen on Carter's hit parade was an original novel by Katherine Kurtz. *Deryni Rising* (1970) developed into a successful body of work for Kurtz, mixing elements of Tolkien and Celtic fable to create something uniquely her own, a series which has continued successfully through the 1990s.

Carter provided an introduction to each book in the Adult Fantasy series, giving readers even more of a history lesson in addition to the book itself. The cover art was an eclectic mix, from the somewhat surreal look of Gervasio Gallardo and the delicately stained-glass-like pieces by Bob Pepper to the antiquated cracked masterpiece look of Robert Lo Grippo's Bosch-like nightmares and David Johnstone's fine, delineated paintings.

George Barr, an artist whose work graced many a cover for Donald A. Wollheim's DAW Books and Ace Books in the 1970s, produced a striking color piece for *Zothique,* and rang in 1971 with a gem of a cover for *The Broken Sword* by Poul Anderson. Originally published in 1954, it was a dark tale of good and evil, played out among the denizens of faerie and their interactions with humans. It brought into play the title object, which was one of those kinds of swords that, once drawn, *must*…well it's not pretty, but it makes for a hell of a story. Barr used an unusual technique combining colored ballpoint pens and watercolor, with brilliant results.

This portent came towards Count MANUEL horribly

For someone who generally worked in the science fiction field, Poul Anderson wrote several pure fantasies, as well as his retelling of the Norse *Hrolf Kraki's Saga* (1973), which won a British Fantasy Award in 1975. *Three Hearts and Three Lions* (1953) was another of Anderson's ventures into the genre but with more of a de Camp/Pratt spin on it.

Carter tried out his sea legs on his next trip out by launching *The Boats of the "Glen Carrig"* by William Hope Hodgson. English author Hodgson, born in 1877, spent nine years at sea as a merchant seaman. The beauty and mysteries of the ocean obviously provided background material for this, his first novel.

THE CREAM OF THE JEST
JAMES BRANCH CABELL
1917 (1971 REPRINT)
BRIAN FROUD

A Cabellian fantasy with an early cover by celebrated British artist Brian Froud.

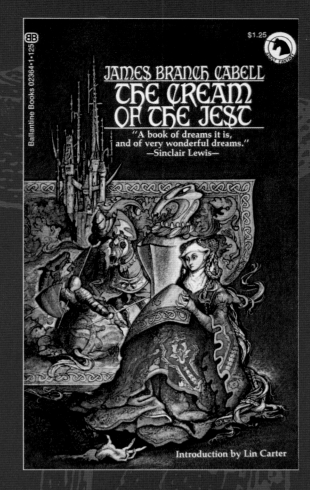

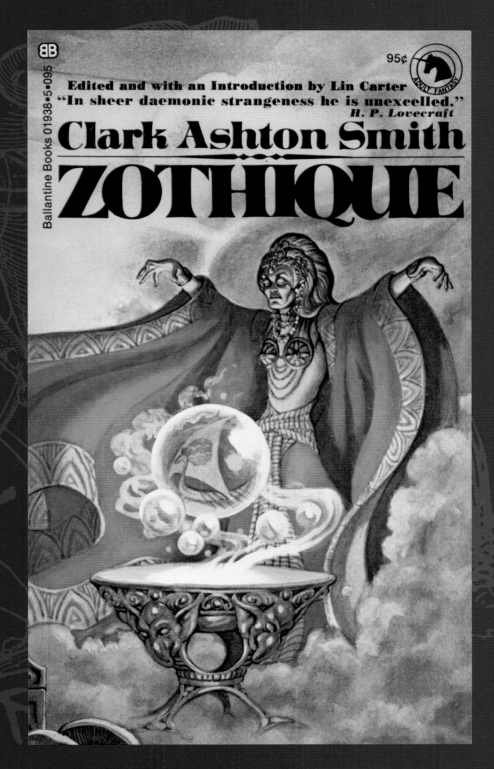

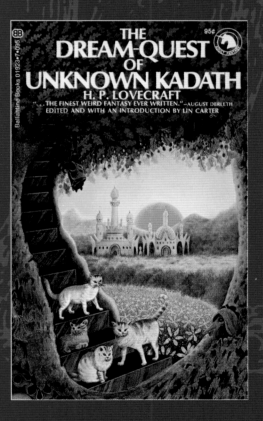

THE DREAM-QUEST OF UNKNOWN KADATH
H. P. LOVECRAFT
1970
GERVASIO GALLARDO

A reprint, but first paperback publication, of Lovecraft's posthumously published dream fantasy, along with similar tales.

ZOTHIQUE
CLARK ASHTON SMITH
1970
GEORGE BARR

A first paperback collection for Smith, reprinting all of his Zothique stories.

THE DREAM OF X
WILLIAM HOPE HODGSON
1912 (1977 REPRINT)
STEPHEN E. FABIAN

An abridged version of *The Night Land*, illustrated in color by Fabian, from small press publisher Donald M. Grant.

THE BROKEN SWORD
POUL ANDERSON
1954 (1971 REVISED REPRINT)
GEORGE BARR

Anderson revised his excellent fantasy novel for its first paperback publication.

16

THE NIGHT LAND
WILLIAM HOPE HODGSON
1912 (1972 REPRINT)
ROBERT LO GRIPPO

Elements of epic fantasy, science fiction, and horror are combined with a love story, resulting in this most unusual work.

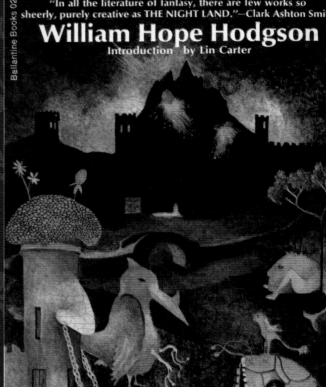

Originally published in 1907, it told a story of the survivors of a shipwreck and the strange terrors they discover as their lifeboats are carried into the weed-choked Sargasso Sea.

Hodgson's next novel, *The House on the Borderland* (1908), was more of a cosmic horror fantasy, the title dwelling being invaded by forces from beyond. Like *The Boats of the "Glen Carrig"*, it is required reading for the fantasy/horror enthusiast and cannot be praised highly enough. Just ask H. P. Lovecraft, who considered it Hodgson's masterpiece (and if you happen to get an answer, please let me know as I'd rather like to talk to him myself!).

The Ghost Pirates (1908) brought Hodgson back to the familiar surroundings of the sea, haunted by decidedly unfamiliar terrors. His mammoth fantasy work *The Night Land* appeared in 1912. Lin Carter added this epic to the Adult Fantasy roster in 1972 but published it in two volumes because of its length. The novel was an ambitious landscape of the imagination, though not as easily traversed as his previous three books. Among other things, it was a love story, set in a dying future world of darkness inhabited by unnatural creatures.

Arkham House, that fine horror and fantasy publishing imprint, going strong since 1939 and known for respecting the classics, had published a hardcover volume of four of Hodgson's novels in 1946, entitled *The House on the Borderland,* which featured a stunning cover by Hannes Bok. Arkham later issued a collection of some of Hodgson's strange sea tales as *Deep Waters* (1967). More Hodgson material subsequently surfaced as illustrated editions from publisher Donald M. Grant.

Carter unearthed another fantasy classic to join the ranks in 1970: *Lud-in-the-Mist* (1926) by British

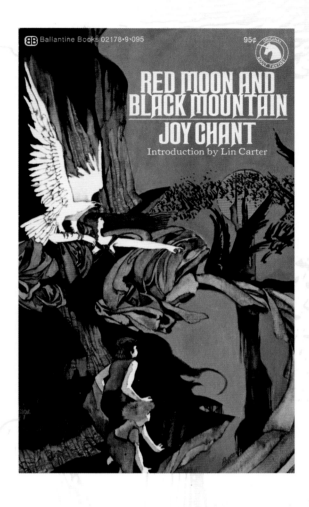

RED MOON AND BLACK MOUNTAIN
JOY CHANT
1970 (1971 REPRINT)
BOB PEPPER

A very good first novel and more than just a children's fantasy.

THE CHILDREN OF LLYR
EVANGELINE WALTON
1971
DAVID JOHNSTONE

Previously unpublished follow-up to *The Island of the Mighty,* based upon the second branch of the *Mabinogion.*

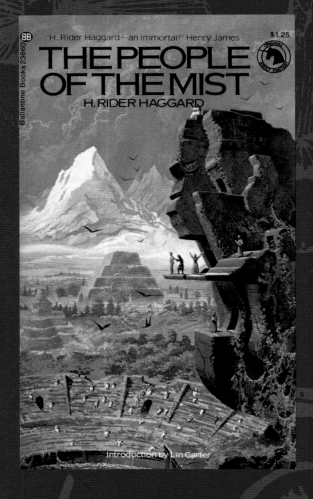

19

THE PEOPLE OF THE MIST
H. RIDER HAGGARD
1894 (1973 REPRINT)
DEAN ELLIS

Carter brings Haggard's
lost race adventure back
for re-discovery.

20

THE WORLD'S DESIRE
H. RIDER HAGGARD AND
ANDREW LANG
1890 (1972 REPRINT)
MATI KLARWEIN

A novel of Helen of Troy,
co-written by the creator
of another strong female
character, Ayesha.

author Hope Mirrlees. In 1971 more works by
Lovecraft, Cabell, Clark Ashton Smith, Lord Dunsany,
and William Morris came off the Adult Fantasy
presses, as well as a few more striking originals.

Red Moon and Black Mountain (1970), a first novel
from British writer Joy Chant, was a juvenile fantasy
—an area garnering increasing respect in the early
1970s.

The Children of Llyr (1971) by Evangeline Walton
was a surprise second book in a series. Carter had
presented the first, *The Island of the Mighty* (1936),
as an Adult Fantasy the previous year, unaware that a
follow-up had been written but never published.
Walton contacted him to let him know that it was
available and went on to complete the story with two
original novels in 1972 and 1974. The series was
based on the *Mabinogion*, the famous cycle of Welsh
myths and legends. Walton also wrote *Witch House*,
published by Arkham House in 1945, and various
historical novels. In 1985 she was honored with a
Special World Fantasy Award and given another
award for Life Achievement in 1989.

Carter edited four more original anthologies and
added H. Rider Haggard and Andrew Lang to the
fantasy blend that included yet more from Smith,
Cabell, Lord Dunsany, George MacDonald, and
Evangeline Walton.

Katherine Kurtz produced another original, *Deryni
Checkmate* (1972) and Carter paid lip-service to the
lost race novel by raising C. J. Cutliffe Hyne's *The
Lost Continent* (1899). He also turned to a series of
oriental fantasies by U.K. author Ernest Bramah,
starting with *Kai Lung's Golden Hours*, originally
published in 1922. The Kai Lung tales spread out
over several volumes, presented by their master storyteller, Kai Lung himself, after the fashion of

21

KAI LUNG'S GOLDEN HOURS
ERNEST BRAMAH
1922 (1972 REPRINT)
IAN MILLER

The colorful tales of an Old China that never was.

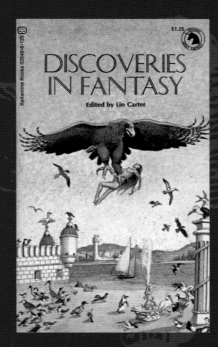

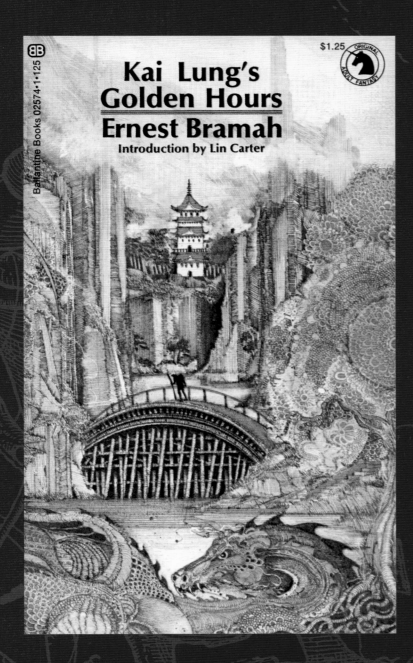

22

DISCOVERIES IN FANTASY
EDITED BY LIN CARTER
1972
PIERRE LE VASSEUR

One of Carter's many anthologies for the series, designed to revive interest in neglected fantasy writers.

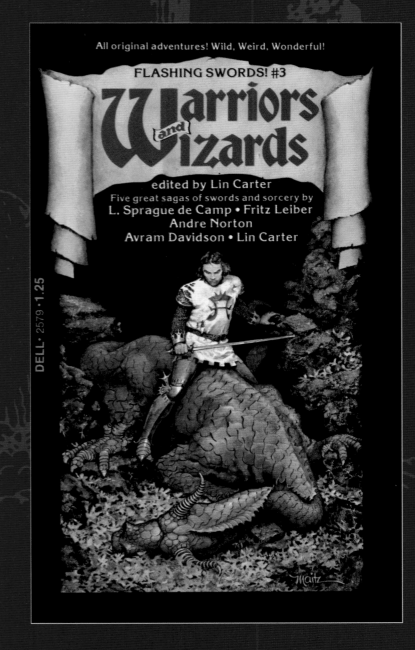

23

THE YEAR'S BEST FANTASY STORIES: 3
EDITED BY LIN CARTER
1977
JOSH KIRBY

As an editor Carter did as much as he could to bring fantasy literature, both old and new, to the fore.

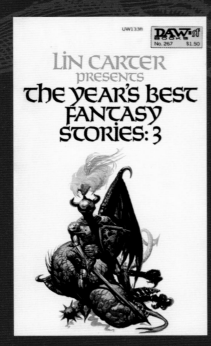

24

FLASHING SWORDS! #3 WARRIORS AND WIZARDS
EDITED BY LIN CARTER
1976
DON MAITZ

An all-new fantasy anthology including stories by favorites Fritz Leiber and L. Sprague de Camp.

25
THE BLACK CAULDRON
LLOYD ALEXANDER
1965 (1980 REPRINT)
JEAN-LOUIS HUENS

The second book in Alexander's
'Chronicles of Prydain' series,
given an animated treatment by
Disney in 1985.

26
THE FACE IN THE FROST
JOHN BELLAIRS
1969 (1978 REPRINT)
CARL LUNDGREN

This established Bellairs, who wrote
several young adult fantasy novels.

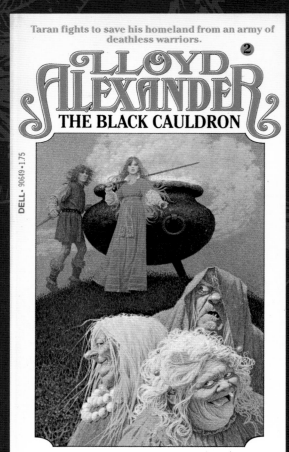

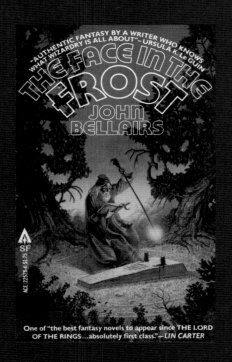

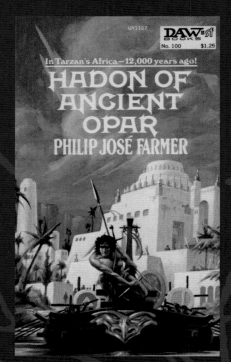

27
HADON OF ANCIENT OPAR
PHILIP JOSÉ FARMER
1974
ROY G. KRENKEL

An established science fiction writer known for
his somewhat John Kendrick Bang's-inspired
'Riverworld' series, Farmer wrote novels based
on Edgar Rice Burroughs' lost city of Opar.

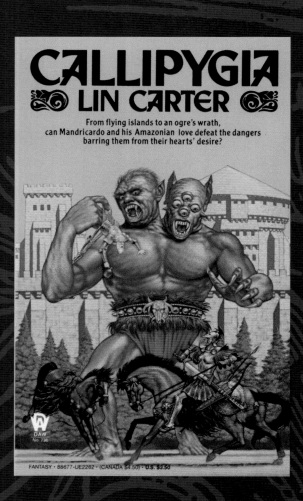

29
THE SHATTERED CHAIN
MARION ZIMMER BRADLEY
1976
GEORGE BARR

Bradley's 'Darkover' books are more heroic fantasy
than science fiction, and she was just one of the many
acclaimed writers published by DAW books during
the 1970s.

28
CALLIPYGIA
LIN CARTER
1988
WALTER VELEZ

Some of the last of Carter's fantasy
writing from his 'Terra Magica' series.

Scheherazade. They remain delightful stories of a China of the imagination.

Considering that a good deal of the material being published *between* the covers of the Adult Fantasy books was of British origin, it made sense that some of the *outsides* be graced with images by British illustrators. Ian Miller and Brian Froud, both respected fantasy artists, contributed some beautiful work.

By 1973 Carter had edited eight new anthologies as part of the Adult Fantasy series, with stories by familiar authors—Morris, Lovecraft, Tolkien, Bramah—plus works by Anatole France, Robert W. Chambers, Rudyard Kipling, and Eden Philpots, enabling him to provide as wide a range of fantasy as possible.

The fifty-eighth book in the series, published in June 1973, was a very special one.

Imaginary Worlds, written by Carter himself, was a love letter to the field and those who gave it life, from its earliest days to some of its modern creators. It also provided a template of sorts for writers of the fantastic and included detailed notes and references.

More titles were added, spreading the Gospel according to Carter throughout 1974.

The World Fantasy Convention was inaugurated in 1975. The convention award, nicknamed the Howard after both Robert E. Howard and Howard Phillips Lovecraft, was a bust of Lovecraft, designed by the macabre cartoonist and writer Gahan Wilson. It is presented in several categories for outstanding work in the genre. That first year, Ian and Betty Ballantine received a special award for the Ballantine Adult Fantasy series.

However, sales of the series had been steadily decreasing. Some of the final volumes, such as Evangeline Walton's *Prince Of Annwn* (1974), were published without the unicorn head logo or Carter's introduction. Five years after it began, the Adult Fantasy series was closed down. Ballantine Books, which had been founded in 1952 by Ian Ballantine, became a division of Random House publishers. Judy-Lynn del Rey became the science fiction editor, while her husband Lester del Rey created his own fantasy list. In 1977 the imprint was renamed Del Rey Books.

Meanwhile, *Fantastic* continued to publish fantasy throughout the decade, as did some of the other paperback houses. Small press publications such as *Whispers* and *Weirdbook* turned out fantasy as well as horror. Fantasy also continued to receive the deluxe treatment from specialty imprints like Donald M. Grant and Underwood-Miller.

Lin Carter went on to edit five volumes of the *Flashing Swords!* sword and sorcery anthology series (1973–81), and, beginning in 1975, DAW Books' annual *The Year's Best Fantasy Stories* (1975–80). He also recognized the adult appeal of so-called juvenile fantasy, with works like the highly praised 'Chronicles of Prydain' (1964–68) series by Lloyd Alexander, about the assistant pig-keeper Taran and his efforts to save Prydain from the Horned King, another series drawing on the Welsh *Mabinogion*. Another favorite was a novel by John Bellairs: *The Face in the Frost* (1969) was a humorous juvenile fantasy and probably the most accomplished of the several series he produced.

Throughout his career, as both author and editor, Lin Carter championed the cause of fantasy, promoting the works of writers past and present in the genre he loved and knew so well. He died at the age of fifty-seven in 1988.

Donald A. Wollheim, science fiction and fantasy pioneer, publisher, editor and even writer, had already played a significant role in developing the

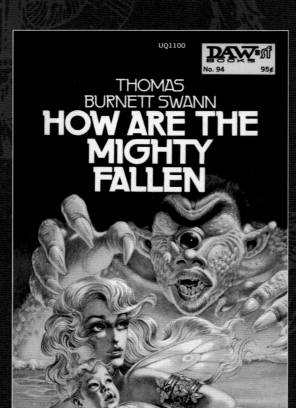

33

HOW ARE THE MIGHTY FALLEN

THOMAS BURNETT SWANN
1974
GEORGE BARR

A lyrical historical fantasy by Swann, who was also a poet and academic.

34

THE RIDDLE-MASTER OF HED

PATRICIA A. MCKILLIP
1976 (1978 REPRINT)
DARREL K. SWEET

The first book in McKillip's heroic 'Riddle-Master' trilogy.

35

THE FORGOTTEN BEASTS OF ELD

PATRICIA A. MCKILLIP
1974 (1996 REPRINT)
CHERYL GRIESBACH AND STANLEY MARTOCCI

McKillip's award-winning young adult fantasy.

writers between hardcovers. In 1978 they published *Born to Exile* by Phyllis Eisenstein. In the time-honored tradition of Michael Moorcock and Fritz Leiber—in regard to both their series characters and publishing histories, as well as the high calibre of the material—portions of the episodic novel were first published in *The Magazine of Fantasy & Science Fiction* between 1971–74. The book concerned the wanderings of Alaric the Minstrel on a journey to discover his true heritage. Artist Stephen Fabian, influenced by both Virgil Finlay and Hannes Bok, provided a cover plus interior work. Alaric's adventures continued in *In the Red Lord's Reach* (1989). *Sorcerer's Son* (1979), another tale of a young man in a world of magic and its follow-up, *The Crystal Palace* (1988), continued to showcase Eisenstein's fine writing skills which, frankly, the genre could use more of.

Between the paperbacks, hardcovers, specialty press publications, role-playing games, conventions, and movies, fantasy was no longer taking a back seat to science fiction. Horror, on the other hand (or rather, claw) was on the rise, thanks to the efforts of newcomer Stephen King and others in scaring the hell out of readers. In the late 1970s terror was big business, and when done effectively, went straight to the top of the bestseller list.

But as the 1980s approached, fantasy was still doing just fine. Tolkien, the revival of Robert E. Howard and the sword and sorcery tale, the persistance of individuals like Donald A. Wollheim, L.Sprague de Camp and Lin Carter, and an incredible number of talented writers and artists, many newcomers among them, all contributed to giving the fantasy field what horror fiction was already experiencing and enjoying—R-E-S-P-E-C-T.

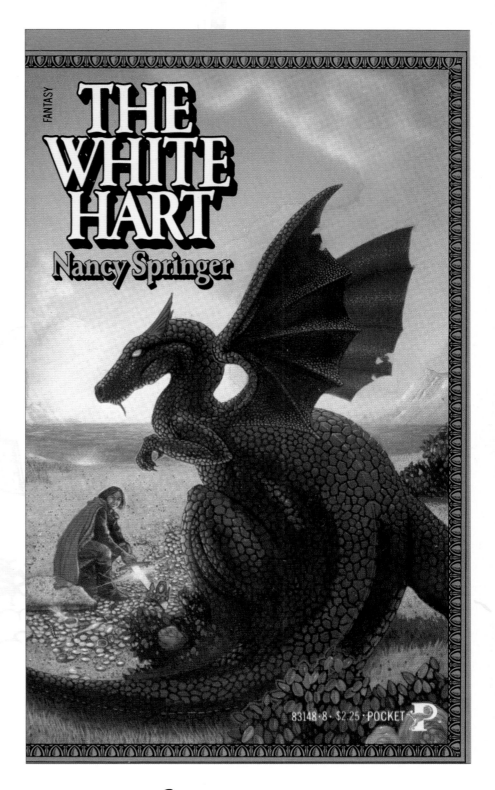

THE WHITE HART
NANCY SPRINGER
1979
CARL LUNDGREN

In addition to her high fantasy work, Springer has also published children's fantasy.

PHYL IS EISENSTEIN

Now it's time for the travelog portion of our program, so please make sure your seat belts are fastened and your seat is in the upright position. On that little white card where it asks the purpose of your visit, please print, as neatly as possible: *To tour the birthplace of fantasy as we have come to know it and see what is going on in its hometown.* That's right, we're going to Britain, an island steeped in the tradition of the imagination, both in literature and art. Fantastic fiction was raised and nurtured in Europe, particularly in the United Kingdom. Think of H. G. Wells, science fiction pioneer, author of *The Time Machine* (1895), *The Island of Dr. Moreau* (1896), *The Invisible Man* (1897), *The War of the Worlds* (1898), and many other flights of fancy. Or how about Mary Shelley, mother of Frankenstein and his abominable creation, stitched

CHAPTER 10

FAERIE 'CROSS

THE MERSEY

FAIRY TALES BY HANS CHRISTIAN ANDERSEN

ILLUSTRATED BY HARRY CLARKE

FAIRY TALES BY HANS CHRISTIAN ANDERSEN
1846 (1916 REPRINT)
HARRY CLARKE

Among the handful of beautifully illustrated books by artist Harry Clarke is this edition of Andersen's fairy tales.

together from dead bodies and brought to life? Or what of that two-faced physician brought to you courtesy of Robert Louis Stevenson in *The Strange Case of Dr. Jekyll and Mr. Hyde* (1886)? Even "ghost writing" became a respectable profession in the capable hands of M. R. James.

The legends and folk tales of Europe gave rise to many of the staples of early horror fiction, as well as the world of faerie. The collected fairy tales of Jakob and Wilhelm Grimm and Hans Christian Andersen, first published in English in 1823 and 1846 respectively, were initially gathered together from stories heard in folklore, although Andersen went on to create brand-new tales of his own.

Much earlier, in France, these magical narratives were introduced by Charles Perrault and Madame d'Aulnoy, with the latter's collection of stories published in the U.K. in 1699 under the translated title *Tales of the Fairys*, thus establishing this story medium forever more as "fairytale".

The mid- to late-1800s saw a renaissance in Britain as fairy tales reached new heights of popularity. *The Blue Fairy Book*, the first of a wonderful series edited by Andrew Lang, was first published in 1889. These collected fairy tales were beautifully illustrated with fanciful pen-and-ink drawings—and in later volumes of the famous sequence, full-color paintings —by Henry Justice Ford, which contributed greatly to the popularity of the books. Ford also provided art for other volumes edited by Lang. His color paintings in the *Fairy* books were very much in the style of the Pre-Raphaelites which, considering his friendship with artist Sir Edward Burne-Jones, is probably no coincidence.

John Batten, another fairy tale artist, worked in a similar pen-and-ink style to Ford; he too illustrated numerous volumes.

Alice's Adventures in Wonderland (1865) by Lewis Carroll (a.k.a. Charles Lutwidge Dodgson) headed more in the direction of a children's fantasy than a fairy tale, a trend that was becoming more popular among Victorian readers. John Tenniel's wonderful illustrations for the book ensured that he would forever be linked with Alice and her creator.

However, some writers persisted in continuing the fairy tale as a separate medium to the children's fantasy story. Oscar Wilde and Andrew Lang were among the last of the Victorian practitioners of faerie.

Quite possibly the first serious adult fantasy novel was *Phantastes* (1858) by George MacDonald, a writer of many children's stories. Subtitled *A Faerie Romance for Men and Women,* it proved to be very popular. Soon H. Rider Haggard was spinning his tales of reincarnation, adventure, and lost cities. And not far behind him was William Morris with his own adult faery tales.

The worlds of faerie and fantasy were very much celebrated by Victorian painters such as the following: Sir Joseph Noel Paton, with his scenes from *A Midsummer Night's Dream;* Pre-Raphaelite artist Sir John Everett Millais; John Anster Fitzgerald; Richard Doyle (uncle of Sir Arthur Conan Doyle); and committed artist Richard Dadd. By committed, I don't actually mean to his craft: Dadd was institutionalized in Bethlem Hospital Asylum after killing his father. He spent nine of his years there creating *The Fairy Feller's Master-Stroke,* an incredibly detailed rendition of the faerie world.

The faerie craze reached its height of notoriety with the publication of "genuine" photographs of faeries in the Christmas 1920 edition of *The Strand Magazine.* The images were checked and corroborated by experts, and more faerie pictures taken by the two young girl photographers were published.

Lang's fairy books were extremely popular
and profusely illustrated by H. J. Ford.

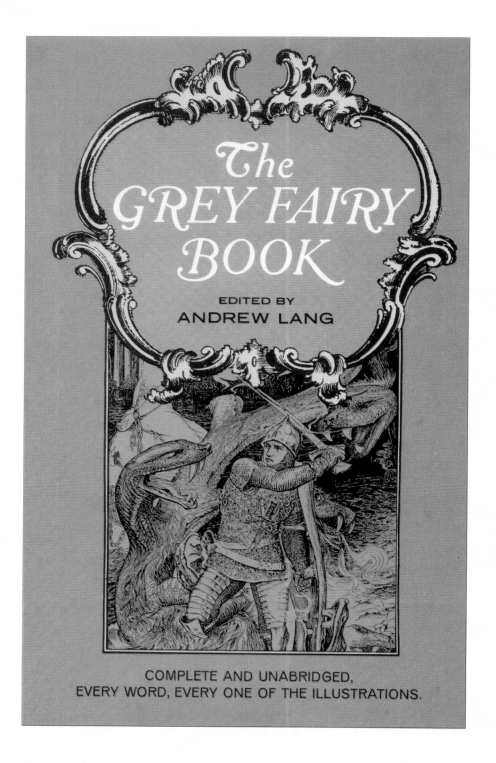

When doubts were eventually raised to their authenticity by the newspapers, Sir Arthur Conan Doyle, creator of Sherlock Holmes, sprang to the girls' defense in his book *The Coming of Fairies* (1922). The photographs were later revealed to be fakes, but for a while there…

Fairy tales and children's books began to receive better and better production in the way of fine binding and illustration. These gift books reached new heights with the publication of *Rip Van Winkle* (1905) by Heinemann, containing *fifty-one* colored plates by Arthur Rackham, England's premiere visual interpreter of faerie. With his distinctive watercolor and pen-and-ink style, Rackham became a favorite, bringing life to the world of J. M. Barrie's Peter Pan and Shakespeare's *A Midsummer Night's Dream*, among many others.

Hodder and Stoughton published the Rackham-illustrated *Peter Pan in Kensington Gardens* in 1906 and began a tradition of holiday gift books, brought out in time for the Christmas season. In most cases the books were produced in two editions: a cheaper, cloth-bound trade edition, and a more expensive limited edition, signed by the artist, beautifully bound in gilt-decorated vellum or leather.

Other talented artists, such as Edmund Dulac, Harry Clarke, brothers Charles and William Heath Robinson, Kay Nielsen, and Hungarian-born Willy Pogány, all provided brilliant artwork for a wide variety of authors and subject matter, ranging from *The Arabian Nights* and *The Rubáiyát of Omar Khaiyam*, to the works of Rudyard Kipling, Edgar Allan Poe, Samuel Taylor Coleridge, and the heroic operas of Richard Wagner. The latter, consisting of

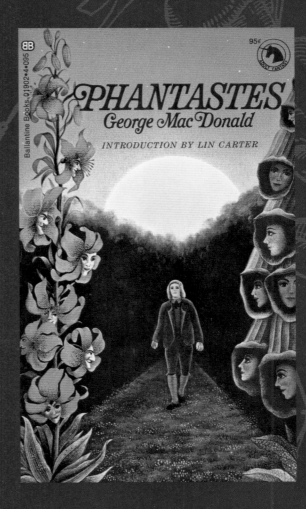

3
THE ORANGE FAIRY BOOK
EDITED BY ANDREW LANG
1906 (1968 REPRINT)
H. J. FORD

This painting for "The Magic Book" shows the influence of Sir Edward Burne-Jones on Ford's work.

4
PHANTASTES
GEORGE MACDONALD
1858 (1970 REPRINT)
GERVASIO GALLARDO

A major fantasy work from MacDonald, who was an influence on both C. S. Lewis and J. R. R. Tolkien.

5
THE ARTHUR RACKHAM FAIRY BOOK
1933 (1975 REPRINT)
ARTHUR RACKHAM

Rackham was the king of the world of faerie, creating goblins, imps, sprites, and lovely ladies for many deluxe editions of fairy tales and fanciful literature.

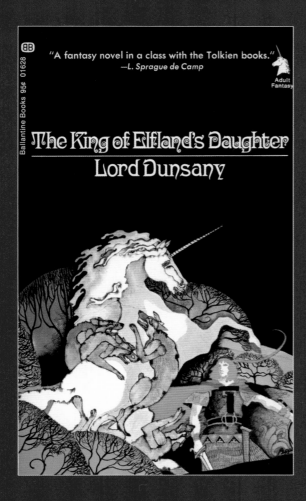

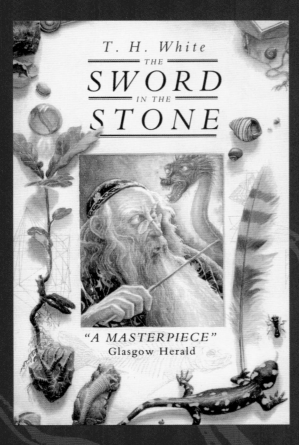

Tannhäuser (1911), *Parsifal* (1912), and *Lohengrin* (1913), along with Coleridge's 1798 poem *Rime of the Ancient Mariner* (1910), represent both book production and illustration at its finest, with their combination of colored plates, pen-and-inks, lithographs and hand-calligraphy text, all by Willy Pogány.

It was the golden age of book illustration, much of it of a fantastical nature. In many cases the artwork was displayed in London galleries prior to publication. The limited, signed, and illustrated editions of fantasy literature that became popular again in the late 1960s and 1970s pale in comparison to the magnificent volumes produced in Britain during that period.

One of the most impressive contemporary productions was the 1998 edition of *The Savage Tales of Solomon Kane*, the complete collected stories about the character by Robert E. Howard, interpreted with paintings and countless pen-and-ink illustrations by Chicago artist Gary Gianni. It was a beautiful production, recalling that golden age of book design, with good reason: it was published by Wandering Star in London, England. The winning formula was repeated in 2001 for the collected stories of Bran Mak Morn, another Howard character, with more beautiful work by Gianni.

The period before World War I saw illustrated books at the top of their form, and it wasn't until the late 1920s that production started to dwindle, especially of the limited, signed, gift editions.

While Rackham, Dulac, and others were bringing faeries, goblins, princes, and princesses to life for children and adults, Sidney Sime was supplying his own unique vision to the weird fantasies of Lord Dunsany and those of another British fantasist, William Hope Hodgson. Writers such as David Lindsay, E. R. Eddison, and Arthur Machen were

THE KING OF ELFLAND'S DAUGHTER
LORD DUNSANY
1924 (1969 REPRINT)
BOB PEPPER

Lord Dunsany's best-known fantasy novel.

THE SWORD IN THE STONE
T. H. WHITE
1938
(REPRINT DATE UNKNOWN)
ALAN LEE

Part of White's masterpiece *The Once and Future King.*

GOBLIN MARKET
CHRISTINA ROSSETTI
THE ILLUSTRATED LONDON NEWS
CHRISTMAS 1911
FRANK CRAIG

Christmas issues featured much in the way of fantasy, by some of the best artists. Here Frank Craig contributes a moody illustration for Christina Rossetti's "Goblin Market".

PHANTOM
VOL. 1, NO. 8
1957
R. W. S.

It was a brief run for this
British weird fantasy digest.

also making major contributions to the field, not to mention the continuing popularity of the supernatural ghost story which had been best exemplified by the work of M. R. James since the early 1900s.

During the 1930s, the British were also responsible for putting two of the most beloved locations on the fantasy map: Shangri-La, from James Hilton's *Lost Horizon* (1933), and Middle-Earth, from the world of *The Hobbit* (1937) by J. R. R. Tolkien. In 1938, *The Sword in the Stone* by T. H. White (later to be part of his complete masterpiece, *The Once and Future King* (1958)) placed a third locale in the public eye: Camelot.

Fantasy and supernatural fiction had been appearing in British magazines as far back as 1786–87 in *New Novelists Magazine*. This trend continued through a variety of publications, among them *Blackwood's Magazine* (1817–1980), *The Strand Magazine* (1891–1950), *The Idler* (1892–1911), and *Pearson's Magazine* (1896–1939). *The Pall Mall Magazine* (1893–1937), during the 1890s, carried stories by some of the best in both fields, including F. Anstey, M. R. James, H. G. Wells, E. F. Benson, Algernon Blackwood, M. P. Shiel, Bernard Capes, and Marjorie Bowen. Material from Europe and Britain was also reprinted in the German magazine *Der Orchideengarten* (a.k.a. *The Orchid Garden*) (1919–1921), the first of its kind to be dedicated wholly to fantastic fiction.

In the U.S. during the same period, the pulp magazines were enjoying their glory days, and one in particular, *Weird Tales* (1923–1954) was soon to corner the market in fantasy and horror. No similarly enduring magazine of fantasy fiction appeared in Britain at this point, although some genre stories were featured in various titles published by Walter Hutchinson in the 1920s. These included *Hutchinson's*

10

SCIENCE FANTASY
VOL. 16, NO. 47, 1961
BRIAN LEWIS

The introduction of the first of the Elric stories of Michael Moorcock, an author new to the pages of *Science Fantasy*.

11

THE TRAVELER IN BLACK
JOHN BRUNNER
1971
LEO AND DIANE DILLON

A revised book of linked stories, originally published in *Science Fantasy*.

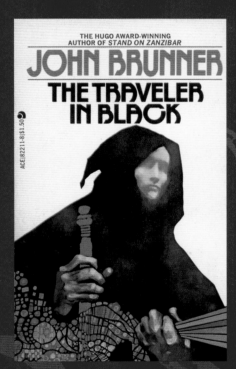

12

THE SAILOR ON THE SEAS OF FATE
MICHAEL MOORCOCK
1976 (1977 REPRINT)
ARTIST UNKNOWN

Elric is unlike any other swordsman, being an albino and a weakling, but his sword is another matter entirely.

Another of Pennington's striking covers, for a familiar face.

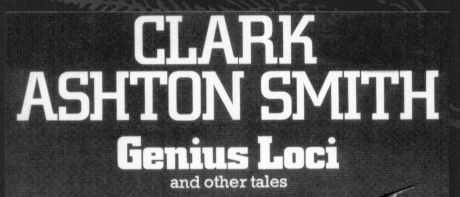

13

GENIUS LOCI AND OTHER TALES
CLARK ASHTON SMITH
1948 (1974 REPRINT)
BRUCE PENNINGTON

Great pulp fantasy was receiving paperback reprints in other countries. For some of the British editions of Clark Ashton Smith, artist Pennington created some memorable work.

15

SEVEN FOOTPRINTS TO SATAN

A. MERRITT
1927 (1974 REPRINT)
PATRICK WOODROFFE

Merritt, who always believed he was even more appreciated in Britain, continued to have his work revived on both sides of the Atlantic.

Story Magazine (1919–1929), *The Sovereign Magazine* (1919–1927), and *Adventure-Story Magazine* (1922–1927). *Mystery-Story Magazine* (1923–1927) featured works by H. Rider Haggard, Achmed Abdullah, Edgar Rice Burroughs, Edison Marshall, and E. C. Vivian. Vivian was both a specialist in "lost race" novels and the editor of *Adventure-Story Magazine* and *Mystery-Story Magazine* for a while.

Phantom and *Supernatural Stories* were two of the very few regular titles to publish fantasy in the U.K. leading up to the 1950s. *Phantom* ran for only sixteen issues in 1957–58, but *Supernatural Stories* held on for longer, lasting from 1954–67.

However, while fantasy was at a low ebb in the U.S. magazine arena during the 1950s, editor John Carnell's *Science Fantasy* found an audience in Britain and kept it through 1966. Publishing the Elric tales of Michael Moorcock, Thomas Burnett Swann's period fantasies, and material by Kenneth Bulmer, J. G. Ballard, Keith Roberts, Brian W. Aldiss, and John Brunner in the same vein as the U.S. pulp *Unknown*, it was the major outlet for fantasy in the U.K. at that time.

Although better known for his science fiction, much of John Brunner's fantasy masterwork—linked stories collected in 1971 as *The Traveler in Black*—debuted in *Science Fantasy* during the 1950s and 1960s. Out of Chaos came order, with a little help from an enigmatic wanderer, garbed in black and carrying a staff of light.

In the late 1950s, horror fiction was rising in popularity, thanks in part to the success of the Hammer horror films, and in 1959 *The Pan Book of Horror Stories* anthology series was launched, edited by Herbert van Thal. It lasted for more than thirty years. But there were still new fantasy classics to be had.

From the pen of Mervyn Peake came the 'Gormenghast' trilogy of *Titus Groan* (1946), *Gormenghast* (1950), and *Titus Alone* (1959). His undisputed epic was made into a mini-series by the BBC in 2000 and was wonderfully recreated for the small screen, with a high level of production. It also contained that precious commodity that seems to be in abundance in the U.K. and is yet another of their contributions to the art of make-believe: fine acting.

In 1954 and 1955, *The Lord of the Rings* trilogy, Tolkien's follow-up to *The Hobbit*, was published. These books built up a tremendous following and, by the latter half of the 1960s, were immensely popular and influential in the revival of fantasy literature.

That revival was already becoming more obvious in the pages of *Science Fantasy*, with new Elric tales by Michael Moorcock and, thanks to Robert E. Howard's Conan and other characters rising from the ashes, more and more heroic fantasy was beginning to appear in print.

Science fiction was still big business but between reprints and new material, much more fantasy was starting to be published. Some British fans reacted to their love of the genre—much in the same way as those in the U.S. or anywhere else for that matter—by producing magazines themselves, containing the type of material that they wanted to read.

Small-press publications were nothing new; they had been around in one form or another since the 1920s. Organizations and fan clubs celebrating a specific genre or author also had their fair share of supporters in other parts of the world, and in 1971 the British Fantasy Society joined that time-honored tradition, to this day holding their own well-attended conventions and presenting the annual British Fantasy Awards.

16
SHADOW
NO. 14 SEPTEMBER 1971
EDITED AND PUBLISHED
BY DAVID SUTTON
BRIAN FROST

Sutton filled *Shadow*
with excellent articles
and reviews and, as you
can see, artwork of the
same caliber.

19
SHADOWS OVER INNSMOUTH
EDITED BY STEPHEN JONES
1997
GEORGE UNDERWOOD

The trade paperback edition of editor Jones' tribute
to H.P. Lovecraft's Innsmouth, with stories by some
of Britain's finest writers including Michael Marshall
Smith and Kim Newman.

18
FANTASY TALES
EDITED BY STEPHEN JONES AND DAVID SUTTON
VOL. 10, NO. 1, 1988
CHRIS ACHILLEOS

The later paperback format anthology version,
still featuring quality stories and art.

17
FANTASY TALES
EDITED AND PUBLISHED BY
STEPHEN JONES AND DAVID SUTTON
VOL. 2, NO. 4, 1979
JIM PITTS

Jones and Sutton proved to be a brilliant combination.
Author Adrian Cole wrote fine planetary fantasy and
gets a great Bok-like cover by Jim Pitts.

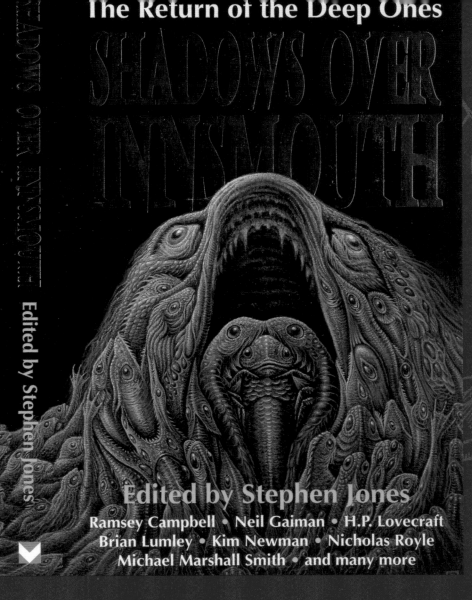

The Return of the Deep Ones

SHADOWS OVER INNSMOUTH

Edited by Stephen Jones

Edited by Stephen Jones

Ramsey Campbell • Neil Gaiman • H.P. Lovecraft
Brian Lumley • Kim Newman • Nicholas Royle
Michael Marshall Smith • and many more

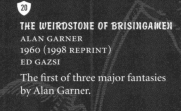

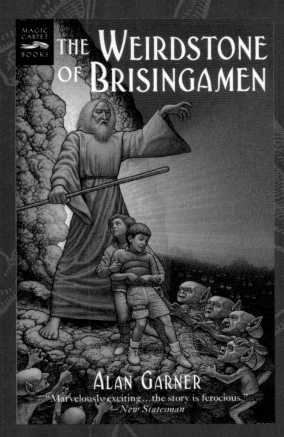

20

THE WEIRDSTONE OF BRISINGAMEN
ALAN GARNER
1960 (1998 REPRINT)
ED GAZSI

The first of three major fantasies by Alan Garner.

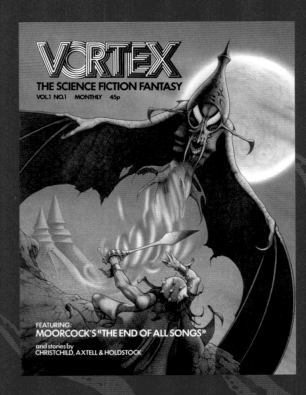

21

VORTEX
VOL. 1, NO. 1, 1977
RODNEY MATTHEWS

Vortex published both fantasy and science fiction with art by some of the best, like Matthews and Eddie Jones.

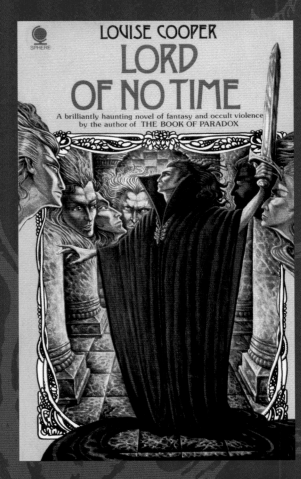

22

LORD OF NO TIME
LOUISE COOPER
1977
ARTIST UNKNOWN

This book by Louise Cooper was revised to form 'Time Master', the first of three connected trilogies.

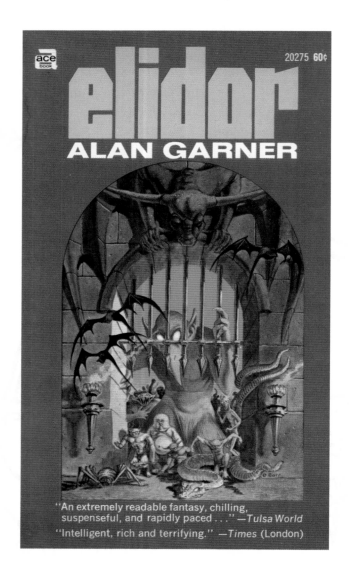

 ELIDOR
ALAN GARNER
1965
GEORGE BARR

Another of Garner's magical worlds.

 THE TOUGH GUIDE TO FANTASYLAND
DIANA WYNNE JONES
1996 (1998 REPRINT)
WALTER VELEZ

Jones is another fine storyteller who has been creating fantasy worlds since the 1970s.

Shadow: Fantasy Literature Review (1968–1974), edited and published by David Sutton, was the first U.K. fanzine to focus on horror and fantasy literature. For all of its simplicity of design, (initially mimeographed like other 'zines at the time) it filled a substantial gap in those days of science fiction and horror movie-oriented periodicals. Regular contributors included Ramsey Campbell, Eddy C. Bertin, James Wade, Brian Mooney, and Kenneth W. Faig.

Sutton knew his stuff, and the magazine ran reviews of new fantasy titles, as well as articles on writers and others in the field. It was a shot in the arm for fans of the fantastic and, in addition to its articles, also featured artwork of a high caliber by Jim Pitts, Brian J. Frost, David Fletcher, David Lloyd, Alan Moore, and Alan Hunter, all of whom produced work that hearkened back to the peak days of *Weird Tales* in both quality and style.

Since *Shadow,* Sutton has played his part for the genre, helping to co-found the British Fantasy Society, editing and publishing numerous books and periodicals, including several horror and fantasy paperback anthologies. As a writer, he has seen much short fiction published on both sides of the Atlantic.

He also served as co-editor on another semi-professional magazine that was a first of its kind in the U.K., publishing fantasy and horror fiction as a paying market. That magazine was *Fantasy Tales* and Sutton's collaborator was Stephen Jones. Jones had already edited several issues of *Dark Horizons,* the journal of the British Fantasy Society, and he was also contributing artwork in the detailed style of Virgil Finlay to various publications, one of the earliest being Sutton's own *Shadow.*

Fantasy Tales was patterned after *Weird Tales* and, like that pulp magazine in its prime, combined a

 25

DARK VOICES #4
1992
LES EDWARDS

Les Edwards has created images of horror and fantasy with a startling sense of reality, as glimpsed here with his painting for the David Sutton and Stephen Jones-edited anthology.

 26

KNIGHT OF THE DEMON QUEEN
2000
LES EDWARDS

Edwards turns on his fantasy charm full-throttle with a real live dragon in this cover painting for Barbara Hambly's novel.

Ramsey Campbell
Far Away & Never

 27

FAR AWAY & NEVER
RAMSEY CAMPBELL
1996
STEPHEN E. FABIAN

A gathering of Ramsey Campbell's early uncollected fantasy tales, four of which feature Ryre the Swordsman.

TERRY PRATCHETT

SOUL MUSIC

 29

SOUL MUSIC
TERRY PRATCHETT
1994 (1999 REPRINT)
JOSH KIRBY

More of Pratchett's magic 'Discworld' madness!

STORM CONSTANTINE
CROWN OF SILENCE

STORM CONSTANTINE

CROWN OF SILENCE

VG

28

CROWN OF SILENCE
STORM CONSTANTINE
2000
ANNE SUDWORTH

Constantine's innovative borderline science fiction/fantasy writing has taken more of a turn to fantasy in her more recent works.

high quality of writing—both new and reprinted—and artwork. Messrs. Pitts, Lloyd, and Hunter added more beautiful illustrations to their portfolios, along with supreme pen-and-ink monster-maker Dave Carson. Winner of the World Fantasy Award and *seven* British Fantasy Awards, *Fantasy Tales* was a triumph of small-press publishing.

Although usually more associated with the horror fiction field, Stephen Jones has continued to support and promote the genre and is one of the U.K.'s leading anthologists. He has had more than sixty books published, including seven *Fantasy Tales* paperbacks (1988–91) plus three *Fantasy Tales* anthologies co-edited with David Sutton; the team was also responsible for continuing *The Pan Book of Horror Stories* series for five volumes as *Dark Voices* (1990–94). More recently, they have co-edited the ongoing *Dark Terrors* anthology series (1995–) and continue to collaborate on various small press projects.

The 1970s brought a major boom in fantasy writing by British authors working in both grown-up and so-called "juvenile" areas. Joan Aiken has contributed many fantasies for young and old, with her 'Willoughby Chase' sequence being perhaps the most famous, beginning with *The Wolves of Willoughby Chase* (1962). Louise Cooper has proved to be prolific in both. Her début novel was the Tarot-based fantasy *The Book of Paradox* (1973) and she continues to write series aimed at the adult and young adult markets. Another U.K.-born Cooper—this time Susan Cooper—wrote five superb volumes in a mythic fantasy cycle, *The Dark is Rising,* beginning in 1965 and concluding in 1977.

Alan Garner began writing fantasy for children with *The Weirdstone of Brisingamen* (1960) and followed it up with several excellent novels, including *Elidor* (1965) and *Red Shift* (1973). Mary Gentle's first novel was the children's fantasy *A Hawk in Silver* (1977). She has gone on to write much imaginative adult fantasy including the epic *Ash* (2000).

M. John Harrison produced a major piece of writing with his 'Viriconium' series of novels. Somewhat in the style of Jack Vance, the cycle began with *The Pastel City* (1971) and continued through *A Storm of Wings* (1980) to *In Viriconium* (1982). A collection, *Viriconium Nights,* was later revised for U.K. publication in 1985.

Diana Wynne Jones is another author who has excelled at both adult and children's fantasy. With early novels in the 1970s such as *The Ogre Downstairs* (1974) and *Charmed Life* (1977), she has gone on to produce several series featuring more traditional fantasy quest elements and parallel worlds, where magic most definitely works, all done with a good deal of humor, shown to excellent effect in the Hugo-nominated *The Tough Guide to Fantasyland* (1996).

Along with great writing at this time came great illustration. A wave of talented artists rose to the challenge of providing imaginative covers. Among them are Bruce Pennington, with his somewhat surrealistic, intensely colored, otherworldly realms; Ian Miller's highly detailed visions; and the delirious fantasies of Patrick Woodroffe. Josh Kirby's darker dreams gave way to the over-the-top orgies-of-the-flesh style he used for Terry Pratchett's novels; Roger Dean is still best known for his vibrant 1960s album covers. Les Edwards has the ability to bring horror to life as well as focusing his attention on the work of Robert E. Howard and others and we should not forget the previously mentioned classic approaches of Alan Lee and Brian Froud.

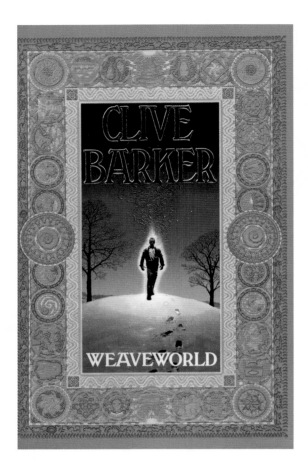

In 1977, science fiction, fantasy, and horror historian and anthologist Mike Ashley compiled *Who's Who in Horror and Fantasy Fiction,* a major reference work at the time. Over the years he has contributed to many similar reference works in the U.S. and Britain. Ashley has also edited several collections of Arthurian and heroic fantasies, as well as compiling fantasy stories for young adults. He continues to support and promote the genre with each new endeavor.

Although primarily writers of horror fiction, both Ramsey Campbell and Brian Lumley have had their share of fantasy encounters. Campbell wrote his Ryre the Warrior sword and sorcery stories and his completion of Robert E. Howard's Solomon Kane fragments. Lumley penned his Lovecraftian Titus Crow stories in the 1970s and his 'Dream-Quest' fantasies of the 1980s with their sword and sorcery Burroughs/Howard elements, exemplified by *Hero of Dreams* (1986), *Ship of Dreams* (1986), *Mad Moon of Dreams* (1987), and the collection *Iced on Aran and Other Dreamquests* (1990).

Storm Constantine entered the arena with a series of futuristic fantasies in the 1980s and has moved into the realm of dark fantasy in her work. Her highly sexually charged writing has breathed new life into a sometimes jaded genre. David A. Gemmell has been spinning action adventure fantasies which show no signs of slowing down, and Brian Jacques has been extremely successful with his Redwall animal fantasies for children and adults, chronicling the adventures of some rather heroic "mice". Another writer putting rodents through their paces and producing some fine fantasy along the way for young and old alike is Garry Kilworth. Jenny Nimmo, Fay Sampson, A. R. Lloyd, Jenny Jones, and Philip Pullman have also done their share for the young-at-heart set.

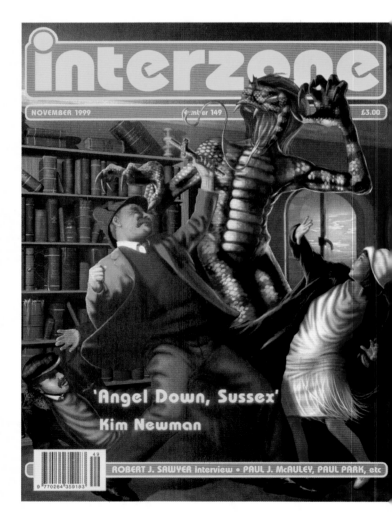

32

LAVONDYSS
ROBERT HOLDSTOCK
1988
ALAN LEE

Part of the 'Rhyhope Wood' sequence,
begun in 1984 with *Mythago Wood*.

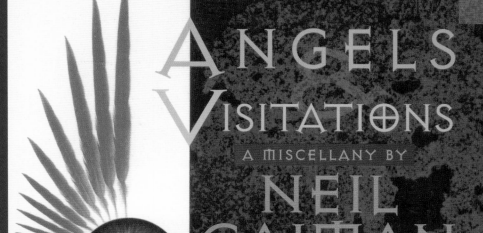

33

ANGELS & VISITATIONS
NEIL GAIMAN
1993
DAVE MCKEAN

From small press publisher DreamHaven
Books comes this illustrated collection of
short fantasies by Gaiman.

BLUE MOON RISING
SIMON R. GREEN
1991 (2000 REPRINT)
JON SULLIVAN

A quest fantasy from Simon R. Green, who earlier wrote detective thriller fantasies.

35

WORLD'S END
MARK CHADBOURN
1999
JON SULLIVAN

A modern-day Celtic fantasy series.

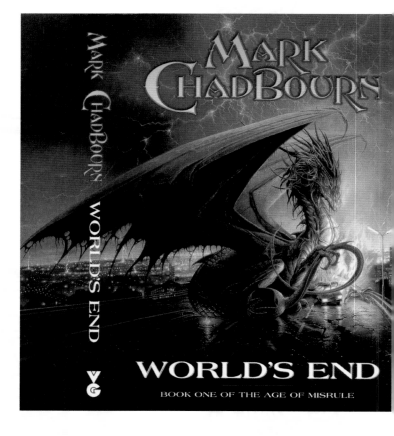

36

THE KING AND QUEEN OF SWORDS
TOM ARDEN
1998
KEVIN JENKINS

The second book of 'The Orokon', a series by one of Britain's newer stars in the fantasy universe.

Terry Pratchett has created a hugely successful cottage industry following the success of his first 'Discworld' book, *The Colour of Magic* (1983) and the nearly thirty subsequent titles. Other U.K. writers of zany fantasy include Robert Rankin, Tom Holt, and Andrew Harman.

Great fantasy sometimes pops up in the least likely places. Stephen King once famously said that he had seen the "future of horror" in British writer Clive Barker. He was only partially correct, for Barker has amounted to much more than that. An accomplished artist, playwright, film director, and producer, many of Barker's works are major fantasies, amongst them *Weaveworld* (1987), *The Great and Secret Show: The First Book of the Art* (1989), *Imajica* (1991), *Everville: The Second Book of the Art* (1994), and the young adult fantasy *The Thief of Always: A Fable* (1992), also illustrated by the author.

Award-winning writer Robert Holdstock explored British mythology in the World Fantasy Award-winning *Mythago Wood* (1984) and its sequel *Lavondyss* (1988), and returned to similar territory in *Merlin's Wood* (1994). Stephen Lawhead has his popular *Pendragon* series; Freda Warrington has her

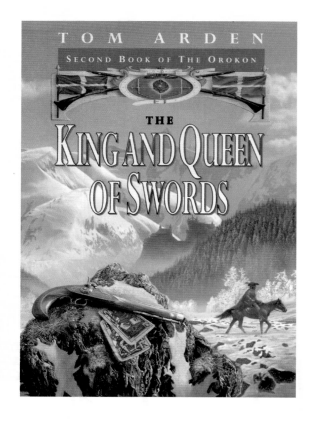

'Blackbird' traditional fantasy series; and husband-and-wife team Mark and Julia Smith (writing as "Jonathan Wylie") have proved that sometimes two heads are better than one, with more than a dozen novels to their credit.

From the medium of the comic book—which, like fantasy fiction, now gets *much* more respect than it once did—came Neil Gaiman. Known for his *Sandman* and *Books of Magic* series among other graphic ventures, his short fantasy fiction was collected as *Angels & Visitations* (1993) while his novel *Neverwhere* (1996) was based on his BBC television series of 1996. *Stardust: Being a Romance Within the Realms of Faerie* (1997–98), illustrated by Charles Vess, was a Dunsanian fantasy with pictures recalling the Golden Age of illustration in Britain. Gaiman and Vess won a World Fantasy Award for Best Short Fiction in 1991 for their *Sandman* installment "A Midsummer Night's Dream"—a first for a comic book.

Among the current crop of notable British fantasy writers, Tom Arden (a.k.a. David Rain) is one of the youngest in the heroic fantasy vein and got off to a great start with *The Harlequin's Dance: Book One of the Orokon* (1997), the first in a five-volume epic series. Others worth looking out for include Mark Chadbourn's contemporary Celtic 'Age of Misrule' series, Simon R. Green's 'Blue Moon' and *Deathstalker* books, and Jan Siegel's *Prospero's Children* series.

Without doubt, the most recent British fantasy success story has to be that of the youngest practitioner of the mystic arts, Harry Potter. With four books to date, beginning with 1997's *Harry Potter and the Philosopher's Stone* (U.S. title *Harry Potter and the Sorcerer's Stone* for those of you thinking you might have missed one) which sold almost 500,000

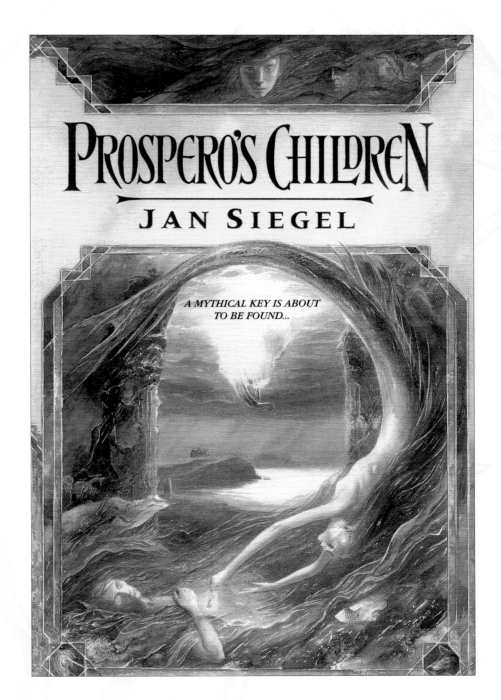

 PROSPERO'S CHILDREN
JAN SIEGEL
1999
ALAN LEE

From deep fantasy waters, an impressive new series has arisen.

FANTASY MASTERWORKS

THE CHRONICLES OF AMBER
ROGER ZELAZNY

THE CHRONICLES OF AMBER
ROGER ZELAZNY
2000
JOHN HOWE

'Amber' omnibus and another well-deserving Fantasy Masterwork.

39

THE WORM OUROBOROS
E. R. EDDISON
1922 (2000 REPRINT)
SIR EDWARD
BURNE-JONES

In the spirit of Lin Carter's Adult Fantasy line comes the Fantasy Masterworks series.

copies in the U.K. alone, author J. K. Rowling has become one of fantasy's highest-ever paid writers. Reader reaction reached an all-time frenzy with the publication of the fourth novel, *Harry Potter and The Goblet of Fire* in July 2000: its staggering 3.8 million first printing in the U.S. quickly sold out, and film and merchandising rights were purchased by Warner Brothers.

Another English woman putting fantasy literature in the spotlight—perhaps not on such a financially rewarding level, but historically speaking, priceless—is Jo Fletcher. Like her sometime collaborator Stephen Jones, Fletcher has long been an active promoter and supporter of the genre that she has loved and worked in for many years. As Editorial Director for Gollancz's fantasy line, she is the guiding force behind the Fantasy Masterworks series for their Millennium imprint. Like Lin Carter's beloved Adult Fantasy series of the 1960s and 1970s, the books in Fletcher's line-up are the classic, influential fantasies that not only deserve to be read but should be required reading for lovers of the field and never be allowed to go out of print. The books speak volumes for themselves. Whether it's *The Compleat Enchanter* by L.Sprague de Camp and Fletcher Pratt, *Time and the Gods* (an omnibus of six collections) by Lord Dunsany, E. R. Eddison's *The Worm Ouroboros,* Jack Vance's *The Dying Earth* stories, Roger Zelazny's *The Chronicles of Amber,* or the two-volume complete Conan stories of Robert E. Howard (and *only* Robert E. Howard—no substitutions please!), fantasy continues to flourish in the country it grew up in, where it not only takes care of its own, but seems to have all our best interests at heart as well.

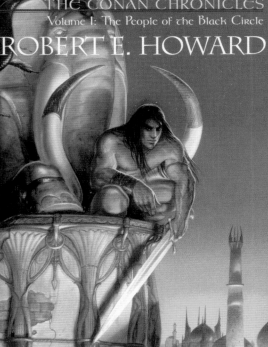

40

THE CONAN CHRONICLES VOLUME 1: THE PEOPLE OF THE BLACK CIRCLE
ROBERT E. HOWARD
2000
JOHN HOWE

Editor Stephen Jones picks up where the late Karl Edward Wagner left off by bringing all of Robert E. Howard's Conan tales—as he wrote them—back into print for a two-volume set in the Fantasy Masterworks series.

THE ROAD
GOES EVER ON
CHAPTER II

In the early 1980s, several interesting writers who had débuted in the previous decade went on to show their stamina in the genre, developing into first-class fantasists. Tim Powers opened *The Anubis Gates* (1983)—a time travel fantasy wherein the hero finds himself stranded in a Dickensian London inhabited by the real and the really grotesque—winning Powers a Philip K. Dick Award in 1984 for his efforts. He then invited us to *Dinner at Deviant's Palace* (1985), a post-holocaust science fiction banquet for the senses and, two years later, put us ashore *On Stranger Tides*, a fantasy adventure like no other—part voodoo magic, part "Pirates of the Caribbean", all Powers. Ten years after bringing together two of my own personal favorites—great beer and great fantasy—in

THE STRESS OF HER REGARD
TIM POWERS
1989
JAMES GURNEY

And you think you know stress…Tim Powers at the top of his game.

ON STRANGER TIDES
TIM POWERS
1987 (1989 REPRINT)
RICHARD CLIFTON-DEY

Rum-soaked voodoo and pirate fantasy as Powers hoists the Jolly Roger for this highly entertaining adventure.

The Drawing of the Dark, his genre début, Powers took us to witness *The Stress of Her Regard* (1989), quite possibly his masterpiece. It was a dark fantasy about the poets John Keats, Percy Bysshe Shelley, and Lord Byron, and their vampiric lovers, the Lamia, who brought personal tragedy along with inspiration. A young doctor, no stranger to personal tragedy himself, joins their group, having in common a similar strange bedfellow. The title of this haunting fantasy was taken from a verse, not, as you might think, by any of the main characters, but rather that of another extremely capable poet, Clark Ashton Smith.

The Last Call (1992), a Las Vegas magical fantasy, *Expiration Date* (1995), an even darker contemporary Los Angeles piece with its concept of a ghostly "high", and *Earthquake Weather* (1997), a follow-up of sorts to the other two, are all set in the "modern world" and it is a bizarre one at that. Powers has continued to write intriguing fantasy, as evident in the more recent *Declare* (2000), published as a limited signed edition by Subterranean Press.

A friend of Powers who also writes along similar lines is James P. Blaylock. Initially the author of somewhat Tolkienesque fantasy, starting with *The Elfin Ship* (1982), Blaylock went on to create a fantastic nineteenth century London for *Homunculus* (1986) and *Lord Kelvin's Machine* (1992) as well as modern fantasies set in present-day California such as *Land of Dreams* (1987) and *The Last Coin* (1988). His other novels throughout the 1990s followed this latter trend.

Elizabeth Lynn, whose late 1970s 'Torner Chronicles' trilogy got off to a great start by winning a World Fantasy Award for the first book, *Watchtower* (1979), turned to no less impressive juvenile fantasy and short stories through the 1980s and 1990s, and she developed a new series in 1998 with *Dragon's Winter*.

TIM POWERS
AWARD-WINNING AUTHOR OF
THE ANUBIS GATES

ON STRANGER TIDES

'AS INTOXICATING AS A SLUG OF SMUGGLED RUM'
NEW MUSICAL EXPRESS

ACE
FANTASY

TIM POWERS

Winner of the Philip K. Dick Memorial Award

THE STRESS OF HER REGARD

TIM
POWERS

THE
STRESS
OF HER
REGARD

GURNEY

ISBN 0-441-79055-0

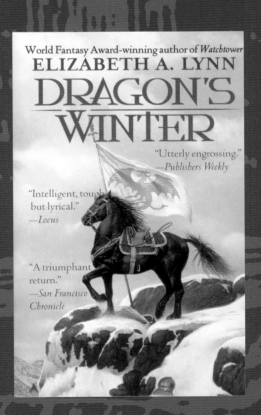

World Fantasy Award-winning author of *Watchtower*

ELIZABETH A. LYNN

DRAGON'S WINTER

"Utterly engrossing."
—*Publishers Weekly*

"Intelligent, tough but lyrical."
—*Locus*

"A triumphant return."
—*San Francisco Chronicle*

♔
DRAGON'S WINTER
ELIZABETH A. LYNN
1998
DUANE O. MYERS

Award-winning writer Lynn started out writing
science fiction before turning her hand to fantasy.

MAGIC CARPET BOOKS

"Exciting." —*School Library Journal*

HEART'S BLOOD

JANE YOLEN

♔
HEART'S BLOOD
JANE YOLEN
1984 (1996 REPRINT)
DENNIS NOLAN

Book II in Yolen's young
adult 'Pit Dragon' trilogy.

MARY FRANCES ZAMBRENO
JOURNEYMAN WIZARD
A MAGICAL MYSTERY

JOURNEYMAN WIZARD
MARY FRANCES ZAMBRENO
1994
CHERYL GRIESBACH AND STANLEY MARTUCCI

Zambreno is another gifted practitioner of young adult fantasy.

Fantasy Masterworks

LITTLE, BIG
JOHN CROWLEY

LITTLE, BIG
JOHN CROWLEY
1981 (2000 REPRINT)
JOHN ANSTER FITZGERALD

Crowley's celebrated faerie tale.

HER MAJESTY'S WIZARD
CHRISTOPHER STASHEFF
1986
DARREL K. SWEET

Humorous fantasy from Stasheff, who has written several fantasy series beginning with *The Warlock in Spite of Himself* (1969).

0-345-27456-3

Christopher Stasheff
A rollicking tale by the author of *We Open on Venus*
HER MAJESTY'S WIZARD

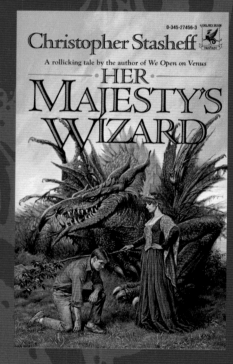

THE FACE OF APOLLO
VOLUME I
BOOK OF THE GODS

a spectacular new fantasy world from the author of *Merlin's Bones*

FRED SABERHAGEN

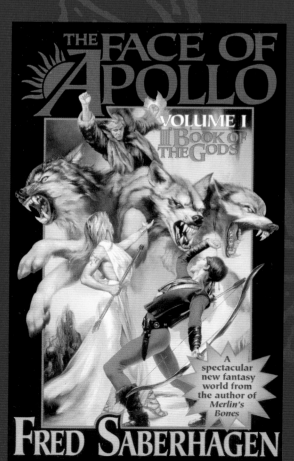

THE FACE OF APOLLO
FRED SABERHAGEN
1998 (1999 REPRINT)
JULIE BELL

A new series of old gods by the author of the 'Book of Swords' series.

Jane Yolen is a prolific writer of fantasy for both adults and children, as well as editing it for other authors. She uses aspects of the fairy tale in much of her work and has written several books in an Arthurian vein. Meanwhile, Ursula K. Le Guin finished her admirable 'Earthsea' series with *Tehanu* in 1990, then moved back into science fiction and literary criticism. She remains one of the field's most respected and influential writers.

Christopher Stasheff started his planetary romance series with *The Warlock in Spite of Himself* in 1969 and he added quite a number of books to the sequence over the next thirty years. He also developed the 'Rogue Wizard' and 'Wizard in Rhyme' series' in the 1980s and 1990s, as well as the more recent 'The Star Stone' series. C. J. Cherryh, predominantly a science fiction writer, had several fantasy and science fiction blends published during the 1970s including *Gate of Ivrel* (1976). She went on to purer fantasy pastures with *The Dreamstone* (1983), *The Goblin Mirror* (1992), and *Faery in Shadow* (1993), among others. Speaking of faerie, one of the most imaginative encounters with that world, and a major fantasy work of the 1980s, was *Little, Big* (1981) by John Crowley. Crowley had previously been known for his science fiction, but this novel was a grand-scale fantasy, wherein the ancestral home of Edgewood shared an attribute with that of the world of faerie: the further you went in, the bigger it got. It certainly did prove to be big, winning the World Fantasy Award for Best Novel in 1982. Crowley continues to write "big" fantasy.

Fred Saberhagen, yet another science fiction author who periodically wrote fantasy adventures in the 1960s and 1970s, began his 'Swords' series in 1983, beginning with *The First Book of Swords* and carried through the 1990s, occasionally dipping into material from Arthurian legend, as in *Merlin's Bones* (1995). *The Face of Apollo* (1998) was the first

THE EYES OF THE DRAGON
STEPHEN KING
1984 (1987 REVISED REPRINT)
ARTIST UNKNOWN

A heroic young adult fantasy from the master of horror.

volume in 'The Book of the Gods' series, which brings the old gods back to earth. Book Two, *Ariadne's Web*, appeared the following year.

Terry Brooks, author of the aforementioned 'Shannara' books, initially brought the series to an end in 1996, for fear of carrying a good thing too far. However, Brooks and 'Shannara' were back in 2000 with a new series to satisfy both old and new fans.

The world's bestselling horror writer, Stephen King, ventured into the realms of fantasy with the publication of *The Dark Tower: The Gunslinger* (1982), a collection of connected stories originally published in *The Magazine of Fantasy & Science Fiction*. A fantastic journey with elements derived from Robert Browning's 1855 poem "Childe Roland to the Dark Tower Came", it has been a unique continuing saga for King, running into four volumes so far. In addition to trade and mass-market versions, the series has also been published in deluxe illustrated and limited signed editions from specialty publisher Donald M. Grant.

In 1984 King collaborated with another talented and successful writer, Peter Straub, on *The Talisman*, a modern-day quest fantasy which was beautifully slipcased in two volumes, containing color paintings by some of the finest artists in the field (Jeff Jones, Rowena Morrill, and Bernie Wrightson, among others). It was another feather in the cap of Donald M. Grant, publisher of both trade and limited signed hardcover editions. A belated sequel from both authors has been announced.

King paid another visit to the kingdom of the fantastic in 1984, looking through the eyes of youth into *The Eyes of the Dragon*, a heroic and entertaining adventure of treachery which kept a rightful young heir from his throne amidst a background light years (or maybe that should be "dark years") away from what one might expect to find in Stephen King country.

While more and more fantasy material was appearing from major publishers such as Donald A. Wollheim's DAW line, Del Rey Books and others, small press publications and magazines, along with specialty house editions, continued to blossom.

The digest-sized *The Magazine of Fantasy & Science Fiction* has enjoyed a long life, starting in 1949 and still going strong today. It has featured some of the finest fantasy writers in the business and continues to do so, in addition to its celebrated science fiction stories.

The venerable Arkham House published fiction by such British talents as Ramsey Campbell, Basil Copper, Brian Lumley, Denys Val Baker, Walter de la Mare, Russell Kirk, M. P. Shiel, and Elizabeth Walter during the 1970s. It also brought out fantasy and horror anthologies, poetry, and collections by *Weird Tales* writers Mary Elizabeth Counselman, H. P. Lovecraft, August Derleth, and Frank Belknap Long to name just a few. Three major excursions into fantasy territory were L. Sprague de Camp's *Literary Swordsmen and Sorcerers* (1976), a non-fiction volume about the writers of heroic fantasy; Phyllis Eisenstein's wonderful début, *Born to Exile* (1978), and *The Black Book of Clark Ashton Smith* (1979). This last book was a new venture for Arkham House; it was a softcover edition containing plot ideas, poetry, and miscellany from Smith's own notebook, along with striking black and white illustrations by Andrew Smith, who raised the quality of interior art in several Arkham House volumes. The editor was poet and writer Donald Sidney-Fryer, whose own collection *Songs and Sonnets Atlantean* (1971) was also published by Arkham.

Throughout the 1980s, Arkham House expanded its horizons under the watchful and insightful eye of

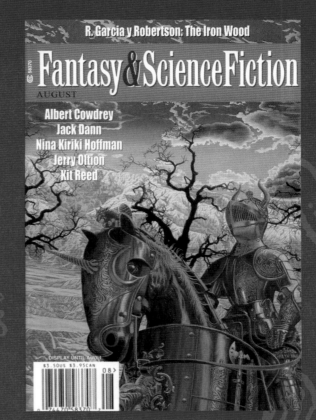
10

WORLD FANTASY CONVENTION 1983
PROGRAM BOOK COVER
ROWENA MORRILL

Program books for conventions can vary when it comes to production. This one hits a high mark!

World Fantasy Convention 1983

11

THE MAGAZINE OF FANTASY & SCIENCE FICTION
AUGUST 2000
KENT BASH

Still going strong since 1949, this issue includes a mediaeval fantasy "The Iron Wood" by R. Garcia y Robertson.

13

DRAGONS OF DARKNESS
EDITED BY ORSON SCOTT CARD
1981
DON MAITZ

The darker side of the scale is examined by Edward Bryant and Ben Bova among others.

WHAT IS COILED IN THOSE HIDDEN
PLACES IN YOUR HEART?

DRAGONS OF DARKNESS

A COMPANION VOLUME TO THE
HIGHLY-PRAISED **DRAGONS OF LIGHT**

Interior Design by
MICHAEL GOODWIN

Edited by
ORSON SCOTT CARD

Edited by
ORSON SCOTT CARD
DRAGONS OF LIGHT

NEVER BEFORE
HAVE STORIES AND ART
BEEN SO PERFECTLY JOINED, TO BRING
TO LIFE THE DRAGONS OF YOUR DREAMS
—AND NIGHTMARES

Interior Design by Michael Goodwin

12

DRAGONS OF LIGHT
EDITED BY
ORSON SCOTT CARD
1980
MICHAEL WHELAN

Dragons have always been popular fantasy creatures. For this illustrated anthology their lighter sides are explored by the likes of Roger Zelazny, George R. R. Martin, Jane Yolen, and Michael Bishop.

14
ARIEL—THE BOOK OF FANTASY
NO. 3, 1978
BARRY WINDSOR-SMITH

There may have only been four issues, but they were all high quality.

15
SHAYOL
NO. 3, VOL. 1, 1979
THOMAS BLACKSHEAR

The World Fantasy Award-winning small press magazine that published fantasy and supernatural fiction.

LARRY NIVEN shows how the "Known Space" series was only a hoax; a "Gormenghast" folio by TIM KIRK; JAMES MICHAEL MARTIN on Tod Slaughter; PHYLLIS EISENSTEIN; RON WILSON

16
TRUMPET
NO. 10, 1969
EDITED BY TOM REAMY AND ALEX EISENSTEIN
GEORGE BARR

Trumpet was a grand fanfare. A slick 'zine of articles and reviews, combined with fine illustration, including artwork by Jeff Jones, Tim Kirk and George Barr, the latter with his beautiful graphic adaptation of Poul Anderson's *The Broken Sword*.

managing editor James Turner, who had been gradually introducing new authors, including science fiction writers, to Arkham's stable. Tanith Lee, Richard L. Tierney, Michael Bishop, Greg Bear, Joanna Russ, James Tiptree Jr., Lucius Shepard, Michael Shea, J. G. Ballard, and Bruce Sterling were among those published by Arkham House during Turner's tenure, which was an extremely innovative period for the publisher. Turner later established his own imprint, Golden Gryphon Press, prior to his premature death in 1999.

The World Fantasy Convention has continued to honor the best in the field each year, and small press publications have done their share of keeping fans aware of the genre. The World Fantasy Award-winning *Fantasy Newsletter* (1978–87), founded by Paul C. Allen and later edited by Robert A. Collins under the title *Fantasy Review,* was a perfect example of this type of informative fanzine.

After co-publishing a chapbook of poetry by Clark Ashton Smith with Clyde Beck in 1962, Roy A. Squires became prolific at producing beautifully handmade chapbooks featuring poetry by Smith, Robert E. Howard, Fritz Leiber, Ray Bradbury, and others.

Ariel-The Book of Fantasy was a slick, large format quality production, which lasted only four issues from 1976–78. It included stories by Michael Moorcock and Roger Zelazny and art by Frank Frazetta, Richard Corben, and Jeff Jones. *Chacal* and *Shayol* were two magazines of the 1970s and 1980s, finely produced with high quality art and articles, published by Arnie Fenner and Pat Cadigan. Today Fenner is responsible for editing, with his wife Cathy, beautiful hardcovers devoted to the work of artist Frank Frazetta and the highly successful annual *Spectrum* series (1994–), which showcases the best of contemporary fantastic art.

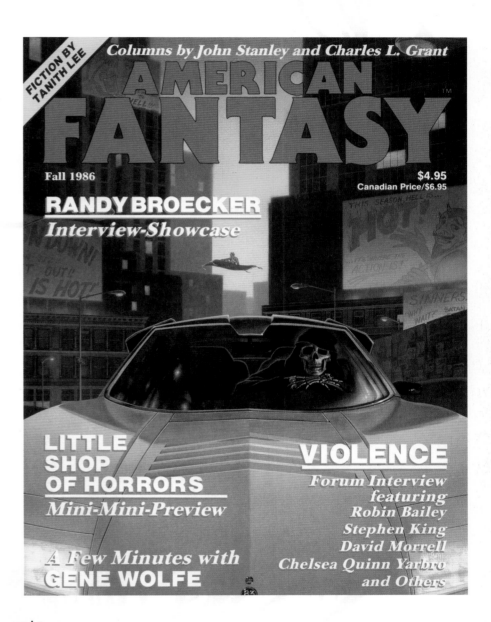

AMERICAN FANTASY
VOL. 2, NO. 1, 1986
MICHAEL WHELAN

Another World Fantasy Award-winner, Robert and Nancy Garcia's magazine published first-rate articles, reviews, author and artist interviews and showcases. Occasionally they lowered their standards.

MARION ZIMMER BRADLEY'S FANTASY MAGAZINE

NO. 46, 2000
OMAR RAYYAN

Ceasing publication after Bradley's death, this magazine published much in the way of fine art as well as fiction by Parke Godwin, Mercedes Lackey, Jo Clayton, and others.

DARK REGIONS

NO. 14, 2000
LUBOV

A horror fiction magazine, but this was a special all-fantasy issue.

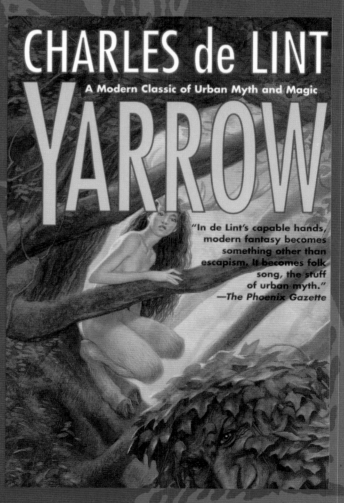

REALMS OF FANTASY

DECEMBER 1998
MICHAEL WHELAN

A slickly-produced magazine publishing fantasy fiction, with work by some of the top writers and artists in the field.

YARROW

CHARLES DE LINT
1986 (1997 REPRINT)
JOHN HOWE

De Lint published his first writings through his own Triskell Press in 1979 and has since gone on to specialize in contemporary fantasies.

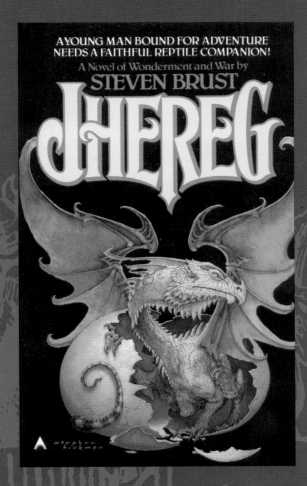

A YOUNG MAN BOUND FOR ADVENTURE
NEEDS A FAITHFUL REPTILE COMPANION!

A Novel of Wonderment and War by

STEVEN BRUST

JHEREG

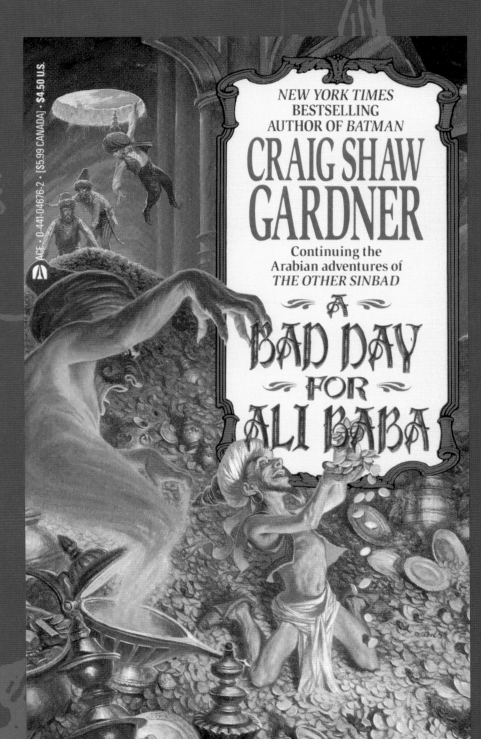

NEW YORK TIMES
BESTSELLING
AUTHOR OF *BATMAN*

CRAIG SHAW
GARDNER

Continuing the
Arabian adventures of
THE OTHER SINBAD

A
BAD DAY
FOR
ALI BABA

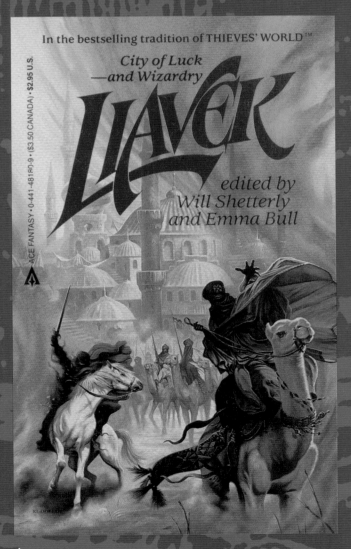

In the bestselling tradition of THIEVES' WORLD™

*City of Luck
—and Wizardry*

LIAVEK

edited by
Will Shetterly
and Emma Bull

22

JHEREG
STEVEN BRUST
1983
STEPHEN HICKMAN

Brust's long-running 'Taltos' sequence
begins with this fantasy novel.

24

A BAD DAY FOR ALI BABA
CRAIG SHAW GARDNER
1992
DARRELL K. SWEET

Part of the Arabian Nights sequence of books by Gardner,
who has written a good deal of humorous fantasy.

23

LIAVEK
EDITED BY WILL SHETTERLY AND EMMA BULL
1985
GARY RUDDELL

The first volume in this shared-world series, featuring stories
by Gene Wolfe, Steven Brust, and Jane Yolen among others.

THE BLACK SWAN
MERCEDES LACKEY
2000
JON SULLIVAN

Lackey utilizes the story of Swan Lake
as the basis for this fantasy novel.

Robert and Nancy Garcia picked up a World Fantasy Award in 1988 for their well-produced and informative *American Fantasy* magazine (1982–88). Garcia previously produced *The Chicago Fantasy Newsletter* (1978–81) and today works at both designing books for publishers like Fedogan and Bremer (who publish horror and mystery fiction along the lines of Arkham House) and for his own American Fantasy imprint.

In 1988 *Marion Zimmer Bradley's Fantasy Magazine* was christened, coming to the end of its run in 2000 after the death of the renowned science fiction and fantasy author the previous year. Since its inception in 1994, *Realms of Fantasy* magazine has consistently published high fantasy stories by the likes of Neil Gaiman, Tanith Lee, Louise Cooper, and Roger Zelazny, along with an emphasis on quality artwork.

While we are on the subject of art, the older professionals of the cover arena such as Michael Whelan, Don Maitz, James Gurney, Stephen Hickman, Boris Vallejo, Rowena Morrill, Darrell K. Sweet and others were joined by newer artistic talents that sprang up in the 1980s. Gary Ruddell, Walter Velez, Richard Bober, Bob Eggleton, and Keith Parkinson were just a few of the individuals bringing dragons, wizards, giants, and other fantastic creations to life on the dust jackets and paperback covers of fantasy books during the 1980s and 1990s.

Many of the authors whose work these artists illustrated have managed to stake and hold onto their claims in the gold mine that the field has become over the past few decades.

Canadian musician and author Charles de Lint wrote several Celtic fantasies in the 'Cerin Songweaver' series published as chapbooks in the 1980s, leading up to his Tolkien-influenced first novel, *The Riddle of the Wren* (1984). However it is the "urban fantasy",

BLACK HEART, IVORY BONES

EDITED BY ELLEN DATLOW AND TERRI WINDLING
2000
THOMAS CANTY

The final volume of six anthologies featuring
original light and dark fairy tales for adults.

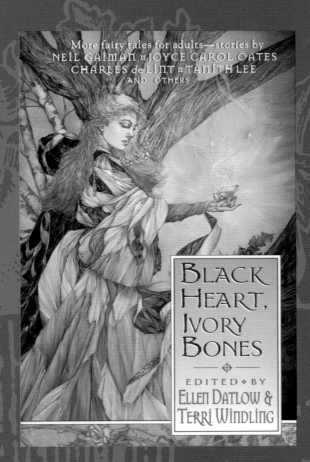

or the merging of the contemporary world with the
fantastic, that he has made uniquely his own in works
such as *Moonheart* (1984), *Yarrow* (1986), *Greenmantle*
(1988), *The Ivory and the Horn* (1995), *Moonlight
and Vines* (1999), and *Triskell Tales* (2000). Steven
Brust began his 'Vlad Taltos' series with *Jhereg* (1983),
and it is still continuing. Emma Bull and Will
Shetterly co-edited the shared-world *Liavek* series of
anthologies they created (1985–90), while Emma
Bull's own first novel, *War for the Oaks* (1987), was a
fine contribution to contemporary fantasy, describing the world of faerie merged with that of our own.
Since that first book, the singer/author played a large
part in helping to turn the city of Minneapolis into
something of a center of fantasy excellence with a
thriving community of writers and artists.

Craig Shaw Gardner started out writing humorous
fantasy, including a parody of the Arabian Nights in

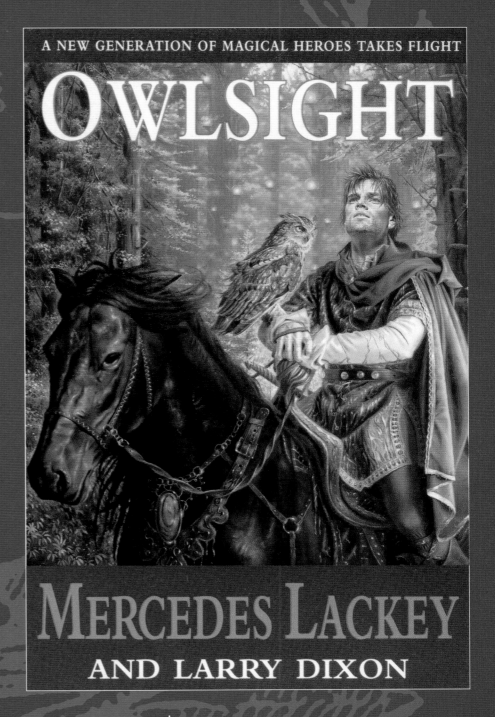

OWLSIGHT

MERCEDES LACKEY AND LARRY DIXON
2000
JON SULLIVAN

Another recent fantasy by Lackey,
co-written with her husband.

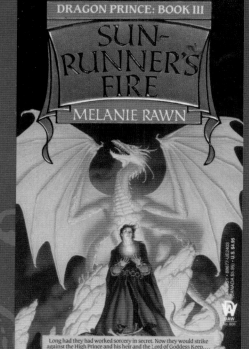

SUN-RUNNER'S FIRE

MELANIE RAWN

1990

MICHAEL WHELAN

Whelan has painted more dragons than you can possibly imagine. Here's another great one for Rawn's third book in the 'Dragon Prince' series.

THE CHRONICLES OF MASTER LI AND NUMBER TEN OX

BARRY HUGHART

1998

KAJA FOGLIO

Omnibus volume of the three books in Hughart's Oriental fantasy trilogy.

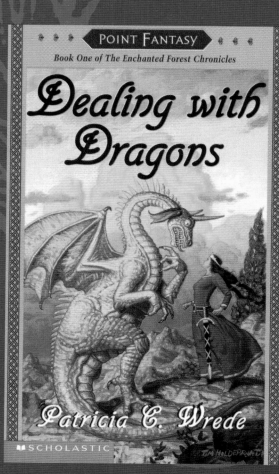

DEALING WITH DRAGONS

PATRICIA C. WREDE

1990 (1992 REPRINT)

TIM HILDEBRANDT

Book One of the 'The Enchanted Forest Chronicles'.

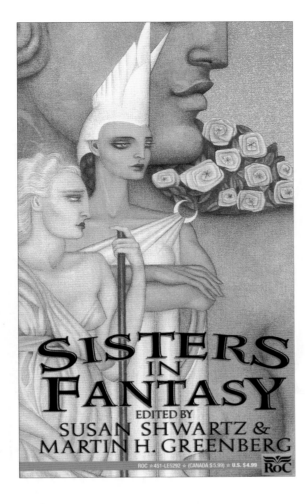

a series in the 1990s, before playing it straight with his 'Dragon Circle' series, beginning with *Dragon Sleeping* in 1994. An Arabian Nights background also set Esther Friesner on a literary journey in 1985 with the start of several comic and urban fantasies which continue today.

Mercedes Lackey has been extremely prolific since her début novel *Arrows of the Queen* (1987), with several fantasy trilogies and novels to her credit, some written in collaboration with and illustrated by her husband, artist Larry Dixon. Elizabeth Boyer and Barbara Hambly are two other women writers who received acclaim early in their careers in the 1980s and have continued to produce fine work during the past decade.

Since 1988, Ellen Datlow and Terri Windling have edited *The Year's Best Fantasy and Horror* annual anthologies, with Datlow handling the horror chores and Windling the fantasy, consistently bringing together some of the finest short works in both fields. As an editor at Ace books, Windling produced the anthology *Faery!* (1985) and began the Ace Fantasy line, publishing early material by Emma Bull and Charles de Lint, among others. She was also responsible for the young adult 'MagicQuest', series and kicked off her 'Fairy Tales' series with *The Sun, the Moon, and the Stars* (1987) by Steven Brust.

There were other anthologies as well, containing material old and new, usually based around the world of faerie for which Windling has a fondness. These included *Ruby Slippers, Golden Tears* (1995), *Snow White, Blood Red* (1993), *Black Thorn, White Rose* (1994), and *A Wolf at the Door and Other Retold Fairy Tales* (2000), all co-edited with Datlow. In 1996 Windling's own first novel, *The Wood Wife,* was published, and in 1999 she collaborated with Wendy

SISTERS IN FANTASY
EDITED BY SUSAN
SHWARTZ AND
MARTIN H. GREENBERG
1995
MEL ODOM

An anthology of fantasy fiction by women including Tanith Lee, Jane Yolen, Jo Clayton, Andre Norton, and Phyllis Eisenstein.

SHARDS OF EMPIRE
SUSAN SHWARTZ
1996
RICHARD BOBER

An historical fantasy set during the fall of the Byzantine empire.

"I enjoyed this very much indeed. It's nice to find a new writer of such obvious merit and vivid imageries."
—Anne McCaffrey

DRAGON AND PHOENIX
JOANNE BERTIN
1999
BOB EGGLETON

Bertin had a bestseller with *The Last Dragon Lord.* This marks a return to that world.

Froud on the elegant picture book *A Midsummer Night's Faery Tale.*

Orson Scott Card, although primarily a science fiction author, wrote the magical *Hart's Hope* (1983), then went on to create 'The Tales of Alvin Maker' series of novels. Beginning with *Seventh Son* (1987) and still continuing, these are considered to be among the best of American fantasy writing. Another fantasy, *Enchantment,* was published by Del Rey in 1999, the same year as Card's fable for adults, *Magic Mirror.*

In 1985 Barry Hughart collected a World Fantasy Award for *Bridge of Birds: A Novel of an Ancient China That Never Was* (1984). This beautiful Oriental fantasy, written in the vein of Ernest Bramah's Kai Lung

books, was the first in a trilogy which also comprised *The Story of the Stone* (1988) and *Eight Skilled Gentlemen* (1991). All three titles were collectively published in limited hardcover and trade paperback editions as *The Chronicles of Master Li and Number Ten Ox* (1998) by The Stars Our Destination, the first book publication from the science fiction, fantasy, horror, and mystery bookstore of the same name in Chicago. Both editions rapidly sold out.

Many female writers were producing novels and series work during this period. Melanie Rawn's 'Dragon' books were extremely popular throughout the 1980s and 1990s. Other writers of note included Patricia C. Wrede, Mickey Zucker Reichert, Jennifer Roberson, Susan Shwartz, Amy Stout, Sheri S. Tepper, Judith Tarr, Paula Volsky, Brenda W. Clough, Diane Duane, Kate Elliott, Deborah Turner Harris, Ellen Kushner, Patricia Keneally-Morrison, Holly Lisle, Nina Kiriki Hoffman, and, more recently, Joanne Bertin, Tanya Huff, Kathe Koja, and Rebecca Bradley.

Those years were not lacking productivity from male authors either, such as John Morressy, James Morrow, Eric S. Nylund, Michael Swanwick, Robert E. Vardeman, L. E. Modesitt, Jr., and relative newcomers James Clemen and David Farland.

The fantasy role-playing games that originated in the 1970s with *Dungeons & Dragons* had also become extremely commercial and were springing up like the proverbial Hydra's heads. Games were based both on existing fictional characters as well as totally new concepts. There are countless game manuals, magazines, and miniature figures catering to various fantasy game worlds and, more importantly, they are quite a major market for original fiction, such as the series of books published under the TSR 'Forgotten Realms' or 'DragonLance' imprints. R. A. Salvatore is

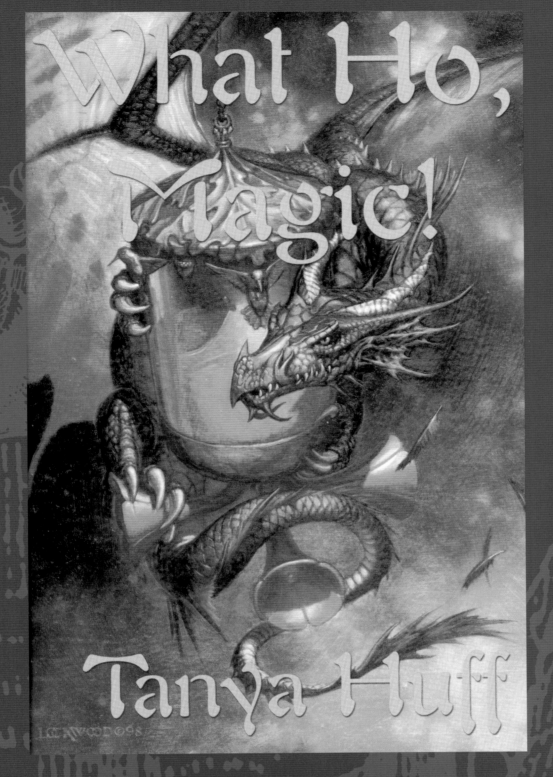

LOCKWOOD ©98

WHAT HO, MAGIC!
TANYA HUFF
1999
TODD LOCKWOOD

A first collection of short stories by Huff.

THE RUNELORDS
DAVID FARLAND
1998
DARRELL K. SWEET

A well-praised fantasy by science fiction author Dave Wolverton under the pseudonym of Farland. A very nice cover by Sweet, surely one of the hardest working artists in this field.

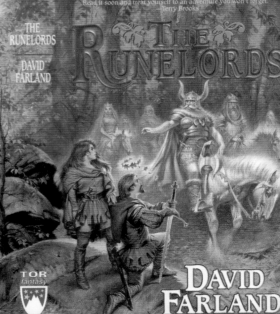

"A first-rate tale, an epic fantasy that more than delivers on its promise. Read it soon and treat yourself to an adventure you won't forget."
—Terry Brooks

THE RUNELORDS
DAVID FARLAND

TOR fantasy

ISBN 0-312-86653-4

DAVID FARLAND

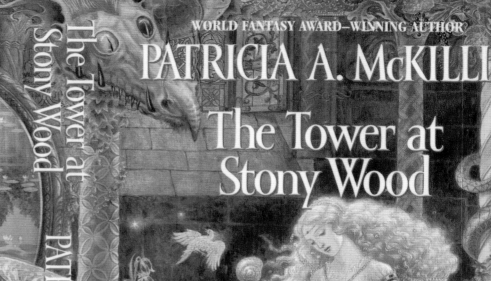

WORLD FANTASY AWARD—WINNING AUTHOR

PATRICIA A. McKILLI

The Tower at Stony Wood

The Tower at Stony Wood

PATRICIA A. McKILLIP

ACE
FANTASY

ISBN 0-441-00733-3

52295>

EAN

9 780441 007332

👑 36

LEGENDS

EDITED BY ROBERT SILVERBERG
1998
GEOFF TAYLOR

Fantasy worlds of several bestselling authors—including Stephen King, Robert Jordan, Terry Goodkind, and Terry Pratchett—are visited via all-new novellas in this huge anthology.

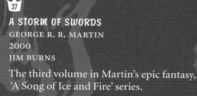

👑 37

A STORM OF SWORDS

GEORGE R. R. MARTIN
2000
JIM BURNS

The third volume in Martin's epic fantasy, 'A Song of Ice and Fire' series.

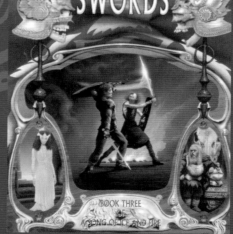

👑 38

SHIP OF DESTINY

ROBIN HOBB
2000
JOHN HOWE

More magic, piracy, and dragons in the final book of Hobb's trilogy.

THE TOWER AT STONY WOOD
PATRICIA A. MCKILLIP
2000
KINUKO Y. CRAFT

A beautiful fantasy of knights and magic by award-winner McKillip, who continues to show why she is one of the most outstanding writers in the field.

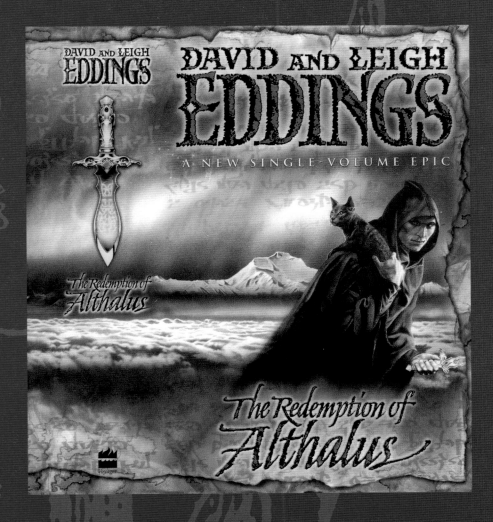

just one of the many popular writers working successfully in this area. Numerous games have proven to be lucrative enterprises: The extremely popular *Magic: The Gathering*, developed by role-playing company Wizards of the Coast in 1993, started the trend of card games.

Fantasy has been a natural for the development of computer games such as *Myst* and *Riven*, with their impressive graphics, and role-playing has been taken to another level with the proliferation of the personal computer.

The five years leading up to the twenty-first century marked the appearance of fine fantasy fiction from a large stable of younger writers as well as a number of respected veterans. The mammoth anthology *Legends* (1998), edited by Robert Silverberg, contained all new novellas by many of the masters of the field, including Terry Pratchett, Robert Jordan, Terry Goodkind, George R. R. Martin, and Stephen King, all dealing with their own fantasy world creations.

George R. R. Martin, who was already very successful in the science fiction field, scored well with his epic fantasy series which began with *A Game of Thrones: Book One of a Song of Ice and Fire* (1996) and continued with *A Clash of Kings* (1999) and *A Storm of Swords* (2000). In 1999 *Reave the Just* was published, a collection by another favorite, Stephen R. Donaldson, as well as a powerful ghost fantasy from Peter S. Beagle, *Tamsin*. The third volume of David Drake's 'Lord of the Isles' series entitled *Servant of the Dragon* also took a bow that year, as did *Into the Darkness* by Harry Turtledove, an author better known for his alternate history novels, featuring yet again a world where magic worked. Jody Lynn Nye's 'Dreamland' series and Robin Hobb's *Ship of Magic* series also débuted at the end of the decade.

The stories continue to be told and we keep reading them. Whether they be about heroes and monsters, barbarians and sorcerers, lost cities and their inhabitants, Arthur and his champions, noble quests and the not-so-noble encountered during them, we are entertained and, as is the case with all good fiction, briefly transported away from our own, often, less-than-fantastic world. And in the capable hands of a good fantasy writer, amazing things can happen during that brief journey.

The thousand-and-one stories that Scheherazade told so long ago have been added to by a multitude of imaginative talents too numerous to count. And there is no end in sight. Better still, unlike that expansive narrator of legend, we can enjoy them at our leisure and still look forward to what the next day will bring.

40

THE REDEMPTION OF ALTHALUS
DAVID AND LEIGH EDDINGS
2000
GEOFF TAYLOR

A recent epic fantasy of the rare, old-fashioned, one volume tells all variety.

BEYOND
THE FIELD I KNOW
CREDITS & ACKNOWLEDGEMENTS

That part of me upon which I sit was saved by the following individuals, without whose generous assistance this book would not be anywhere near as entertaining nor as informative.

First on the list of people I would like to thank is my wife Sara. I simply couldn't have done this book without her.

I am also indebted to Stephen Jones and Jo Fletcher, old friends and respected editors, for not only giving method to my madness but also much in the way of visual support.

I would also like to thank Robert Weinberg (whose beauty of a book on horror from Collectors Press preceded this volume) for his help and advice and for allowing me to plunder his extensive collection.

My appreciation goes to my older brother, Jay, for sharing his books and pulps with me so many years ago and for doing the same again on this project.

Ronald V. Borst of Hollywood Movie Posters provided me with transparencies for many of the movie images, as well as copies of rare related items, for which I am extremely grateful.

I have known my good friends Alan Wong and Lou and Sue Irmo for more years than any of us care to remember, and yet they *still* generously loaned me items for this book!

Further thanks are due to the many other individuals who gave of their time or their collections: Marcello Anciano of Wandering Star; Peter Atkins; David Barraclough of Titan Books for listening and listening; Ray and Shirlann Boghosian; Dorel Dittmann; Les and Val Edwards; Alex and Phyllis Eisenstein; Frank Eisgruber; Doug Ellis; Neil Gaiman; Robert and Nancy Garcia; Paula Grainger of HarperCollins; Peter Krupkowski for a last-minute barbarian fix; Kim Newman; Mandy Slater;

①

FANTASTIC ADVENTURES
MAY 1946
H. W. MCCAULEY
McCauley knew how to paint glamour girls, and his pulp covers gave him ample opportunity to do so.

Andrew Smith; Michael Marshall Smith; Alice and Berianne of The Stars Our Destination; David Sutton; Alex Wald for the Japanese lesson and answering his phone, and Robert K. Wiener of Donald M. Grant, Publisher, Inc. for supplying various dust jackets designed by Donald M. Grant and Thomas Canty.

Special thanks to Frank M. Robinson, the man who set the ground rules and paved the way, and an extra-special thanks (and a king-sized Dewey button) to Dennis Etchison, my favorite straight man. I should also mention Richard Perry, my patient publisher, and John Gunnison for his technical assistance.

Last, but certainly by no means least, I would like to acknowledge the love, support, and encouragement of my late mother and father, Jim and Dorothy Broecker, and also my mother- and father-in-law, Violet and Jim Jones, who graciously assumed their role, at great personal risk to their own sanity.

While researching this present volume, I used several excellent reference books and would heartily recommend them for further reading: the indispensable *The Encyclopedia of Fantasy* (Orbit, 1997) edited by John Clute and John Grant; *The Ultimate Encyclopedia of Fantasy* (The Overlook Press, 1999)

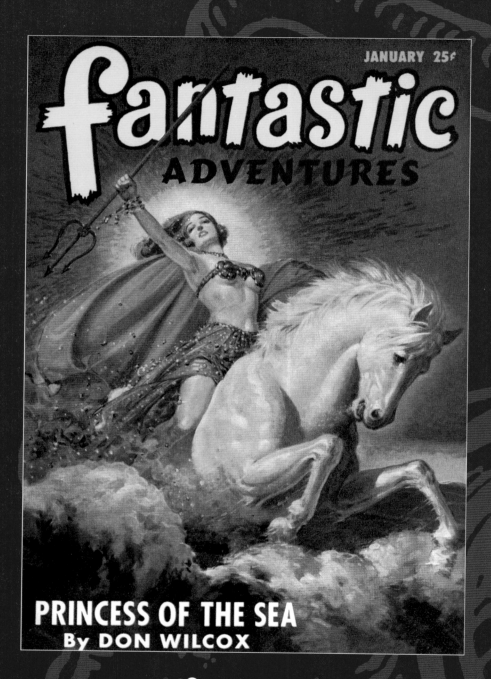

JANUARY 25¢

fantastic
ADVENTURES

PRINCESS OF THE SEA
By DON WILCOX

②

FANTASTIC ADVENTURES
JANUARY 1947
ROBERT GIBSON JONES

A different kind of
Gibson Girl was an added
attraction on some of
the covers of this pulp.

edited by David Pringle; *Fantasy: The 100 Best Books* (Carroll and Graf Publishers, 1991) by James Cawthorn and Michael Moorcock; *Who's Who in Horror and Fantasy Fiction* (Elm Tree Books, 1977) by Mike Ashley; *Imaginary Worlds* (Ballantine Books, 1973) by Lin Carter; *Literary Swordsmen and Sorcerers: The Makers of Heroic Fiction* (Arkham House, 1976) by L. Sprague de Camp; *A. Merritt: Reflections in the Moon Pool* (Oswald Train: Publisher, 1985) edited by Sam Moskowitz; *Reference Guide to Fantastic Films* (Chelsea-Lee Books, 1972, 1973, and 1974) three volumes compiled by Walt Lee; *Famous Fantastic Mysteries* (Gramercy Books, 1991), a reprint anthology of some of the best stories published by the pulp, edited by Stefan R. Dziemianowicz, Robert Weinberg and Martin H. Greenberg; *The Collector's Index to Weird Tales* (Bowling Green State University Popular Press, 1985) by Sheldon R. Jaffery and Fred Cook, and *The Weird Tales Story* (Fax Collector's Editions, 1977) by Robert Weinberg, recently given an over-size softcover reprinting.

Looking for that hard-to-find fantasy fix? (You could look up "fantasy" in the Yellow Pages, but you might get more than you bargained for! Sounds like the start of a de Camp and Pratt *Unknown* story…) Or, you could try the following dealers that have made it their business to keep people like me "supplied" over the years: The Stars Our Destination (705 Main Street, Evanston, IL 60202, USA), The Aleph Science Fiction Book Shop (831 Main Street, Evanston, IL 60202, USA), The Gallery Bookstore (923 W. Belmont Avenue, Chicago, IL 60657, USA), Toad Hall Books (2106 Broadway, Rockford, IL 61104, USA), DreamHaven Books (912 W. Lake Street, Minneapolis, MN 55408, USA), Adventure